MANCHESTER CITY
THE GENUINE SOAP OPERA CLUB

Published by
Legends Publishing

E-mail david@legendspublishing.net
Website www.legendspublishing.net

'It's been an extraordinary way to do it! But Manchester City are there! They are the genuine soap opera club. Cliffhangers upon cliffhangers ...'

Rob Hawthorne calling the 1998-99 Division Two play-off final between Manchester City and Gillingham

'How wonderful is football, so capable of fucking us all. What a great lesson!!!'

Pep Guardiola, writing about the 2006 World Cup quarterfinal match between Germany and Argentina

For my dad. He's not a big football fan, but he does love great stories.
Thanks to him, I do as well.

CONTENTS

Prologue: More Painful Than Childbirth

The Impact of Event Scale-Revised (or IES-R) is an easy-to-administer questionnaire that evaluates distress following a traumatic event. Typically used in the assessment of post-traumatic stress disorder, the IES-R provides a structured way for an individual to communicate distress when he or she does not have the words to do so. A 2001 study utilising the IES-R asked 65 participants who had suffered the same trauma to rate how distressed or bothered they were in the week after the event. Respondents were also asked to rate the frequency of intrusive thinking and avoidance tendencies related to the event. When the participants' trauma scores were totalled, they were similar to the scores for survivors of an avalanche. What was the traumatic event these 65 individuals suffered? The relegation of their favourite football club from the Premier League. Fitting, really. For what supporter has not felt like they were swept away and buried under an avalanche of anger and anguish when their beloved club suffered the drop?

Relegation is a cruel, remorseless beast, one that gives no quarter and offers no mercy. If you are a long-time supporter of an English club – League or non-League; professional, semi-professional, or amateur – chances are you are acquainted with the acute trauma it delivers to the sports fan psyche. And as any fan of a relegated club can attest, it does not matter how early or late into the season it occurred or how mentally prepared they were, or how many times it happened in the past. When the sharp axe of relegation falls, the pain is raw, real, and unremitting.

'I've seen childbirth twice and relegation five times', wrote Pete May, a freelance journalist and West Ham United supporter. 'Childbirth does look very painful, but it lasts only a few hours. The pain of relegation lasts all summer and beyond. Plus, childbirth at least results in something positive. With relegation, you're always worried that it's going to get worse'.

For many clubs and their supporters, it does in fact get worse. On April 29, 1980, Bristol City fell 5-2 to Southampton to tumble into the final relegation spot in the old First Division – 747 days later, the Robins took to the pitch for their first-ever game in the fourth tier. Wolverhampton Wanderers also suffered the ignominy of three successive relegations in 1984, 1985, and 1986.

However, these free-falls were topped by Luton Town's calamitous spiral. Relegated from the English Championship in 2007, the Hatters suffered the same fate one year later; a ten-point deduction for entering administration did not help their

Relegation is a cruel, remorseless beast.
Just ask Georgi Kinkladze.

cause. This was followed by a double-whammy deduction at the start of the next season: ten points for being guilty of misconduct for paying agents via a third party and 20 points for failing to satisfy the League's insolvency rules. The combined 30-point deduction was the most for a club in Football League history.

'Thirty points – who gives a fuck?' went a popular chant that season at Kenilworth Road. 'We're staying up'.

They didn't. A 0-0 draw with Chesterfield condemned the Hatters to a third consecutive relegation.

'If any football club had lived through what we have lived through over the last year', said Luton Town managing director Gary Sweet during that final relegation campaign, 'then we should have known better, but no football club has'.

No football club has stumbled through the relegation debacle that Middlesbrough experienced during the 1996-97 season. Bryan Robson's star-laden side – which featured Brazilian stars Juninho and Emerson, former Juventus striker Fabrizio Ravanelli, and club legend Robbie Mustoe – backed out of a match at Blackburn Rovers because their roster was decimated by illnesses, injuries, and suspensions. Boro's snap postponement earned the ire of the Football Association, and the club was fined £50,000 and docked three points.

In a tight Premier League table – eight points separated ninth through 19th – these three points made all the difference. Middlesbrough entered the final match needing a win to stay up. Hosts Leeds United went ahead before Juninho equalised. The 1-1 draw left Boro in 19th with 39 points. In 17th was Coventry City with 41.

Reflecting on the match years later, Juninho confessed to the magazine *FourFourTwo*, 'That was the only time I cried because of sadness'.

Yes, players cry. Openly and unashamedly. Or privately, a jersey pressed to the face to conceal the tears and anguish. Gaffers stare silently, hands clasped on their heads. Assistant managers wrap their arms around the shoulders of distraught players. Opponents shake hands with the relegated and offer quiet condolences. Then the pitch empties, and the players slowly file through the tunnel to the dressing room, a cortege of bowed heads and grave countenances.

Supporters cry, too. From the fresh-faced, freckled lad who is grieving over his first relegation, sobbing into his newly purchased scarf, to the flat-capped, grey-haired chap who can recall his very first: at a ground since demolished, his club donned in spartan kits long since retired, in the days before premierships and promotion playoffs and parachute payments. They cry because of what their club has lost, because they are already considering the uncertainties next season will inevitably deliver, because they do not know when – if ever – their club will return to such heights.

For many supporters, grief is not the day's go-to emotional response – it is frustration. The final whistle sounds, and the past season's disappointments replay in their minds: missed sitters, goalkeeper howlers, foolish red cards, head-scratching managerial decisions, hair's-width VAR offside calls, needless points dropped. A football season is made up of an infinite number of moments, countless instances in which the outcome is balanced on a knife edge, and had a few, possibly more, gone their club's way, maybe the drop is avoided. For a football fan, 'what could have been' is what gnaws at you, hollows you out.

Roy Hattersley, MP, said as much in a piece for *The Guardian* in December 1977. On the relegations of his beloved Sheffield Wednesday, the Labour politician wrote (with more than a hint of bitterness): 'I know that if Wednesday go down to the Fourth Division it will be the direct result of matches unfairly lost, penalties unjustly given and cruel injuries inflicted on key players by the desperate tackles of less gifted opponents'. In the end, Hattersley needn't have worried about such travesties that particular season, as Sheffield Wednesday avoided the drop.

Also in the stands on relegation day, there among the mournful and the vexed, are the proud. They clap with vigour, sing with passion, cheer with lumps in their throats. When their club's anthem echoes throughout the ground, it is not regarded as a funeral dirge, a heartbreaking coda to a break-your-heart season, but instead, a soaring hymn of unbroken devotion and unyielding resilience. They beam with the satisfaction of knowing their boys fought and fought bravely and fought until the final whistle.

Such scenes play out at football grounds every spring across the land. Relegation is modern English storytelling at its most dramatic, a very public spectacle during which the unexplainable, the fantastic, the tragic, the bizarre, and the comical make regular appearances. The most infamous relegation tales are probably only appreciated by the most dedicated supporters, who know the potential for the improbable, for wild misadventure, for sheer letdowns in a football match.

Relegation's stage, teeming with all-too-human characters and narratives, is also the ideal setting for better understanding the brevity of sporting glory and the strength of the athletic spirit. And much like theatre, relegation is an exploration of the human experience. Only in this case, the typical experience is of feeling like utter shit.

'The football fan is not just a watcher', wrote Arthur Hopcraft in his seminal book *The Football Man*. 'His sweat and his nerves work on football, and his spirit can be made rich or destitute by it'.

For over 120 years, supporters have savoured the richness of promotion and suffered the destitution of relegation. Journey all the way back to the Football League's early days and one discovers that it was not always this way. During the League's first four seasons, the bottom clubs were not relegated but instead, sought re-election during the League's annual general meeting. Other clubs yearning to become members were invited to apply.

After the 1888-89 campaign, the League's first, four clubs were up for re-election – Stoke, Burnley, Derby County, and Notts County – and all four were voted back into the League. This arbitrary voting-in process continued for the next three seasons with the occasional club failing re-election and being replaced by another from the Football Alliance, the progenitor to the Second Division.

The Football League restructured the format prior to the 1892-93 campaign, adding the competitive element that it was previously lacking. The bottom three

First Division teams now faced off against the top three Second Division clubs in what were deemed test matches. If a Second Division club prevailed, it was considered for First Division membership through an election process. Losing Second Division sides remained in the Second Division.

However, the test match system was not without its flaws as evidenced by a showdown between Stoke and Burnley in 1898. Having started out as winner-take-all ties, the test matches evolved into a mini tournament of sorts with clubs facing sides from the other division twice and not playing teams from their own division. Stoke and Burnley went into the final test match knowing a goalless draw would guarantee them both First Division football the next season. According to various reports, the 0-0 slog did not feature a single shot on goal. Both teams were 'devoid of interest and energy', according to one spectator account.

An editorial in *The Manchester Guardian* was significantly less kind: 'It is impossible to ignore the fact that these Test games have proved an utter farce. A change of some kind is absolutely necessary if the contests are in future to be regarded with any seriousness'.

Unsurprisingly, the act of collusion caught the attention of the Football League. Dramatic changes were forthcoming. For the 1898-99 campaign, the Football League introduced the concepts of promotion and relegation that are still in use today. And ever since the system's creation, clubs have tortured their supporters with new and inventive ways to suffer relegation. One such instance was in 1909.

It was not the club's first relegation, and it would not be the last, but it was the first relegation that unfolded in such an outlandish manner it is difficult to determine if the season's final weeks should be classified as a straight-up farce or a complete catastrophe. Perhaps it was both.

On the morning of April 9, 1909, Manchester City sat in 15th, four places above the relegation zone. Liverpool (31 points), Nottingham Forest (30 points), and Bury (29 points) were the buffer between City (32 points) and 19th Bradford City (24 points). With six matches to play, staying up was not a certainty but only a collapse of the most ambitious variety would see the club succumb to relegation.

City kicked off their run-in with a loss to Sunderland on April 9 and then another to relegation favourites Bury the next afternoon. Three days later, they moved up to 34 points with a 2-1 victory over Forest. However, any momentum was stalled when the club fell to Sheffield United 3-1 in the April 17 home finale at Hyde Road. Next was an April 26 away defeat to Aston Villa that was exceedingly cruel: the hosts nabbed the winner during the final five minutes from a free kick that remained 'in the air for an eternity before it dropped a fraction under the bar'.

For City, taking points in the last match at mid-table Bristol City was essential since relegation-threatened Liverpool and Bradford were playing their final fixtures after City's season concluded. Thanks to an exemplary effort by the defence, a much-needed point was all but clinched. Yet, much like the defeat at Villa, City failed to see out the match; the Robins netting the winning goal just two minutes before the final whistle. City's fate was sealed over the next two days when both Bradford

and Liverpool prevailed by 1-0 scorelines. City and the Bantams finished level on points. The tie-breaker at the time was goal average and because the latter had the advantage, 1.000 to 0.971, City were headed to the Second Division.

When a club suffers relegation, the tendency is to examine and pick apart the season's closing chapter: a final decisive moment, the final day, or – much like City in 1909 – the final weeks. When Sunderland went down in May 1977, it was a decisive moment that did them in: Coventry City managing director Jimmy Hill delayed the kick-off of his club's season-ending home match against Bristol City and then announced the score of the Black Cats' game over the Tannoy system at Highfield Road. Once the players from Coventry and Bristol City learned of Sunderland's 2-0 defeat, they knew a draw ensured both clubs' survival (the score was 2-2 at the time). During the final ten minutes, neither side made a competitive effort to win the match.

On Sheffield United's final day in May 1994, the moment that sealed their relegation fate took place 287 kilometres away from the Blades' match against Chelsea in West London. Down 2-1 at home to Wimbledon with just over 20 minutes remaining, fellow relegation-battlers Everton grabbed two late goals, including a wonder strike from distance by Barry Horne. The result meant that a Sheffield United defeat consigned them to the second tier. The Blades were tied 2-2 with hosts Chelsea and appeared to have pulled off a great escape – until a 90th-minute cross by the Blues' Dennis Wise was not cleared and found teammate Mark Stein at the far post for the match-winner. Remarkably, the Toffees had been in the bottom three for all but nine minutes that day.

But the Hill and Goodison Park dramas lacked the iconic imagery and instant lore associated with Manchester United's relegation in April 1974. With two matches remaining, United visited rivals City needing a victory and a Birmingham City defeat to stave off relegation. United's quest to evade the drop was one of two compelling pre-match stories this afternoon; the other was the return of legend Denis Law to Old Trafford following his free transfer to City ahead of the season.

After a scoreless 82 minutes, City's Francis Lee made a diagonal run from the penalty arc and played the ball to Law, who was standing on the edge of the six-yard box with his back to goal. Instinctively and in one fluid motion, the Scotsman back-heeled the ball through the legs of United keeper Alex Stepney for a shock match winner.

Law's iconic goal proved to be inconsequential. United went down to the second tier anyway on account of Birmingham's defeat of Norwich City. Three-hundred thirty-three goals for both club and country, and this was the tally for which Law was forever remembered.

For many clubs, relegation is a season-long creation born from countless instances of ineptitude, misjudgment, and poor luck. It is the result of dropping points to lower-table clubs in September and October, a dodgy refereeing decision in December, an unsuccessful transfer attempt in January, and the injury of a star player in March. Sometimes suffering the drop is a meticulously constructed thing.

Nottingham Forest's 1992-93 relegation campaign was comprised of one unfortunate event after another. Striker Teddy Sheringham desired a move to London for family reasons and was sold to Tottenham for £2.1 million. Left-back Stuart Pearce battled injuries. The Forest board announced that legendary manager Brian Clough was stepping down at season's end. Des Walker, a star for England during the 1990 World Cup, departed for Sampdoria, leaving the club to lean heavily on fellow centre-back Carl Tiler, a £1.4 million debacle of a signing from Barnsley. Wrote Clough in his autobiography, *Walking on Water*: 'If I hadn't been boozing to excess already, Carl Tiler might have driven me to it'. Clough's final acquisition for the club was Robert Rosario, who arrived from Coventry City in March 1993. He scored only once in ten Premier League outings that season.

Even the laws of the game conspired against Forest. The back-pass rule, implemented to reduce time-wasting and provoke more attacking play, was rolled out during the 1992 Summer Olympics and then introduced to the Premier League that autumn. 'We couldn't slow the game down anymore', said right-back Brian Laws. 'In the last 15 minutes of games we were knackered, and very average teams were starting to put us under pressure'.

Clough's one and only Premier League jaunt met its relegation conclusion during the penultimate match of the season, the manager's last at the City Ground. Forest were beaten by Sheffield United 2-0. After the result, a reporter cornered Clough for a post-match soundbite. 'Can I have a word from you, Brian?', he asked. 'Of course', Clough replied. 'Goodbye'.

Forest's relegation was a dream season when contrasted with Doncaster Rovers' 1997-98 disaster. The club trotted out 45 players and cycled through an astounding four managers. Kerry Dixon was sacked after just three matches, one of which was an 8-0 rout by Forest in the League Cup. Mark Weaver was at the helm in December when Rovers notched their first three points of the season: a 2-1 victory over Chester City in front of 846 supporters. Fan apathy reached a pinnacle in March when only 739 showed up at Belle Vue for a 2-0 loss to Barnet – Doncaster's lowest-ever attendance in the Football League.

Disastrous results on the pitch were mirrored by calamitous events away from it. The club entered administration in October. Wages were delayed or never meted out. And in what was perhaps a world football first, Doncaster's owner hired a man to burn down the main stand at the club's ground in the hope of forcing the club to move to a new stadium. Owner Ken Richardson was arrested and charged with conspiracy to commit arson. His forthcoming trial haunted Rovers throughout the season.

The final numbers were appalling enough to make a neutral observer cringe: a Football League-record 34 defeats, four victories, 20 points, 113 goals conceded, and a goal differential of -83. The relegation ended the club's 75-year stay in the Football League.

Years later, Adie Mike, one of Rovers' most popular players, shared a memory that captured the utter dysfunction at the club. 'There was no set place where we'd train', he said. 'Sometimes we'd train on the pitch when we could, but the majority of the time it was at a local school or a local park ... I remember training at one park, and it was full of dog stuff'.

Shit as far as the eyes could see – and everyone stepping in it. The image was the perfect metaphor for Doncaster's entire season.

Manchester City: The Genuine Soap Opera Club is about such shit. A book on relegation must be, of course. There will be no shortage of melancholy, turmoil, and defeat. But this book is also about much more: the highs that balanced the lows, the instances of calm amid the chaos, the victories that accompanied the losses, the personalities, settings, narratives, and events that comprise a football season. Relegation is more than just the very moment a club is sent down; relegation is not the enduring image from a club's season. My aim is to recount with much detail and colour the long, eventful journeys Manchester City undertook before arriving at their final-day denouements.

City have suffered the drop 11 times in their history, and this book explores five of these relegation campaigns. Five stories with their own unique sets of characters, match results, opportunities, and obstacles. Five stories with painfully similar endings. The stark differences in how each of these five teams arrived there demonstrates that there truly is no single path to relegation.

Finally, I do not consider this work to be a book about relegation. It is a history book, and on the succeeding pages you will encounter City's most well-known and successful past players, be taken pitch-side to many of the club's most calamitous (and in some cases, celebrated) matches, and become acquainted with the board-room decisions that contributed to being sent down. You will also discover how much suffering the drop – particularly more recent relegations – impacted the club's overall health as well as the collective psyche of fans.

'Sometimes you win and sometimes you learn' goes the adage. If losing does indeed provide wisdom, then City may just be the wisest of the wise. And if the act of being relegated is, indeed, akin to the trauma associated with surviving an avalanche, then you City supporters are undoubtedly the most resilient in all of England.

1937-38:

'Many of City's Supporters Were Growing into Old Men Before Their Time'.

Their early form was inconsistent and error-filled, equally unexpected and maddening for a club that closed the previous season with a 22-match unbeaten run and a coronation as champions of England. An opening loss to Wolverhampton Wanderers ended the undefeated streak and following successive clean-sheet victories, there was a 4-1 away loss to Everton – a side that finished only five points above the relegation zone the season prior – and a 3-1 defeat at Sunderland. The media had grown critical, and supporters were voicing their displeasure.

So, in September 1937, during an era before mundane post-match television interviews, mindless talk radio chatter, and the unfettered madness of social media, Manchester City captain Sam Barkas staunchly defended his teammates and their paltry early form the only way he could: He penned a letter to a local newspaper. Writing to *The Manchester Evening Chronicle*, which was considered the City paper at the time, whereas *The Manchester Evening News* was regarded as the Manchester United paper, Barkas described the bullseyes him and his teammates carried on their backs after their First Division title: 'Somebody builds a fine structure without certainty of permanence – a football team, of course – and the other fellows say: "Let's have a shot at knocking it down". Every week somebody has a shot at taking the Champions down a peg or two'. And then later in his letter: 'The opposition is keener to begin with. Teams pull out just that "little bit extra" for the satisfaction of beating the Champions'.

Responding to criticism that City's squad had grown too old for the rigours of top-tier football, the left-back wrote: 'I do not suppose there is more than a year or two in the aggregate between us and any other team in the League. If our average age in the City team were in the neighbourhood of 30, I should say we were too old to have a chance of the big honours in football. But it is not – and I do not'.

SAMUEL BARKAS, Manchester City F C — Topical Times.

Finally, Barkas reminded the media and fans that the previous season's squad – a title-winning one, mind you – also started poorly: 'Last season, we won only two matches out of the first five and we won the Championship. This season we have three wins in six matches and our chances of winning the Championship are as good as anybody else's ... I will go so far as to say that individually the team, for the most part, is playing just as well as it did last season. But the ball has not run quite so kindly for us. Every athlete knows what that means'.

Barkas' positive attitude was justified, considering how the title-winning squad dramatically turned their season around – they were as low as 16th in the table at the end of October – and played championship-level football for the final five months. Barkas did not know in the opening weeks of 1937, when he passionately supported his teammates, as any trusted, loyal captain would, an extraordinary rebound akin to the previous season's would not transpire.

On the day Barkas' letter was published in *The Evening Chronicle*, he and his teammates thumped Derby County 6-1. But then, to use Barkas' words, the ball continued to run not so kindly. Over the next 10 matches, City managed only three victories: at home against Blackpool, Birmingham City, and Sunderland. At season's end, the club became the first – and still only – top-tier champion to suffer the drop the next spring. Theirs was a two-year emotional rollercoaster ride unlike any other.

A historically large crowd was expected to descend upon the warren of terraced-home-lined streets surrounding Maine Road – so large that a notice ran in *The Manchester Guardian* the morning of the match detailing the police measures put in place to control and expedite Manchester City and Arsenal supporters. Officers were on duty at specific road junctions; one-way traffic systems were implemented on nearby streets.

Saturday, April 10, 1937: Only a month remaining in the season, and top-of-the-table Arsenal were visiting number two City, in what would have been dubbed a dream 'four-pointer' in the newspapers had the term been popular at the time. The hosts were in imperious form, having last suffered a league defeat on Christmas Day at Grimsby Town. They closed February with a 5-0 away thrashing of Derby County and a 4-1 win over Wolverhampton Wanderers at Maine Road – centre forward Fred Tilson was the star, nabbing hat-tricks in each – moving them up to third in the table with a match in hand.

City stumbled in the FA Cup on March 6 against Millwall, the Lions' 2-0 shock victory earning them the distinction of becoming the first Third Division side to make the competition's semi-finals. All newspaper and supporter speculation on whether the poor form would carry over to the league was put to rest after a 3-0 win over Huddersfield Town one week later. Then came City's most prolific goal-scoring stretch of the season. Host Liverpool were dispatched 5-0 on Good Friday with outside-left Eric Brook netting three goals. A 2-2 home draw with Bolton Wanderers was followed by a 5-1 victory vs. Liverpool during which City's corps of clinical finishers put on their most impressive display thus far: a seven-minute period in the second half that featured four goals. Five days later, they crushed Brentford 6-2, scoring three times in eight minutes.

'There was not a flaw in the City machine', enthused the writer of the February 25, 1937, match report in *The Manchester Guardian* after a 5-0 win over Derby. 'Each cog contributed its appointed part with exemplary accuracy'. And what cogs they were – equally capable of match-changing individual brilliance and unmatched group genius. Captain Sam Barkas' defensive play was so dominant this season it was said he seemed to fill the whole of the penalty area. The left-back also had a flair for spearheading attacks: galloping up field, the ball at his feet, he shouted orders to his half-backs and forwards, words of instruction and encouragement, before firing off an accurate pass, linking the defence and attack superbly. His leadership qualities made him an obvious choice for captain after Matt Busby's departure for Liverpool near the conclusion of the previous season.

Brook was similarly versatile and selfless. When injuries bedevilled City during their 5-1 victory over Liverpool, the outside-left moved to full-back and turned in an admirable performance; he did the same earlier in the season in the Manchester Derby when Barkas withdrew hurt. When he was not playing out of position (he could also fill in at goalkeeper), Brook was attacking opposing penalty areas and firing powerful left-footed shots. He finished with 20 league goals during the title-winning campaign, including a vital match-clincher against Brentford in early April.

Opposite of Brook was speedy outside-right Ernie Toseland, renowned for his thrilling runs, mazy dribbling, and pure inventiveness. Durable and ever-dependable – he only missed nineteen league games out of a possible 368 between April 1929 and March 1938 – Toseland was also highly skilled at distributing the ball to attacking teammates. Much of his best passing work came during the club's 22-match unbeaten run.

During their playing days at Barnsley, Brook and Tilson, an inside-left, struck up an electric partnership on the wing – one that continued upon the pair's arrival at City in 1928 for a joint fee of £6,000. Tilson was renowned for his lightning-quick attacks and flair for positioning. He also possessed an eye for goal (he could fill in at centre forward), scoring 15 times in the league this season, including back-to-back hat tricks against Derby and Wolves in late February.

Another essential City cog was inside-forward Alec Herd, who also finished with 15 league goals. A terrific shooter and accurate distributor, Herd was both proficient at aggressively attacking or feeding the ball to teammates. He also possessed a reputation for being deadly accurate on long-range shots and free kicks. Herd's goal in a crucial 1-1 tie with title contenders Charlton Athletic was a candidate for City's goal of the season. From the February 15, 1937, match report in *The Manchester Guardian*: 'A quick little stamp, a neat little touch, and he was past one man; within a yard he had tricked another and there, 20 yards out, for a split second he had free view of the goal; he hit the ball a sledgehammer blow and [Samuel] Bartram's groping fingers could not stop its smashing its way through just under the crossbar'.

Peruse those *Manchester Guardian* match reports from the 1936-37 season and you quickly gain a sense of how slick and intricate City's link-up play was. Nifty combos and even niftier triangles: Toseland to Herd to Brook; Brook sending Toseland through and Toseland doing the same for Herd; Brook, Herd, and Toseland passing and moving, perfectly in sync; Herd on the right wing, smoothly connecting with Tilson and Toseland; Tilson receiving a well-timed cross from Toseland. And on and on and on.

Many of their well-timed and well-placed passes and crosses ended up on the boots or head of an inside-forward City manager Wilf Wild nabbed for a club-record fee of £10,000 the previous season. Deft with both feet, terrific in the air, and a clinical finisher, Northern Ireland's Peter Doherty was enjoying one of the most memorable goal-scoring stretches in the club's history. The way he carried City on his broad shoulders during the final 12 matches of their title-winning season was nothing short of remarkable.

He could vividly remember the pressure that came with being the club's record signing, the heavy burden of expectation every time he stepped on the pitch. In his debut, at home to Preston North End, he was shut down and shut out by right-half (and future Liverpool manager) Bill Shankly. 'I must have been a grave disappointment to the thousands of Manchester City fans who had come along to see the club's expensive capture', Peter Doherty wrote in his autobiography, *Spotlight on Football*. 'During a quiet spell, I heard one of them voice his disapproval very clearly. "Ten thousand pounds?" he shouted scornfully. "You mean ten thousand cigarette cards!"'

Failure was never an option for Doherty, as throughout his career he exhibited an unflinching determination to succeed – no matter where he was playing. A quality that was evident during the second replay of the 1933 Irish Cup final, when he reinjured a severely sprained ankle, returned with a hastily executed tape job, and netted a goal in Glentoran's 3-1 victory. (He also fired the shot with his injured foot – and immediately lost consciousness from the pain.) His trademark resolve was also there prior to his stint with Glentoran, during his days with a local junior team, Station United, when he was just 'a leggy, slightly-built youngster' battling against 'older and bulkier opponents'.

And it was present growing up in Coleraine, Northern Ireland, during World War I, one of six children, running on daily errands while kicking a tennis ball, slowly wearing away the toes of his shoes.

'My life seemed to be dedicated to the game', Doherty said, 'and I was never happier than when I had a ball at my feet'.

He transferred from Glentoran to Blackpool in November 1933, barely twenty years old, his first extended trip from home leaving him buzzing and bewildered. He slowly adjusted to the club's meticulously planned training routines – a far cry from the informal sessions he grew accustomed to in Ireland – and settled into life at Bloomfield Road. His description of the dressing room and a standard training session in *Spotlight on Football* is a neat, little snapshot of a largely forgotten and forever-gone era of English football:

> *Players arrived at the ground at ten in the morning, signed the 'arrival' book, and trained until noon – perhaps lapping or sprinting under the supervision of Jimmy Stewart and [second team trainer] Jack Charles. After lunch, there was more intensive work until 4 p.m., with perhaps a round of golf or brine baths. No smoking was the rule during these training periods, and punctuality was insisted upon. The dressing-room was a model of neatness, with numbered pegs and lockers, and an orderly array of kit. You could sense an air of workmanlike efficiency about the whole place.*

When it came to the game and the men who played it, Doherty was a sharp observer and deep thinker. Natural-born talent does not guarantee great results, he believed. The essentials for achieving success were stick-to-itiveness, self-belief, and experience acquired through hard work and with much humility. 'Average ability, plus exceptional keenness and constant practice', he wrote in *Spotlight on Football*, 'has pushed more men to the top than has hereditary genius. The remedy lies mostly in our own hands; footballers can be, and generally are, 'made''.

After the conclusion of his playing career, Doherty became a strong advocate of innovation and reform. He criticised clubs for failing to evolve on the training grounds. The methods put into practice a generation ago – sprinting, lapping, minimal ball practice since it was believed players would be 'hungrier' for the football on Saturday if they touched it very little during the week – were still commonplace when he played and later managed. The changes he pushed for would not be considered radical today but certainly were by the close-minded football establishment of the 1940s: instituting drills that involved running with the ball, refining a player's decision-making skills and sense of timing with games of volleyball and basketball, constructing indoor training facilities.

But what was perhaps Doherty's most revolutionary proposal was one he made while still a player. He submitted a coaching scheme to the Irish Football Association (IFA) that called for the creation of football centres near Irish League clubs, places where boys of all ages would receive instruction from qualified coaches, partake in physical training sessions, and participate in other healthy, recreative activities. Doherty's proposal covered everything: from how construction and upkeep of the centres would be funded (by the IFA and participating clubs as well as proceeds from pre-season matches and member subscriptions) to where youngsters would land once their development was completed (clubs would have first claim on any player attached to their centres; participants could play for another club if their 'parent' club gave permission) to what would happen to these young men if they were rejected as professionals. 'By the time a boy has worked at the centres and has reached the age when he may enter professional football', Doherty proposed, 'he will have a sound basic trade to his name ... If he fails as a footballer, he must have other work to turn back to'.

What Doherty was outlining was a youth football academy – years before clubs began opening their own. And even though his primary objective was to improve the overall quality of Irish football and the national team, the IFA was not interested. The entire scheme was deemed too expensive.

For the Doherty of 1936, the pain of this rejection was several years away. This Doherty was dealing with a different variety of rejection, one that came from the terraces and from the throats of City supporters. After his less-than-stellar debut against Preston, he came up empty-handed once again – this time in a 2-2 away draw with Everton. But on March 7, Doherty finally opened his goal-scoring account for City, netting one in a 6-0 demolition of Middlesbrough at Maine Road. He tallied three more goals this season, including a brace in a 7-0 home rout of Bolton Wanderers. Four goals in nine league appearances: It was a tantalising preview of things to come.

According to local newspapers, 50,000 supporters already filled the Maine Road terraces 45 minutes before the kick-off of the April 10 Manchester City-Arsenal showdown. Fans spilled over to the running track around the pitch and set up in front of the ground's white perimeter wall. Mounted constables patrolled the touchlines.

After all the hype and hyperbole, the predictions and prognostications, the debates and discussions, the First Division's biggest match of the 1936-37 season was seconds from kicking off. Or was it?

Second placed City and top-of-the-table Arsenal were on the Maine Road pitch, primed and ready for battle, when an observant eye noticed neither squad was wearing mourning armbands for William Isiah Bassett, the West Bromwich Albion chairman who passed away two days earlier. 'It was rather as if the curtain had gone up', went the April 12 match report in *The Manchester Guardian*, 'and discovered the leading lady powdering her nose'. As the crowd of 74,918 waited patiently, City trainer Laurie Barnett tracked down the missing items and quickly brought them to the pitch. The whistle sounded, and the match was finally underway.

Arsenal wasted no time in asserting their dominance. The Gunners opened in magnificent form and kept City on the back foot for the match's first 30 minutes. Robert Davidson nearly put the visitors ahead with an acrobatic overhead kick.

Teammate Alfred Kirchen's volley almost found the back of the net as well. But the best chance was by Ray Bowden, who pounced on a miskick by City's Jack Percival three yards from his own goal and fired from close range – only for the ball to be stopped by the body of diving goalkeeper Frank Swift. *The Manchester Guardian's* match report captured the tension evident in the Maine Road terraces: 'Many of City's supporters were growing into old men before their time'.

City gradually eased their way into the match and despite being outplayed, were the first team to score. Midway between his own goal and the halfway line, the ever-resourceful Eric Brook beat a tackle by Jack Crayston and lobbed the ball toward the Arsenal penalty area. Gunner Bernard Joy botched the clearance and speedy Fred Tilson gained possession on the left wing. Tilson steered a pass to Peter Doherty, who then, running at full speed and from the narrowest of angles, poked the ball into the roof of the net. '[Frank] Boulton, the Arsenal keeper, looked amazed', wrote Doherty in a match story for a local newspaper. 'As well he might, for I was very nearly on the goal line when I shot'. And from *The Manchester Guardian's* story: 'The expression on Boulton's face was that of a man who saw a giraffe for the first time'. It was the 35th minute, and City had seized the lead.

The second goal was not as audacious and inventive as Doherty's, but it did effectively kill the match. Brook bombed forward and deftly crossed to Ernie Toseland, who drove a shot past Boulton. Desperate for a breakthrough, Arsenal juggled their forwards. But the change in tactics was all for naught as the home side defended resolutely. The 2-0 result pushed City to the top of the First Division table with 50 points (and a match in hand), one above Arsenal and Charlton Athletic.

Four matches remained on the fixture list, including three on the road, but City were playing with a confidence and a cohesion that made a first-ever top-flight title appear to be a certainty.

To state that the English football landscape on the eve of Manchester City's maiden championship was dramatically different from what current supporters are accustomed to would significantly undersell the differences. Virtually unrecognisable may be a more apt descriptor.

Let's start with wages. In Arthur Hopcraft's landmark book *The Football Man*, the author provides details on the typical earnings of a professional footballer in the 1930s. A First Division player earned no more than £12 a week, even with bonuses for winning matches and for appearances in the senior side. Hopcraft cited the case of Stan Cullis, later a successful manager with Wolverhampton Wanderers, who joined the West Midlands club in 1934 and earned a basic wage of £2 10s to £3 during his first two seasons.

There were material extras, sure – a free house for a married man, for example – and the bonus payments. Hopcraft described how the bonuses broke down in the late 1950s, a few seasons before the Football League abolished the maximum wage in 1961: £1,000 to be shared among players who made first team appearances for the First and Second Division champions, £880 to be distributed among the runners-up, £660 for the clubs in third, and on and on. Additional payments were handed out for victories in the FA and European Cups. 'Whereas smaller sums paid before the war had kept professional footballers generally up alongside the skilled workers of industry', Hopcraft wrote, 'and well ahead of the unskilled, to say nothing of the legion of unemployed – a wage like this was small beer to what could be earned on the production lines of some of the country's post-war, streamlined factories'.

The enormous disparity in pay between today's professional footballer and the average labourer did not exist in the 1930s. 'It was a time of the survival of the fittest', Cullis remembered. 'There was a feeling of great insecurity. If you didn't make the grade, you were on the dole'. The tenuous hold on your job, the humble wages, the power the clubs' bosses held over the players – added up, it meant the average footballer who partook in the 'ballet of the working class' every Saturday afternoon was not unlike the working-class man who applauded him from the terraces. One could identify and sympathise with the plight of the other. A footballer 'came from these streets where the spectators lived', Hopcraft wrote. 'The spring grass and the winter mud on the other side of the stadium wall were within walking distance from where he played, kicking at makeshift balls, perhaps just bindings of rags, against doorways for goals'.

The other vital difference between today and the football of yesteryear is the connection between club and supporter. It's a bit of an exhausted statement, one that has been asserted countless times by fans who can measure the length of their fandoms in generations. But there is little doubt a supporter's bond with their club has irrevocably changed – or been modernised, to be more precise, football fans recognising that a club's aims and objectives have been modified and that continuing to be an ardent follower means modifying your own dreams and expectations. In today's age of streaming matches, foreign television rights, and social media platforms, clubs drop 'FC' from their badges, hatch plans to launch elite super leagues, and build new stadia far away from the grim factories, smoking chimneys, and terraced houses that surrounded their former grounds. (What would L.S. Lowry – a City supporter, it must be noted – have painted had he visited ... say, Bolton Wanderers' new stadium, which is located more than four miles from the city centre?)

For the biggest clubs, the entire world is regarded as a single market. Detractors of modern-day football have argued that the more clubs think globally, the less they think parochially, that building a brand portfolio is as essential as getting tactics right on the pitch. Consider past and more recent sponsorship deals for Nottingham Forest and Stoke City. In 1989, the former was sponsored by a local ceramic tile maker, the latter a local brewery. Fifteen years later, Stoke's were an online betting company, Forest's the company run by their billionaire Kuwaiti owner.

Team loyalty was fed by family tradition or regional pride in the 1930s. Your club gave you a sense of who you were and where you were from. 'You felt a part of your club', wrote David Conn in *Richer Than God: Manchester City, Modern Football, and Growing Up*, 'that it still belonged to you, you were involved in your soul with its story, however mismanaged it had been'. Of course, tradition and pride still play a role in turning folks into fans, but there is now the all-consuming goal of attracting a wider audience, both socially and geographically. The supporter in Thailand is just as significant as the supporter in Nigeria, who is just as essential as the supporter in Moss Side. The global game has become the ultimate representation of globalisation.

On April 24, 1937, Moss Side supporters – as well as those from Hulme, Ardwick, West Gorton, and countless other sections of Manchester – descended on Maine Road by foot and bus and in tram cars and automobiles. Tingling with anticipation, buzzing with nervousness (or likely both), they crowded onto the terraces in the hopes of seeing their beloved Manchester City – more neighbourhood club than English giant in these days and one not that far removed from their humble church club roots – reach the country's football pinnacle for the first time.

After the April 10 victory over Arsenal, manager Wilf Wild and his men in sky blue notched back-to-back away wins over Sunderland (3-1) and Preston North End (5-2). Peter Doherty was in superb form in both, tallying a brace in the first match and a hat trick in the second. The four points gave City 54 for the season, three more than second-place Arsenal. Both clubs had two games remaining, which meant a victory against Sheffield Wednesday – a side battling to stay in the top flight – on this spring Saturday would clinch the First Division crown for City.

Much like they fared against Arsenal, City were sluggish from the start. Wednesday's attack was relentless, and goalkeeper Frank Swift was pressed into service early, making two marvelous saves. But this City side was renowned for its perseverance and spirit. After a sixth-round defeat in the FA Cup to third-tier Millwall the previous month, a *Manchester Guardian* write-up made this assessment: 'Manchester City, as we have often remarked in these notes, are a jack-in-the-box type of side; they take their fair share of knocks right on the chin, but nobody ever sits on their chest'. Against Wednesday, City took their knocks for 19 minutes before finally counter-punching. And it was Eric Brook who delivered the blow, scoring from a thunderous strike that he later confessed to teammates was his hardest hit shot in several years.

The goal opened the offensive floodgates for City. Five minutes after Brook's goal, Doherty zigzagged through the Owl defence with ease before pushing the ball to Fred Tilson, who first-timed it past the Wednesday keeper. Then, at the 31-minute mark, came a goal that *The Manchester Guardian* match report crowned 'the gem of the season'. Doherty certainly agreed, as he dedicated a hefty passage to it in his autobiography, *Spotlight on Football*:

> *I myself believe that I have never, in my whole career, taken part in such a perfect, goal-crowned moment. It was I who put the ball into the net, but equal credit must go to Freddie Tilson. It all started from one of Frank Swift's lofty clearances. I gained possession from just about the centre of the field, and Freddie and I went through the Wednesday defence with a rapid interchanging of passes which carried us over 40 yards, and well into the Wednesday's penalty area. It was a precision movement, a slick passing shuttle which the Sheffield defenders were powerless to intercept, and the ball finally came to rest in the corner of the net, after Freddie had made the final pass and I had whipped it through.*

In a mere 12 minutes, City scored three times, seized control of what had been a tightly contested match, and put themselves on the doorstep of a First Division title. Wednesday pulled one back in the second half before Brook placed an exclamation point on the championship-clinching win with a goal in the final minute.

At the final whistle, a joyous bedlam descended upon Maine Road. Thousands of spectators stormed the pitch in celebration. Countless attempted to chase the City players down the tunnel to celebrate with the champions before they were halted by police. Fans gathered in front of the main stand and belted out a terrace favorite from this season: 'Who Said City Couldn't Play?'

'Who said City couldn't play?
City couldn't play, City couldn't play
Who said City couldn't play?
City couldn't play football?'

More than half a century had passed since City's founding. More than half a century since members of St. Mark's Church in West Gorton started organising sporting activities (first cricket, then football) to keep bored young men out of pubs and beer houses and belligerent young men away from the 'scuttling' conflicts that pitted neighborhood-based gangs against one another. Sporting activities that became more competitive, better organised, and increasingly popular among spectators – before St. Mark's fledgling football club held their first-ever match on a tiny scrap of land that was part of the old Brooks & Doxey's Union Ironworks complex in West Gorton.

During the 50-plus years that followed this debut match, City claimed two Second Division titles, edged Bolton Wanderers in an FA Cup final, nabbed two more second-tier crowns, and nipped Portsmouth for another cup win. But never had City stood atop the summit of English football. Never had the club's supporters been able to peer down on rivals and other top-flight clubs from unseen heights. Until this Saturday afternoon in late April, shortly after half past four, in front of more than 50,000 supporters. 'We have pulled together', said captain Sam Barkas. 'We have been a happy family, and that is one of the secrets of our success'.

City were First Division champions, first-time title-holders, and first in the blue-tinged hearts of their supporters.

And now that it was over, the celebrating began. Four days after the victory over Sheffield Wednesday, Manchester City played Second Division champions Blackpool in the Victoria Hospital Cup at Bloomfield Road. After the visitors' 1-0 win, manager Wilf Wild and City directors, officials, and players attended a banquet and dance hosted by the Blackpool Corporation in the Empress Ballroom, an event that honored both clubs' titles.

Two days later, on Friday, April 30, City chairman Robert Smith led the celebrations at the Manchester Town Hall. One hundred guests attended the dinner, including the Lord Mayor, Alderman O'Toole, and the club's players and directors and their wives and guests.

Football fans, foreign or domestic, could not get enough of the English champions; the celebrations and honors continued through the spring and into the summer. After several weeks of respite, City spent a few weeks in May playing a series of friendlies in Germany. The biggest match of the tour was in front of 70,000 spectators at the Olympic Stadium in Berlin. Battling a combined German side, City were nipped 3-2. In June, Blytheswood Shipbuilding Company in Glasgow named a new vessel the Manchester City in honor of the First Division champions.

It was no surprise that the 1936-37 squad captured endless imaginations. City's entertaining attack-minded style of football produced 107 goals in league 42 matches – still a top-flight record for the club – and 117 overall. In both league and cup games, they tallied five or more goals seven times, four or more 13 times. During the season's home stretch, when City were battling with Arsenal and Charlton Athletic for the First Division crown, no Saturday afternoon stage was too big, no opponent too formidable. City nabbed victories in 11 of their final 14 matches; overall, they were unbeaten after Christmas.

The club also had a legitimate superstar in Peter Doherty, who proved to be worth every penny of his record £10,000 transfer fee. The Northern Irishman led the squad with 30 league goals (32 in all competitions), the most any City player scored in the top flight for the next 35 years, when Francis Lee netted 35 goals in all competitions in 1971-72. During the season's final two months, whenever goals were needed – whether to shift a match's momentum, put an opponent on their heels, or drive the dagger into the hearts of a title challenger – Doherty delivered. The Northern Irishman scored 15 times in City's final 12 matches, including goals in the final seven. During this period, he recorded braces against Huddersfield Town, Brentford, and Sunderland and a hat-trick versus Preston North End. As a goal scorer, Doherty was more than reliable that season – he was simply automatic.

An illustrious forward, a glittering attack, a penchant for delivering big results when big results were needed. City's future was indeed promising. Heading into the 1937-38 season, Wild and his men in sky blue were kings of the First Division and had no intention of relinquishing their crown.

Among Manchester City's managerial greats, Wilfred Wild is the forgotten man. Pep Guardiola is currently overseeing the most successful period in the club's history: an astounding 14 trophies in seven seasons. Joe Mercer nabbed six trophies of his own, including City's first European title, and forged an unforgettable partnership (for both the triumphs and the tempestuousness moments it produced) with assistant Malcom Allison. Les McDowall managed a club-record 592 matches and was behind one of the most tactically daring innovations in post-war football: the Revie Plan. Roberto Mancini ended the club's 35-year trophy drought and then one season later, was in charge for the most dramatic finish in the history of English top-flight football. Even Tony Book, who has just the 1976 League Cup victory on his CV, received greater acclaim than Wild, primarily because he made the direct jump from City player to City manager and notably logged four spells as caretaker.

Wild's anonymity is central to his narrative. Little is known about his life beyond the pitch. He was a half-back with Reddish and Heaton Chapel and manned every position except goalkeeper for Stockport County reserves – yet no record of his matches played or goals scored exists. His tenure as manager ended nearly a decade before the BBC started bringing the sport's faces and personalities into the country's sitting rooms through its highlight packages. Wild exists in only a few grainy, black-and-white photographs.

His brief obituary in *The Manchester Guardian* following his death on December 12, 1950, does not paint a portrait of the man but pencils a light sketch. There is no mention of his 158 wins – third all-time for the club, seven more than Ernest Mangnall and nine more than Mercer – but instead, admiration for Wild's 'strength of will' and 'force of character'. Just as many words are dedicated to his detached demeanor: 'In his later life, Wild tended to shield himself behind a stern – almost a glum – exterior'. Much of the praise for his trophy-winning sides is lavished on his players:

> *It was his good fortune during his secretary-managership to be instrumental in fielding a side which helped itself liberally to most of the honors which Association football can offer: a side which from the incomparable Swift right down to the irrepressible Brook had personality and character written all over it.*

In his 1969 book *Manchester City: Meredith to Mercer and the FA Cup*, longtime *Manchester Evening News* correspondent Eric Thornton provided a behind-the-scenes look at the club. Thornton's football vignettes (some captivating, some not-so-much) described the countless moments in a season that take place away from the Saturday afternoon pitch: practical jokes in the dressing room, rides on the team coach to away matches, dust-ups on the training ground, heated discussions within the club's board room. Over the course of the book's nearly 200 pages, Thornton shared just one anecdote in which Wild was the central character – but it was revealing.

The tale begins with a 3-0 away victory over Leicester City to open the 1946-47 campaign. On the journey back to Manchester, coaches, players, and media members assembled at the Midland Hotel in Derby for a celebratory post-game meal. After drinks were served, out came the soup course, and in the rush of feeding the hungry patrons, one member of the serving staff tripped on the carpet and sent steaming-hot pea soup onto Wild's lap. 'It brought him leaping into the air like a wounded animal', Thornton remembered, 'and crying out, 'What the hell's the game?''

Perhaps Wild believed that soup-tossing was a form of sport in the East Midlands. The embarrassed waiter had no answer to the manager's unusual query and to make amends, offered to wash Wild's jacket. Beyond furious now, Wild barked, 'I suppose you're after giving me pneumonia next?'

Walter Smith, one of four travelling directors on the trip, attempted to diffuse the situation with a bit of cheek, suggesting that on his next meal at the Midland Hotel, Wild could protect himself from projectile foodstuffs by wearing his overcoat and turning up the collar. 'Even if I did', the manager snarled, 'the so-and-sos would probably stuff red-hot potatoes down my neck'.

The pea-soup episode encapsulated everything Wild was as a football manager: pragmatic, stern, buttoned-up, imposing, proud. When City's goalkeeper situation descended into shambles during the 1933-34 season – regular Len Langford was sidelined with an injury and back-up James Nicholls was a sieve between the posts, allowing eight goals in an embarrassing December 23 loss to Wolverhampton Wanderers – Wild went with a rather unconventional replacement: a teenager who was not even the regular keeper for the City reserves but was starting for the A team. Wild rang the goalkeeper on Christmas Eve to inform him that he was starting the next day at Derby County. His name was Frank Swift.

What Swift later learned during his City career was that Wild was not just comfortable with defying convention and making bold moves – he made difficult ones as well. When the club found itself in the Second Division for the 1938-39 season, Wild knew that a strong start would be a major boost to their promotion hopes. But two big wins in August were followed by three consecutive losses. Swift allowed 10 goals in the defeats, and the keeper was summarily benched by Wild for the upcoming home match against Millwall. Back-up Jack Robinson fared no better – he let six go past him in another City loss – and Swift was back as the starter a week later against Blackburn Rovers.

The message to Swift and every other member of the City squad was crystal clear: performance matters more than tenure. When you make mistakes, own them – otherwise your mistakes own you. And if there was a need to relegate a starter to the bench or release him from the club outright, it was not personal.

During his 14-plus years in charge, Wild was all business, as evidenced by this memory from former player Johnny Hart:

> *I remember the chief scout Albert Kavanagh coming in at about 11. Wild asked him where he was going. Albert said, 'I was thinking about going to watch some lads on Hough End'. Wild said, 'No. I want you to go to Halifax'. Albert pointed out the time and how difficult it would be to get there on time, but it was no use. Then he said, 'I'll have no dinner', so Wild leans over. I thought he was going to get some money to give to him, but he opened up his own lunchbox, pulled out a scrappy sandwich, and handed it to Albert: 'Here have this. Now get off to Halifax'. I couldn't believe it.*

When Wild was running City, no task was too big or too small. After thieves broke into the club's offices at Maine Road, Wild purchased a German shepherd dog for security – a disciplined, well-trained beast that was allowed to roam the grounds at night. No further break-ins occurred.

Wild joined the club in 1920 to assist then manager Ernest Mangnall with administrative duties. He eventually moved up to club secretary and performed so superbly in this role that when manager Peter Hodge departed for Leicester City in 1932, Wild was selected to be his replacement. Wild accepted, and to further demonstrate his dedication to the club, chose to stay on as secretary. The dual role meant Wild was often pulled away from managerial duties to scout British cities, towns, and villages for new talent. Philip Neale's book on the 1936-37 title-winning season, *Who Said City Couldn't Play!*, details Wild's near constant pursuit of the next big City star and how regularly it pulled him away from managing. Thirteen matches into the championship campaign, Wild was present on the touchline for only three of them. The previous season he managed only a dozen.

After Hodge's nearly six years in charge, Wild's maiden 1932-33 season was expected to be one of transition. City finished 16th in the table, four points above the relegation zone. But a memorable FA Cup run demonstrated that the first-year manager possessed the vision, mindset, and determination necessary to succeed in English football. In the third round, City braved the winter mud and grinded out a dreary 1-1 draw at Gateshead. The replay could not have been more dissimilar. Led by Fred Tilson's three goals, City cruised to an easy 9-0 win. Wild's men dispatched visiting Walsall 2-0 in the fourth round and then rode an Eric Brook hat trick to a 4-2 away victory over Bolton Wanderers in the fifth.

The announced attendance of 69,920 remains Bolton's record home crowd. The scenes before the cup tie were allegedly the inspiration for L.S. Lowry's famous football painting Going to the Match.

The quarterfinals sent City to Burnley's Turf Moor, where a lone goal from Tilson was all the visitors needed to secure a spot in the semis. At Hudderfield Town's Leeds Road, Wild's side took on Derby Country, an opponent that thrashed City in the league back in October. Five months later, the result was very different. Goals by Ernie Toseland, Tilson, and captain Jimmy McMullan gave City a 3-0 lead before two late Derby goals turned a blowout into a nail-biter. But City hung on to book their first trip to Wembley since the FA Cup final loss in 1926.

Disappointingly, Wild's maiden campaign ended in similar circumstances – but not before the manager defied convention once again. On the morning of the final, Wild shocked his squad, not to mention supporters and the attending media, when he announced that Tilson (who scored a team-leading six FA Cup goals that season) was not playing. The inside-left suffered a nerve injury in his leg and although he passed a fitness test, the club doctor witnessed Tilson wince when his leg was examined.

In the final, Tilson-less City fell to legendary centre forward Dixie Dean and his Everton teammates 3-0. But the run to Wembley kicked off a golden period for Wild and his squad. City improved to fifth in 1933-34 and made amends for the previous season's loss in the final by nipping Portsmouth 2-1 to secure the FA Cup. What followed was a finish in fourth and then two years later, the club's first top-flight title.

Wild not only proved that he could adeptly oversee the dual role of manager and club secretary – he also demonstrated that from this unique position he could bring trophies back to Maine Road. As the 1937-38 season got underway, Wild was aiming for further glory.

Did memories of the previous season's unprecedented triumph ease the despair of relegation? Or did the heartbreak of suffering the drop take the sheen off their trophy-winning campaign? Which was the more enduring memory: When the title was gloriously clinched or when a season in the Second Division was assured?

These are questions only one side in the 135-year history of top-flight English football can answer.

The 1937-38 Manchester City team is an anomaly, an outlier, a misfit. Calling them champions with an asterisk is indeed unfair, but the ineptitude and mismanagement was so glaring, it is difficult not to believe the title was tainted slightly. They are the first – and still only – reigning title holders to be relegated from the First Division the next season. From lofty heights to a hellish low, they are the lone members of England's inglorious first-to-worst club. Well, technically not *the* worst. West Bromwich Albion finished below Manchester City in 22nd this season. But the point stands.

Clubs flirted with this ignominy in previous years. After their 1897-98 title-winning campaign, Sheffield United finished in 16th, just four points separating them from relegation. (They did win the FA Cup.) Everton similarly slumped to 16th after their 1914-15 title – and was a mere two points from suffering the drop – but the Toffees' abysmal performance can be forgiven since the Football League suspended play during the First World War and they, along with the rest of the top flight, were returning to legitimate competition for the first time in five years. However, there were no extenuating circumstances when Everton won the league in 1927-28 and then plummeted to 18th the next season. This marked the furthest a reigning champion had fallen. Until City's ill-fated 1937-38 season.

(In the post-war era, Ipswich Town finished as top-flight champs in 1961-62 and nosedived to 17th the next season. Leeds United fell to a similar spot after their title in 1991-92 – the final season of the old First Division. In the Premier League era, the two biggest drops were by Chelsea [10th after their 2014-15 championship] and Leicester City [12th following their improbable 2015-16 crown].)

A new season brought new rules and new regulations. The penalty arc was introduced to stop the unfair encroachment of opponents when a penalty kick was taken. Another major change in the laws was that the previous year's amendment to the goal-kick rule, which forbid the tapping of the ball back to the goalkeeper for the latter to punt from his hand, was extended to all free kicks taken within the penalty area by a defending side. Additionally, if the ball did not travel beyond the 18-yard box, the free kick was retaken.

During the close season, much ink was also dedicated to whether Manchester City could break Burnley's record of playing 30 straight league matches without a defeat, a mark the club set during their title-winning 1920-21 campaign. Sitting at 22 games unbeaten, manager Wilf Wild and his squad could shatter the Clarets' mark on October 2 when they travelled to north London to face Arsenal.

Breaking this record – and completing the much larger, more important task of navigating the First Division's 42-match grind and repeating as champions – would be formidable undertakings. Runner-up Charlton Athletic and the third placed Gunners, both powered by stingy defences, were expected to compete for the title once again. Brentford was bolstered by the signing of inside forward George Eastham from Bolton Wanderers. FA Cup winners Sunderland rounded out the contenders.

City were given a taste of how unpredictable and fiercely competitive the top flight would be when it was outrun, out-passed, and outclassed in a 3-1 loss at Wolverhampton Wanderers. Alec Herd put the visitors in front when he wove through a cluster of defenders and scored from close range. Four minutes later, Wolves' Gordon Clayton equalised and then tallied two more before the halftime whistle.

Late in the first half, City had their first experience with the penalty rule change and the newly implemented arc. Eric Brook lined up for the kick, but his attempt to slice the lead in half was unsuccessful when his left-sided shot was saved. Missed opportunities, lapses in concentration, defensive breakdowns, a lack of cohesion in attack, defeat on the road – they all afflicted City that afternoon and would be the common themes of the club's ill-fated 1937-38 season.

City followed up their first loss in eight months with clean-sheet home victories over Everton and Leicester City before dropping a pair of away matches. These setbacks prompted captain Sam Barkas to pen his previously mentioned letter to *The Manchester Evening Chronicle*, in which he defended his teammates and their early form. His missive's impact was immediate. On the day Barkas' letter was published, City broke a 1-1 deadlock against Derby County with five second-half goals. Brook and Peter Doherty were the match heroes, each player recording a brace.

One week later, during a 2-2 draw with hosts Portsmouth, City were undone by a pair of ill-timed goals: the first three minutes from halftime and the second right before the final whistle by Scot Symon, a two-sport athlete who played cricket in addition to football. Up next was Arsenal, a title contender City notably vanquished during the home stretch of their championship campaign. Without Fred Tilson and Herd, City's attack lacked a cutting edge, and the result was a 2-1 defeat. These results kicked off a two-month run of patchy form: a 4-0 embarrassment at Middlesbrough, back-to-back 2-0 victories over Birmingham City and Sunderland at Maine Road, 2-2 away draws to Preston North End and Chelsea, and a 3-1 home win over Grimsby Town.

During this stretch was a scoreless draw with Stoke City during which Barkas had a notable showdown with one of the era's all-time greats: Stanley Matthews. From the match write-up in *The Guardian*:

> *Barkas had an eventful afternoon what with one thing and another, and particularly with Matthews, who won again and again a most fascinating battle of wits, and, curiously, won it nearly always with the same gambit. He would feint to cut in for goal, instantly flick the ball the other way, catch Barkas on the wrong leg, and be steaming for the horizon by the time the back recovered.*

The match write-up also praised Barkas for his ability to spearhead City's counter-attacks and how during the match's final seconds, he led an assault on Stoke's goal that nearly produced the game winner. During an era of kick-and-rush defending, the England international was a left-back well ahead of his time. Simply clearing his lines held no appeal to him – he played the ball out from the back with complete purpose, commanding City's charges as they barrelled up the pitch and into opposition territory. In photographs, he strikes an intimidating pose: hair slicked and parted on the left, thick arms crossed, collar turned upwards, eyes cold and penetrating, face expressionless. Going shoulder to shoulder with Barkas and attempting to win the ball was undoubtedly a frightening endeavor.

A match write-up from the championship season (covering a January home victory over Manchester United) captured Barkas' on-the-pitch aptitude, pure ferociousness, and leadership qualities in two colourful sentences:

> *It is a stimulating (not to say alarming) sight to see Barkas plunge forward, take the ball on his chest, leave his immediate opponents strewn in attitudes rather suggestive of a nasty road accident, and gallop upfield, roaring orders to his half backs and forwards, the light of battle in his eyes. Normally Barkas goes about his business with the stolid dignity of a commissionaire, so that these occasional bursts are as startling as the sight of a runaway steam-roller.*

Born in South Shields, South Tyneside, Barkas was one of four boys – all of whom played league football. Perhaps it was sibling competitiveness that shaped his playing style: that unrestrained desire to hold onto the ball, lower his head, and charge down the pitch, for with siblings kicking at you to reclaim it, who knew when – or even if – you would get it back. He came to Manchester from Bradford City in April 1934 for a reported fee of £5,000. Over the next four seasons, Barkas was ever-present in the starting XI, making a total of 153 league and cup appearances. When City clinched the First Division title, the proud captain heaped all the praise on his fellow men in sky blue: 'Towards the end of the season the team more or less captained itself. I sometimes thought that I was needed only to spin the coin before the game!'

Like countless other footballers, Barkas lost prime playing years to World War II. He served with the British Army and upon his discharge, returned to City, his familiar left-back position, and the captaincy. It was in this role that Barkas led City to the 1946-47 Second Division title, a season during which the England international turned 37 and made a club-leading 37 total appearances.

By that season, only three players remained from the 1936-37 championship side: Barkas, Herd, who still showed a bit of scoring pop at age 35 (11 goals), and a veteran keeper who was nearing the end of his storied career with the club.

On a February afternoon at Bloomfield Road in Blackpool, four-year-old Margaret 'Iris' Swift watched her father play football for the first time. Iris frequently attended matches at this ground accompanied by her uncle, Alf, who was confined to a wheelchair. Alf was permitted to watch on the pitch, close to the touchline and the players' tunnel. On this day, the position allowed Alf to catch the attention of Iris' dad as he jogged onto the field prior to the match, gesture to the little girl, and ask him, 'Do you know who this is?'

'As far as I can remember', recalled Iris, 'he said, "I think so" before giving me a hug'.

Iris could recall other memories of her footballing father, such as sneaking a bus ride to Manchester and asking a neighborhood milkman to escort her to Maine Road, where her father procured her a last-minute ticket to the match. ('My grandmother was very, very angry', she said.) There were warm-hearted memories as well, unforgettable moments away from a football pitch. 'As I got older and became a young girl, then he would hold my hand, but even when you were with him you rarely had his full attention as people were always asking for autographs or to have their photograph taken with him. There was always someone there'.

Iris' father was Frank Swift, the first in what would be a series of standout goalkeepers for Manchester City. He made nearly 400 appearances for the club – City's official website lists him at 375 appearances; *Bluemoon-MCFC.co.uk*, which relies on the research of football historian Gary James, has him at both 376 and 378 appearances – was the first keeper to captain England in the 20th century, and notably fainted in the goalmouth at the final whistle when City won the FA Cup in 1934. Yet when his name is spoken of or written about, it's typically his hands that are mentioned first. The hands that made saves of all varieties: diving, full-length, scrambling, comfortable, remarkable. The hands that held his daughter Iris when she was an infant, that caught her up in a hug when she was an adolescent.

City fan Geoff Ireland shared a memory of a young Swift popping into a bakery in his native Blackpool 'for a loaf and his hands were so big you couldn't see the bread when he picked it up'. 'Frank was a giant of a man', said Preston North End legend Sir Tom Finney, 'capable of picking the ball off the ground with one hand and then, quite effortlessly, tossing it half the length of the field and beyond'. From Sir Matt Busby, City wing-half and right-half and after his retirement, Manchester United manager: 'He was the first goalkeeper I saw who threw the ball out, accurately and over great distances, to a colleague, instead of merely punting it up the pitch and giving the other team an equal chance of getting it. He would pick it up one-handed and throw it like a cricket ball'. But the most poignant (and perfect) assessment came from Swift's teammate and captain, Sam Cowan: 'Big man, big hands, big heart'.

When these celebrated hands were not punching away corner kicks or tossing the ball to a teammate to start a break, they were ... Directing local traffic? One of the most amusing anecdotes from the keeper's autobiography, *Football from the Goalmouth*, involved Swift serving as a special constable in Manchester during World War II. On his first day of traffic control duty, his hand signals confused drivers, bringing the intersection to a standstill, his knack for directing centre-halves and full-backs clearly not extending to automobiles. Remembered Swift: 'I got everything so muddled that, on the advice of a colleague, I walked away, leaving the traffic to sort itself out'.

Born on Boxing Day in 1913, Swift took to goalkeeping at an early age, recalling childhood matches in his native Blackpool during which the goalposts were players' jumpers. Playing football at school, he injured his right instep during a collision in the penalty area and from that point forward, delivered goal kicks with his left. He mastered the skill of throwing the football by mimicking the motion of water polo players and through endless practice with medicine balls that weighed as much as six pounds.

After leaving school at age 14, Swift signed for the team at Blackpool Gasworks and took a job as a coke-keeper. 'That occupied five days of my week', he wrote in *Football from the Goalmouth*. 'On the sixth day I played football, and on the seventh day talked about it'. He earned a trial at Fleetwood Town thanks to a boastful letter he wrote to the club ('After one match when I must have been impressed with myself for not having given a goal away', he confessed). After a successful trial, he joined the Lancashire side as an amateur and made his debut in September 1931 for the club's reserves. He totaled 12 appearances that season, started for the reserves in the Richardson Cup final, and showed steady progress with each passing match.

The gradual improvement in form is what certainly caught the eye of City, and when he signed with the club in October 1932, it was the kind of unsavory deal that became all too common in modern football's fast-moving, shadowy transfer market. Swift wrote in his autobiography that Jimmy Haslam, later to become chairman at Blackpool, heard City needed goalkeepers, so he escorted Swift to Maine Road for a try-out. Fleetwood did not learn of Swift's departure until he was unavailable to play for them against Barnoldswick Town. Club secretary Harold Colley penned a letter of complaint to City. The response from manager Wilf Wild came with a hint of condescension. 'I am very sorry to hear of the trouble you were put to in order to find a substitute for him', he wrote. 'The question of being reimbursed for the cost of the taxi [to shuttle the keeper who filled in for Swift to the Barnoldswick match] I will have to mention to my board. We have again selected Swift to play in our A team for Saturday and you may rest assured that if the lad makes good, your club will not be forgotten'. Wild held true to his word, but the amount City ultimately paid for the goalkeeper was a pittance: £10 10s.

Swift spent the 1932-33 season as goalkeeper for the club's A team while continuing in his role as coke-keeper. When City travelled to Wembley Stadium for the FA Cup final in April 1933, the keeper was there – even though he was not part of the first team. Swift made the trek with a work mate, stuffed into the sidecar of a motorcycle, and when the final whistle sounded and City's defeat was confirmed, the keeper turned to his friend and said half in jest, half in earnest, 'If City ever get to Wembley again, I shall be in goal'. He could not have known how prophetic his words would be.

The gift was not wrapped in glittering paper, topped with a bow, or even placed underneath a Christmas tree. But Frank Swift still insisted it was the best he ever received. What Swift was gifted was an unexpected phone call on Christmas Eve from Manchester City manager Wilf Wild, who informed the goalkeeper that he would be making his first team debut on Christmas Day, 1933 – one day shy of his 20th birthday. The change in net occurred so quickly – Wild made the decision after an embarrassing eight-goal defeat to Wolverhampton Wanderers one day prior – that Swift's name was missing from the match day programme.

Derby County were the opponents, a side known for their attacking prowess. Centre forward Jack Bowers was the star – the Englishman was the First Division's top scorer during the 1932-33 season and was in the process of repeating the feat – and he quickly spoiled Swift's debut with two goals as the Rams stormed to a 4-0 lead.

In the second half, the City goalkeeper learned that the perils of his profession involved more than just stopping a heavy leather football. To prevent a fifth Derby goal, Swift dived at the feet of Bowers and was knocked unconscious. As Mark Metcalf explained in his biography on the keeper, *Frank Swift: Manchester City and England Legend*, 'Leather football boots in the 1930s were much heavier than today, had metal studs or tacks hammered into the sole, and contained a steel front toecap. A keeper kicked – accidentally or not – by a forward's boot was much more likely to be badly injured and/or knocked out'.

A cold sponge was applied to Swift's face and after regaining consciousness, he was hauled to his feet. Since substitutions were not part of football's *Laws of the Game*, the goalkeeper continued playing.

The incident was evidence of Swift's courage and confidence and of his exemplary pitch awareness, positioning, and decision-making. 'Don't be afraid to go out to meet a forward making a lone raid', he wrote in *Football from the Goalmouth*. 'Try to make him do what you want him to do ... By staying 'at home' you are almost sure to be beaten ... By going out you've got a chance of saving'. His daring save was largely forgotten four months later when Swift fell unconscious on the pitch a second time.

Frank Swift was a compelling figure, one whose contrasts become more intriguing the closer they are examined. He took his craft hyper-seriously, sketching diagrams of goals he allowed to determine if he had wrongly positioned himself. His biography contained a chapter devoted solely to the mechanics and fundamentals of goalkeeping. 'All the top-class footballers', he wrote, 'will tell you that the most important points to remember are possession and position. The goalkeeper can help the rest of his team to both'. But for all his seriousness, Swift also understood that professional football was an endeavor to be treasured and enjoyed, and so he played with a smile and a wittiness to match, happily chatted to supporters behind the Manchester City goal, and shared jokes and moments of laughter with teammates in the dressing room. Swift recognised that the football competitor was also an entertainer. Recalled Ian Niven, City director from 1973 to 1996, who watched the keeper during his playing days: 'Frank wasn't against making a comfortable save into a diving one. There was always a bit of showmanship'.

Listed at six-foot-two, Swift was a physical presence between the posts, a well-built keeper who utilised his size to cut down opponents – and on occasion, inadvertently, a teammate – to win aerial balls in the penalty area and his height to save corner shots other keepers could not reach. Yet for all his physical gifts, the goalkeeper was similarly admired for the cerebral side to his game and praised for his ability to instruct his centre-halves and full-backs on where to position themselves on the pitch, quite often with merely a shake of his head.

During the 1933-34 season, Swift's first with the club, he was complimentary of opposing keepers, applauding their efforts after victories and defeats, even as he was conscious of his own deficiencies and anxious over his place in the starting XI. Able to recognise the talent in others, he was uncertain of his very own, a consequence of his young age.

City's FA Cup campaign that season kicked off with a solid performance from Swift and a 3-1 home win over Blackburn Rovers. (Said Swift of opposing goalkeeper Cliff Binns: 'No one could have kept a better goal'.) In the fourth round at Hull City, Swift's heroics – the highlight: a glorious one-handed save on a dangerous header in the first half – helped his squad to a 2-2 draw. City prevailed in the replay 4-1 and again needed two matches to dispatch Sheffield Wednesday in the fifth round. The keeper's clean sheet in the replay against the Owls – only the second of his young career – was followed by another at home to Stoke City (1-0) and a one-goal performance versus Aston Villa (6-1) in the semifinals. Swift helped City survive an early Villa onslaught by making two excellent saves.

FRANK SWIFT, Manchester City F.C. TOPICAL TIMES

On the eve of the FA Cup final against Portsmouth, despite enjoying an unbroken run of 27 league and cup starts between the posts, Swift's fretting over his place in the goalkeeper hierarchy recommenced. Former first-teamer Len Langford had fully recovered from a knee injury and was among the reserves accompanying the team to Wembley Stadium. However, manager Wilf Wild remained confident in the fledgling keeper he named his No. 1 four months earlier. One year after Swift declared that if City returned to the FA Cup final he would be in goal, his prediction came to pass.

In the most memorable passage from his autobiography, Swift described in rich detail the walk-up to the stadium for the April 28 final:

> *Then Wembley, the long run up from Wembley Park Station, and the hustling, hurrying, excited masses of people. The sudden bursts of cheering as some of the more observant in the throng recognised us as we slowly edged our way through the crocodile line of traffic; the sharp roar of an aeroplane zooming over ... and then the giant sweep up to the imposing stadium, surely the greatest sight in the world to a young footballer.*

Sheer wonder quickly turned to outright anxiety in the dressing room. Trainer Alec Bell was the individual who calmed Swift – and in a way that was so 1930s English football, it feels like parody: he hauled the keeper into the washroom, slapped his face, and gave him a nip of whiskey from his flask.

Nerves settled and head buzzing, Swift took to the pitch and was untested until nearly half an hour had gone: a Sep Rutherford shot across goal slithered through the keeper's outstretched right hand and into the net. The self-reflective and ever-critical Swift blamed his decision to mimic Portsmouth keeper Jock Gilfillan, who was not wearing gloves in the Wembley rain. In the dressing room at halftime, he was inconsolable.

Swift's despair continued into the match's final 20 minutes – then City caught a much-needed break. With 17 minutes to go, Pompey centre-back Jimmy Allen left the pitch with an injury. Playing with a man advantage, City equalised: Eric Brook flicked the ball through to Fred Tilson, who fired a left-footed shot past Gilfillan.

Allen returned to the pitch after a five-minute absence and was quickly caught flat-footed on City's second score. Ernie Toseland played the ball to Alec Herd, whose cross-field pass to Tilson beat the centre-back. Tilson's second goal mirrored his first: left footed, corner of the net.

One last moment of drama transpired before the match's conclusion: a long cross from Rutherford was nodded down toward the post by Freddy Worrall, and Swift, stretching every bit of his six-foot-two-inch frame, palmed the ball away. When the final whistle sounded, Swift promptly fainted in the goalmouth, the afternoon's amalgam of emotions having left him weary and dazed. Much like when he was knocked lifeless during his debut against Derby County, the goalkeeper woke to a wet sponge being dabbed on his face. Only this time, Swift regained consciousness for a City victory, one that still ranks as of the most memorable in the club's history.

In the leadup to Christmas during the 1937-38 campaign, Manchester City had taken 20 points from 19 matches. The holiday period delivered further misery: back-to-back losses to Brentford then a 4-2 home defeat to Wolverhampton Wanderers. Then came what appeared to be a season-saving run of form: a four-match unbeaten streak, including a 7-1 away hammering of Derby County. 'The outstanding performance of the day was credited to Manchester City', went the match report in *The Observer*, 'whose revival, although coming a little later than it did last season, appears to be equally striking'.

Only the revival was fleeting. City lost their next four league matches with the low point a 6-1 home defeat to Middlesbrough. The club stanched the bleeding on March 12 with a 2-2 draw at Birmingham City, but the run of dropped points left City in 21st, one spot above bottom-of-the-table Portsmouth. Predictable with their results, City were unpredictable with their blundering. Disorganised on the attack, careless with their passing, weak in possession, inept when finishing – each match brought a different concern. As with any relegation side, it was not one problem, it was a dozen.

Fred Tilson battled injuries and saw his overall goal total drop from 18 the previous season to only one. Alec Herd was also hurt; Eric Brook missed time recovering from an appendectomy. Their replacements typically played poorly. Northern Irishman Albert Barr, who partnered with Brook in a 2-2 draw at Portsmouth, was given this assessment in a *Manchester Guardian* write-up: 'Barr has the ideal build, but his football instinct has not yet been trained to respond with sufficient alacrity'. Bristol native Jack Milsom, signed from Bolton Wanderers to play centre forward, was 'cumbersome and out of touch' in a 1-1 draw at West Bromwich Albion on March 16. But the most scathing *Guardian* appraisal was reserved for 24-year-old Maurice Dunkley, who brought the mischief typically reserved for the training ground to a league match when he flaunted his skill for juggling the ball: 'Lack of stature does not automatically prevent a wing from achieving greatness, but in the hard school of experience, Dunkley and City will find it a handicap until he comes to maturity'. Manager Wilf Wild sought help through the transfer market, signing wing-half Les McDowall from Sunderland for approximately £7,000.

Three days after the draw with West Brom, 'City fought despairingly to the end but with no real strategy' in a 2-1 defeat to eventual FA Cup winners Preston North End. April opened with wins over Chelsea, highlighted by a bit of goal-keeping genius from Frank Swift, and Charlton Athletic (according to *The Guardian*, a supporter succumbed to a 'heart too weak' during the match). But the relegation chatter began anew after losses to Grimsby Town and Bolton. Locked in a remarkably tight race with half a dozen other clubs to avoid the drop, City nabbed a vital 7-1 home victory over West Brom on April 16 – vital for the two points and the boost to City's goal average, which was the first tie-breaker in English football at the time. The formula was a simple one: goals scored divided by goals allowed. During the 1937-38 season, City tallied 80 goals and allowed 77 for a goal average of 1.039.

During the season's final act, a packed fixture list proved to be City's undoing. Playing in their third match in four days (and fifth in less than two weeks), the reigning champions fell 2-1 to a Bolton side with just one regular first-team forward in the lineup. With three games remaining, City sat in 21st with 33 points. Four clubs were clustered above them with 34 each. Five days after facing the Trotters, City grinded out a scoreless away draw at Charlton. Two much-needed points were picked up a week later at home to Leeds United along with six goals to boost their all-important goal average.

On May 7, the season's final day, seven sides were in danger of being sent down. City were slated to play at Huddersfield Town. Both clubs needed a point to remain in the First Division – a draw would be the dream result. Such an outcome appeared likely when the match remained scoreless deep into the second half. Stung by Preston in the FA Cup final one week earlier, the Terriers were intent on ending the season victorious. The home side scored in the 78th minute and held on for the win.

In the dressing room at Leeds Road, the City squad waited for results to filter in from across England. Needing only one of the relegation-endangered group of Grimsby, Portsmouth, Birmingham City, and Stoke City to lose to ensure their safety, players and staff were devastated when they heard all four prevailed. The added humiliation was the final table revealing that Second-Division-bound City scored more goals than any other top-flight side.

In his autobiography, *Spotlight on Football*, Peter Doherty penned the obituary:

> *Our goal average was better than that of a dozen clubs above us. But points count first, and we had dropped far too many of these. Injuries, of course, had handicapped us severely, and luck, which had sometimes stood us in*

good stead the previous season, deserted us completely. Some apologists blamed the hard grounds, caused by long spells of fine weather, which certainly didn't suit our style of play. But whatever the cause, we were in Division II and the road back was going to be a hard one. There were no delusions on that score.

No delusions, no excuses, no complaints, and sadly, no First Division football the next season.

The 1937-38 campaign's postscript came 20 years later, when tragedy took one of the side's greatest players on a slush-covered German airstrip. Two decades after – almost to the day – watching her father trot onto the football pitch at Blackpool's Bloomfield Road, Margaret 'Iris' Swift was with her grandparents and aunt when she learned that her father has passed away, one of the victims of the Munich air disaster. 'I later found out', Iris recalled, 'he had lived for a short period of time, his strength having pulled him through a crippling series of injuries'.

On February 6, 1958, 23 people perished when a plane carrying Manchester United players and staff and print journalists crashed on the runway at the Munich-Reim airport in West Germany. Among those who lost their lives was Frank Swift, who covered United's European Cup match in Belgrade for the *News of the World*.

Eleven football writers were on board – a reflection of the prominent role newspapers played in the days before extensive television coverage and the Internet – one-quarter of the passengers and crew. Swift was one of eight who perished. Before the plane took off on its fateful flight, he nicked fellow journalist Donny Davies's jacket and was trying to playfully squeeze his 6-foot-2 frame into the garment. (Davies was a foot shorter and wrote for *The Manchester Guardian* under the penname 'An Old International'. He covered numerous matches during Manchester City's 1936-37 title-winning campaign and their 1937-38 relegation season. Much like Swift, he was an ex-footballer, having played for Port Vale and the now-defunct Northern Nomads.) Right to the very end, Swift was a warm and vivacious presence, a man who was perpetually happy in the company of others, whether footballers, writers, or otherwise.

'I was badly hit when I saw TV coverage of the return of the coffins', Iris remembered, 'as it was obvious, because of its size and length, which one my dad was in'.

The funeral was held on February 12 at St. Margaret's Church in Whalley Range, Manchester. Former teammates attended: Jackie Bray, Fred Tilson, Alec Herd, Eric Brook. Iris stood outside in the church gardens with hundreds of other mourners. After the funeral and burial, she visited the cemetery to pay her respects. But the girl who once found the courage to slip away on a bus to watch her father play at Maine Road only made it as far as the gates before turning around and heading home.

1962-63:

'When Youngy plays, City play'.

The neighbourhood kid was from Fallowfield, just off Platt Lane, and could see the Maine Road stands from the window of his childhood bedroom. He was still a teenager, a regular on the terraces on Saturday afternoons, cheering on his beloved Manchester City, when he caught the eye of scout Harry Godwin. So, when it was time to sign apprentice forms, spurning Manchester United for City was an easy decision. He was only three months past his 15th birthday. The neighbourhood kid was typically a left-winger, but in his league debut, a 2-1 away loss to Aston Villa on November 25, 1961, he played at outside-right. Later in his career, much later, he moved to inside-left, and was admired for his elegance and grace on the pitch, feared for his powerful left foot, and scored several of the most important goals in the club's history.

The fresh-faced kid joined the club as an apprentice in July 1961. He made his first appearance on April 11, 1962, in a 4-1 home loss to Birmingham City. At age 15 years, 314 days, he became the youngest player to participate in a league match for City – even though he had yet to turn professional. There is a black-and-white photograph of him taken the morning after his debut. He is tucked into breakfast, staring admiringly at his mother, who is pouring a cup of tea. He is smartly dressed, a curl of hair atop his head, apple cheeked. The fresh-faced kid started his first match in the number nine position but in time he moved to left-back – a right-footed left-back to be precise – and thanks to his strong tackling abilities and excellent passing skills was praised as one of the best players of his generation to never win a cap for England.

The ever-dependable kid was the cousin of the fresh-faced kid, and he landed at City when he signed as an amateur from Mid-Cheshire Boys. Among his early duties were scrubbing the boots of legendary goalkeeper Bert Trautmann. He debuted on November 14, 1959, in a 1-1 home draw to Chelsea – the first of a club record 680 appearances. A tenacious and unfailing defensive midfielder, he became the heart of the City sides of the 1960s, a tireless worker who was more than capable of dispossessing an opponent and then firing a 60-yard pass out wide to a teammate with his marvellous left foot. He was described as the consummate professional by both teammates and opponents.

They were Neil Young, Glyn Pardoe, and Alan Oakes. Football glory would eventually be theirs – Oakes himself earned six winners' medals, the most for a City player until the Sheikh Mansour era – but before trips to Wembley, victories in headline matches, and the hoisting of trophies, the fledgling trio was given sharp lessons on the pitfalls of First Division football. And when their fateful second season together concluded, all three club legends were handed their only relegation in City sky blue.

This is the story of the 1962-63 campaign.

Manchester City's relegation in May 1938 ended a ten-season spell in the First Division. A decade passed before they returned. During the 1938-39 season, City finished a respectable fifth but was handed an early exit in the FA Cup, losing to Sheffield United in the fourth round. City's second attempt at returning to the top tier ended three matches into the next season when the entire football league programme was halted on account of World War II and remained suspended until August 1946.

By the time of football's return, longtime manager Wilf Wild had stepped down as manager to assume the role of club secretary. In a massively popular decision, the board replaced him with Sam Cowan, the former captain and centre-back who represented City in three FA Cup finals. His relationship with the club directors was strained from the start. Cowan managed a successful physiotherapy practice in Brighton and insisted on commuting to Manchester. George Smith, who played for Cowan during the 1946-47 season, remembered the arrangements that were made to accommodate the first-year manager: 'We'd have training sessions and meetings certain evenings so that Sam could arrive and talk with us. I don't think we thought there was anything strange. We just went along with it'.

Reluctantly, the City board did as well, primarily due to the club's success on the pitch. City topped the Second Division in Cowan's first season in charge, securing promotion back to the top tier. He won a trophy and, just as essential, earned the respect of the men in the dressing room. 'Sam was a great favourite with all the players', wrote Eric Thornton in *Manchester City: Meredith to Mercer*. 'Probably because he was a players' man. He forgot the old saying, if ever he knew it, that managers have not only to build winning teams but have also to please directors'.

Not fulfilling the latter responsibility was his undoing. Thornton's book detailed several bizarre quarrels between Cowan and the club's board, including one that involved City's players consuming all the post-match sandwiches on the club's coach before the directors had a chance to eat. 'Apparently, [Chairman] Bob [Smith] had impressed on him that managers also have to attend to the needs of directors and not just players', wrote Thornton. 'Sam told me he didn't entirely agree with that opinion'.

Their patience worn thin, the club's directors considered the final straw to be Cowan's decision to stay with his family – and not his players – during an April trip to Southampton. Cowan submitted his resignation after the season's conclusion and left the club in June.

Wild served as caretaker for the first 16 matches of the 1947-48 campaign before the club directors found their man: former Everton stand-out Jock Thomson. He guided City to respectable finishes of 10th and seventh before an eight-win disaster in 1949-50 sent the club back to the Second Division – although that was a relegation Thomson never witnessed as he was dismissed before the season concluded.

Among City managers who were in charge for more than 100 matches, Thomson has the ignominy of recording the worst win rate: 30.43%. Fittingly, his next gig was taking charge of a hotel in Dundee.

(For comparison's sake, Brian Horton nearly bettered/worsened Thomson with his 30.21% win rate, but he only managed in 96 matches. Wilf Wild's win rate was 44.29% [including his 16 matches as caretaker], Joe Royle's was 43.27%, Joe Mercer's was 43.82%, Roberto Mancini's was 59.16%, and at the time of this writing, Pep Guardiola's is an astounding 72.64%.)

For chairman Bob Smith and the rest of the City directors, the task was clear: Hire a man with the managerial acumen to get the most out of full-backs and centre-backs, not bellhops and busboys.

He stood six feet tall, was the son of a Scottish minister, and during his teenage years, worked as a draughtsman in a Wearside shipyard. When Manchester City manager Wilf Wild signed him from Sunderland during the 1937-38 campaign for the tidy sum of £7,000, there was a bit of grumbling from supporters, as he made only 13 appearances in his three seasons at Roker Park.

But Les McDowall proved he was worth the sizable transfer fee. The versatile wing-half was eventually named captain and served in this role until the outbreak of World War II. During Cowan's one season in charge, he was moved to centre-back, a tactical tinkering credited with helping spur City to the 1946-47 Second Division championship. In the autumn of 1949, his playing career coming to an end, McDowall considered a return to draftsmanship when Wrexham offered him the role of player-manager. He had one unspectacular season under his belt (a finish of 20th) when City came calling.

McDowall once again quickly justified his acquisition. During the close season, he signed wing-half Roy Paul from Swansea Town for £25,000 – a deal that turned out to be a tremendous bargain for the club. The Welshman played in 42 out of a possible 43 matches in 1950-51 as City secured second place and promotion back to the First Division. Paul was a regular on the club's team sheet for the next six seasons.

McDowall was only getting started. In October 1951, already on the good side of City's directors (unlike his predecessor), he was permitted to break the club's transfer record twice: first to sign inside forward Ivor Broadis from Sunderland for £25,000 and then to secure the signature of fellow inside-forward Don Revie from Hull City for the same figure. The former was a stand-out contributor during his two-plus seasons with City, the latter became the focal point of one of the most important tactical innovations in the history of post-war English football.

The individual who inspired the Revie Plan was not its namesake or even the manager who implemented the formation at the senior club level. He was an obscure

Manchester City 1962/63 squad: a club-record 102 goals were scored.

centre forward from Manchester by the name of Johnny Williamson. During a relatively meaningless reserves match in the Central League, Williamson grew bored of his usual duties up top and began drifting down the pitch behind the other forwards to receive the ball and feed it to his teammates. 'This style of play completely upset the opposition', Don Revie wrote in *The Autobiography of Don Revie: Soccer's Happy Wanderer*. Assistant trainer Fred Tilson, star centre-forward on Manchester City's 1936-37 title-winning team, was watching, took note of the impact of Williamson's re-positioning, and mentioned it to Les McDowall.

Manchester City's reserves continued to play with a deep-lying centre forward and went unbeaten over their last 26 matches of the season.

At the international level, a deep-lying centre forward was famously used by Hungarian sides that humiliated England twice in the span of five months. On November 25, 1953, Hungary defeated England 6-3 in what later became known as the Match of the Century. The Three Lions suffered a 7-1 defeat in the return fixture on May 23, 1954, in Budapest.

At the domestic club level? Such an approach was ground-breaking. McDowell employed a deep-lying centre forward in practice sessions and much like the reserves match, the results were impressive. However, with the 1953-54 campaign winding down, McDowall did not have an opportunity to try out the formation until the following season.

The manager instructed the squad to report to training two weeks earlier than normal. Workouts were arduous; Manchester City coach Laurie Barnett pushed the players to excel in their game awareness and physical fitness. Revie remembered how one speech from McDowall resonated:

> *Les McDowall, our manager, called us together. He is not usually a man of many words, and he told us simply: 'We are going to play football this season. By football I mean football. Keep the ball down; no big kicking; no wild clearances from the defence. We want to aim for a smooth link-up from defence to attack, letting the ball do the work, and not leaving chaps to chase a long ball when a short and more accurate pass would suit the situation better'. The lads listened in some astonishment.*

The Revie Plan – as it was soon known – made its introduction to English football on August 21, 1954, during an away match against Preston North End. The results were disastrous. Only a valiant performance from goalkeeper Bert Trautmann kept the scoreline mildly respectable. 'Tom Finney and his henchmen had cut our team to ribbons', recalled Revie, 'and I spent most of the afternoon running around with my tongue hanging out trying to get the ball and never quite getting there'.

But McDowall was not to be deterred, even after losing 5-0. He had complete faith in the system and Revie, who was handling the deep-lying centre forward role. In *Manchester: The City Years*, football historian Gary James recounted how McDowall took Revie aside in training and broke down his complex positioning into the simplest of language.

> *I want you to play deep, and I want the other lads to play to you in the open spaces. It's going to need a lot of stamina on your part to chase about all over the field, but the other lads will have to do just as much running about, too. I want a man as midfield schemer who is prepared to wander about all over the field ... And I think you are the man who can do it!*

Revie was born in Middlesbrough on July 10, 1927, almost within the shadow of Ayresome Park. Like countless other footballers who turned professional during the post-war era, he grew up destitute during the Great Depression, honing his skills without proper boots, his football a tied-up bundle of rags. Revie later befriended a neighbourhood boy named George Tinsley, who owned a real football. 'We could afford one because my father had the general store', Tinsley remembered.

Years later, while playing at Leicester City, Revie befriended right-half Septimus Smith, not for his leather football but for the vast knowledge of the sport he possessed. It was said that the veteran Smith could split open an opposing defence with just one intelligent pass. He taught the teenaged Revie four essential football principles: when not in possession, get into position; never beat a man by dribbling if you can beat him more easily with a pass; it is not the man on the ball but the one running into position to take the pass who is the danger; and aim to have a man spare in a passing move. These principles were to become the foundation of City's tactical reorganisation during the 1954-55 season.

Revie [pictured left] traced his passion for formations and strategy to his days with Middlesbrough Swifts playing for manager Bill Sanderson. Strict and demanding and without a need for temperamental star footballers, Sanderson gathered his players at his home to dissect matches and analyse set-piece positioning. On a model pitch, the manager placed corks to represent players. Revie savoured these kitchen chalkboard sessions, developing a highly cerebral approach to the game that he took to City and then later to Leeds United.

Four days after the defeat to Preston, McDowall attempted the Revie Plan a second time – and on that afternoon, it worked to perfection. Led by braces from Revie and Johnny Hart, City romped to a 5-2 victory in their first home match of the season. Key to the formation's success was Revie doing precisely what he was instructed: dropping deep into City's own end and letting his teammates feed it to him in the open spaces; roaming as a provider and receiver of balls played to his feet. But it also worked magically due to the insertion of Williamson's reserve colleague, Ken Barnes.

Unable to secure a regular place in the first team since his arrival in 1950, Barnes was selected by McDowall that afternoon to play as an attacking wing-half. His link-up play with Revie was exceptional, and from that day forward, he was a fixture in the starting XI. Simply put, Barnes' stamina and passing ability proved vital to Revie's development as City's fulcrum.

'Ken had never commanded a regular first-team place', Revie remembered. 'He is essentially an attacking wing-half with a wonderful sense of distribution. In our style – although it might not have been appreciated at the time – we needed an attacking wing-half who was not only clever in possession but who had plenty of stamina and an ability to bring the ball up and use it intelligently. At first he might not appear to be a man of terrific stamina because he does not carry much flesh. He never spared himself; he was the link-up man with me'.

Barnes' support play was akin to how József Bozsik was tasked with feeding deep-lying centre forward Nándor Hidegkuti during Hungary's victories over England in the 1950s. 'Other sides had no idea how to combat it', remembered Barnes in 2004. 'They tried to get their wing-half to mark Don, but it still seemed to leave a man spare somewhere else. The plan worked like a dream. It was a true team effort'.

Enthused with this cutting-edge approach to attacking, the press dubbed City 'The Magyars of Maine Road', a reference to Hungary's influence on their style of play. But Barnes set the record straight in his biography, vehemently dismissing the connection:

> *It had fuck all to do with the Hungarians. We were playing a deep-lying centre forward in the City reserves before they turned England over at Wembley. Johnny Williamson was a smashing inside forward in the reserves and he got moved to centre forward. Johnny had an inside forward's instincts to come deep and link up with the half backs. Back then, a centre-half expected to mark a centre forward and a centre forward meant a spearhead, someone looking to get in the box at every opportunity – not someone disappearing towards the half-way line. Back then, I suppose, roles were a bit more regimented, and when Johnny dropped off, the opposing centre-half didn't know whether to stick or twist. It suited me down to the ground. I could push forward and try to exploit the confusion. Traditionally, a wing-half had been seen, first and foremost, as a defender. Now I had the chance to do what I was best at. I wasn't the best defensively, but I like to think I could create things going forward. That was my strength or at least I believed it was.*

Here is how the Revie Plan worked: when Bert Trautmann made a save, he held onto the ball. Once Revie, dashing back toward the goalkeeper, was free and clear, the German delivered him a long, accurate throw. As soon as Trautmann shaped to throw, Barnes ran into position to take a short pass from Revie. Barnes held the ball until Revie bolted past the opposing wing-half into open space and then pushed a ten or 15-yard pass down the right touchline. An unmarked Revie – now deep in the opponent's half, beyond the half-back and with the opposing left-back some distance away – either dashed forward with the ball to attack the goal or sent a pass through to a teammate. The scheme looked simple on the training room chalkboard yet was devastatingly effective on the pitch.

'People used to go on about the Revie Plan', Williamson said, 'but Don used to tell them it wasn't his – it was the team's. In particular, he used to tell them how vital Ken was. It wouldn't have worked without Ken, and Don made sure they all knew that'.

'As soon as Ken came into the team', Revie recalled, 'it was obvious where we had gone wrong at Deepdale. It was imperative to have an attacking wing-half to combine with the deep centre forward, and at the same time we had to have mobility in defence to cover up for Ken. Yes, that was the answer: mobility in defence as well as attack'.

After the 5-2 win over Sheffield United, City lost once in their next ten matches and briefly topped the table. The highlight of this stretch was a 3-2 home derby victory over Manchester United and three of their vaunted Busby Babes – Duncan Edwards, Roger Byrne and Tommy Taylor. But just when it appeared the Revie Plan would take City all the way to the First Division championship, their fluidity and rhythm were undone by foul weather and heavy pitches. The club saw out 1954 with four victories in 12 matches.

Yet throughout this run of bad results, McDowall remained committed. He was a man with a seemingly insatiable appetite for new ideas and philosophies. Besides, too much time and effort had been devoted to the Revie Plan – endless discussions and re-discussions in the dressing room, tiring training sessions at the club's reserve pitch in Urmston – for it to be abandoned. So, McDowall and his players persisted.

After a defeat at Burnley on New Year's Day, City lost only five league matches the rest of the season. The stellar run of form included another impressive derby win – this time by five goals and at Old Trafford; said United captain Allenby Chilton: 'Revie roams so much from midfield and wing to wing that putting one man on him to mark him only results in upsetting the balance of your own side' – as well as four-goal outings against Cardiff City, Bolton Wanderers, and West Bromwich Albion. City finished a respectable seventh, tied for their highest post-war finish. Meanwhile, Revie was the club's first player to be awarded the Football Writers' Association Footballer of the Year.

The story of the season was an FA Cup run that ended with City in the final for the first time since 1934. The club allowed one total goal in cup victories over Derby County, rival United, Luton Town, Birmingham City, and Sunderland. But at Wembley, the defensive stalwartness abandoned them. Newcastle United's Jackie Milburn scored 45 seconds into the match – a Wembley cup record that stood for 42 years until Chelsea's Robert Di Matteo scored 42 seconds into the 1997 FA Cup final. City were dealt another blow in the 17th minute when Jimmy Meadows caught his studs in the grass and tore his cruciate ligaments – an injury that would ultimately end his career. Since substitutes were not permitted in English football at the time, City were forced to continue with ten players. Bobby Johnstone equalised just before the break. 'I scored one of the best goals I think I ever scored in my life in that Final', Johnstone recalled years later. 'With a header, and it was from about 17 or 18 yards out, and how I got a header that far I don't know. It was just one of them things'.

Playing a man down ultimately doomed McDowall's squad. An exhausted City allowed a pair of Newcastle goals in during the second half and fell by a 3-1 scoreline. After more than eight months of dizzying success, the Revie Plan met an inglorious end.

Once a pastime, football has become another national anomaly: an institution that is less and less recognisable even as it grows in age and familiarity. Today's headline-grabbing, eight-figure signing arrives to his new ground in a luxury automobile, holds up a freshly printed kit to a crowded room of journalists and television cameras, poses for photographs with the club's manager and top executives, and then meets the club's fitness coach, nutritionist, physiotherapist, masseur, public relations specialist, and any other individual – right down to the kit manager – who will have a day-to-day impact on their career.

Now, consider Ken Barnes' introduction to Manchester City when he joined in May 1950 for £750. The 20-year-old disembarked at Piccadilly Station in Manchester, his meagre possessions packed in a pressed cardboard case. He caught a bus to the corner of Lloyd Street and Platt Lane, where he met his host family, the Claytons, and the two other young City players he was rooming with, Dave Ewing and Spencer Evans. Boarding arrangements such as this were common in English football at the time. From teammate Bobby Johnstone's biography, *Bobby Johnstone: The Passing of an Age*: 'Initially, Bobby was provided with club lodgings at the eastern end of Claremont Road in Rusholme, very near to the ground, in a terraced house the club used to board players. He was looked after by an elderly landlady, who took footballers in to supplement her income'.

The next morning, Mr. Clayton pointed Barnes in the direction of Maine Road before departing for his job at Reynolds Chains. The new signing then made the 15-minute walk to the stadium. 'The ground looked bloody massive', Barnes remembered, 'towering above everything else around. Just for a second, it took my breath away. It was certainly exciting and maybe a little bit daunting if I'm honest'.

Barnes was born on March 16, 1929, in the Small Heath area of Birmingham. His uncle, John Shepherd, played for Birmingham City in the 1920s. As a child, Barnes attended matches at St. Andrew's, his father paying for one ticket and then squeezing his son through the turnstile with him.

Between the wars, before the prevalence of automobiles, the streets were seized and occupied by England's adolescents, with football typically the most popular sport among boys. Barnes learned to play at these 'street academies', participating in after-school and weekend kick-abouts that started at two-a-side and grew to include dozens. 'We practiced all day every day – we really did – and never realised we were doing it', Barnes remembered. 'Mind you, you had to learn quickly. When you play 20-a-side and you make a mistake, you don't get another kick for half an hour'.

In 1943, the aspiring footballer took a factory job on Fordrough Lane in Bordesley Green, where he assembled switchboard components and played for the works team. 'There were no such things as age groups back then', Barnes said. 'You were 14, out in the adult world, and you had to compete on those terms. You played because you wanted to play and it was the old adage: if you were good enough, you were old enough'. Within a year, Barnes was asked to compete for Moor Green, the leading amateur side in the Midlands; he became a fixture in the first team by 16. Stints with Birmingham's Colts side and Bolton Wanderers' 'A' team led to a move to non-league Stafford Rangers, which is where City grabbed him amid fierce competition from Aston Villa, Birmingham, and Sheffield Wednesday.

Barnes progressed from playing with the 'A' team to the reserves but was still frustratingly low in the wing-half pecking order, primarily due to an ongoing row with manager Les McDowall. 'We were very different animals', Barnes said. 'I really believe that he did spend a lot of time thinking about the game, but the trouble was, he didn't bother to tell you what he was thinking'.

The long-awaited first-team debut arrived in January 1952: he wore the No. 4 shirt in a 4-2 win over Derby County at Maine Road. Barnes did not make another appearance that season or the next two. The wing-half had accepted his fate as a permanent reserve when McDowall came calling at the start of the 1954-55 campaign. The fledgling Revie Plan earned him a regular spot in the starting XI, one he would rarely relinquish over the next seven seasons.

Barnes' footballing skills and vision were evident from the beginning as well as his fanatical desire to prove that he was not just a reserve player. He was a superbly accurate passer, a tenacious ball winner (despite being a poor tackler), and a provider of occasional scoring punch (11 goals during the 1957-58 season). But what truly set him apart from his contemporaries was his innate ability to read the game, anticipate moves, and time his reactions. 'Ken was a great player with unbelievable know-how', praised teammate Paddy Fagan. 'I always believed that you could have blindfolded Ken, stuck him out on the pitch, and he would have known where to go by instinct'. 'I can still see him now', said Mike Summerbee, who watched Barnes and the Revie Plan in action during his teenage years. 'City would be defending and as soon as a cross went into their box and Ken knew Bert Trautmann was going to get it, he'd be heading the other way, waiting for Bert's clearance, and looking to get something going forward. He always wanted to be setting up attacking moves'.

This tremendous instinct for the game made him first-team manager material, but Barnes wanted no part of running sessions at the training ground, delivering dressing room orations, and barking instructions from the touchline. However, he did wish to remain involved with football during his retirement years, so when a chance encounter with City manager Joe Mercer during the summer of 1970 led to an invite to join his coaching staff, he gladly accepted. Four years later, manager Ron Saunders appointed him as chief scout, replacing the legendary Harry Godwin. 'I was happy to get out of coaching', Barnes confessed. 'They were bringing in psychologists and bleeding ballet dancers. Not my cup of tea at all'.

For 25 seasons, he stood in the terraces at countless grounds assessing footballers, whether they were budding teenagers for City's youth system or experienced professionals for the first team. The highlight of his scouting career was the 1986 FA Youth Cup-winning side that featured eight players – all signed by Barnes – who later made first-team debuts for the club. One of the eight was Ian Brightwell, who explained the indelible impact Barnes made on himself and fellow young players. 'His first question after a game was always, "Did you enjoy it?" He wanted us to be happy. You really felt he wanted you to do well, and that made you want to do well for him'.

Youth footballers knew they had truly arrived at Maine Road when they were brought into Barnes' office, which was equal parts football laboratory, support group, and social club. 'It was quite a thing to get invited in there', remembered Paul Lake, another eventual first-teamer from the 1986 side. 'Once the smoke cleared, it always seemed to be full of ex-players and to get in to join them was brilliant'. Managers and backroom staff remembered the energetic atmosphere of Barnes' office just as fondly. 'You had to earn your spurs with Ken to get in there', said long-time City scout Eric Mullender', 'but no wonder former pros and visiting managers and coaches made a beeline for the place'. 'The hub of it all was Ken's office at Maine Road', recalled Tony Book, who worked closely with Barnes during his five-year stint as City manager. 'When I think of the good times we shared in there, I really do feel it was a special period for a lot of people. The first thing that comes to mind is laughter. It was a happy place to be'.

Barnes was a lifer – every football club had one. They were the passionate, knowledgeable, trustworthy, caring individual who bled the colours, tackled any task with pure enthusiasm, was familiar with every name and face, and locked up the place at the end of the day. And much like numerous other facets of the game, the club lifer has been driven to near extinction, one more casualty of progress and modernity.

At the urging of manager Les McDowall – and with the promise of a £35 weekly pay rise – Bert Trautmann signed a new contract before the 1962-63 campaign. Centre-back Dave Ewing, who made 303 appearances for the club, departed during the close season, leaving just Trautmann, Bill Leivers, and Joe Hayes as the remaining players from the 1956 FA Cup-winning side.

After years of moderate success, the atmosphere at Maine Road was grim. The club finished 20th, 16th, 13th, and 12th in the previous four seasons. Early exits from the FA Cup and the newly formed League Cup were all too frequent. Attendance in 1961-62 regularly dipped below 20,000; only 15,971 turned out for a dreary 4-2 loss to Blackpool on December 2.

The last campaign of note was in 1957-58, one of the most extraordinary in the club's history, when City became the only side in the annals of the First Division to both score and concede 100 goals in a season. The club finished fifth in the table and were on the winning and losing ends of several astonishing score lines: a 9-2 hammering against West Bromwich Albion on September 21, a 5-4 victory over Sheffield Wednesday on December 21, and an 8-4 defeat to Leicester City on February 22.

Ever the master tactician, McDowall tinkered with City's formation once more. Eventually dubbed the Marsden Plan, it was a distant relative of his Revie Plan: striker Keith Marsden, described as a 'workmanlike but ungifted inside forward', dropped back to play alongside Dave Ewing, giving City two centre-halves. Alan Rowlands' book *Trautmann: The Biography* makes the claim that this was the first time a back four was employed in British club football. McDowall was one of the leading football thinkers of his era, a manager ever willing to experiment with new plans and systems when most of his colleagues were too fearful or too rigid to attempt the same. 'I sometimes worry that soccer is taking up too much of my thinking life', he once confessed. But the Marsden Plan was a disaster from the moment McDowall employed it on the pitch. The formation's death knell was the seven-goal loss to West Brom. Marsden was dropped from the starting XI and never played for the club again.

Trautmann said its chief fault was obvious: lack of talent. 'I could see McDowall's idea', the goalkeeper said, 'but in all honesty, we did not have players with enough skill or intellect to make it work. Beaky [Ken Barnes] and I urged the manager to buy more talented players, but he always said the board would not provide the money'.

Trautmann also admitted that his physical limitations played a role in why City's defence was so porous during the 1957-58 season.

> *I had to become more wily in dealing with forwards. It was apparent to me I could not perform with the same agility. Not just from the neck problem but because age was creeping up on me. I learned to develop my anticipation more and worked hard on my positional stance. I gave forwards less to aim at and tried to force them into errors.*

Trautmann classifying his injury as a 'neck problem' is a testament to his physical toughness as much as his humility. The German's shocking injury, possibly the most discussed in FA Cup history, was a cracked second vertebrae that he suffered when colliding with Birmingham City centre forward Peter Murphy. Seventeen minutes from time in the 1956 final, the goalkeeper dived head-first at the feet of a charging Murphy, won the ball, and took a blow to the neck from the forward's right knee. Trautmann was knocked unconscious – yet remarkably – held onto the ball. Trainer Laurie Barnett rubbed Trautmann's neck and revived him with smelling salts.

'He was reeling around the goalmouth like a drunk', remembered captain Roy Paul, who considered putting right-back Roy Little in goal. Trautmann demanded to continue playing. Sensing an advantage, Birmingham surged forward. An attack from the left ended with the German diving at the feet of Eddie Brown and snatching away possession. Astonishingly, a groggy Trautmann made a second notable intervention: a high cross floated in from the right and the keeper raced from his goal line to catch the ball and prevent it from falling to a charging Murphy. Shortly afterwards, the final whistle blew, and City were FA Cup champions for the third time.

Trautmann's post-injury performance during the match's final act was either an act of astounding bravery or sheer madness. 'Trouble was', Barnes said, 'he could remember sod all about it'.

'Unfortunately, I only have a vague idea of what happened in the closing stages', Trautmann wrote in his autobiography, *Steppes to Wembley*. 'I was completely knocked out when I dived to check a Birmingham raid and finished the match in a dazed condition. I know I owe a great debt to [centre-back] Dave Ewing and company for their wonderful covering during that spell'.

What Trautmann did recall was the stabbing pain from his teammates' congratulatory backslaps on the pitch and from supporters during the long climb to the royal box at Wembley Stadium to receive his medal. Physically supported by his roommate for away trips, Bill Leivers, the keeper shook hands with Queen Elizabeth II and when asked how he was faring, responded famously with: 'I'll be fine, ma'am. Thank you'.

Except he was not. After a night of celebrating and anaesthetising with champagne, wine, and aspirin, Trautmann and Barnett taxied to St George's Hospital in London, where X-rays failed to reveal his broken vertebrae. The next morning, Trautmann painfully dragged himself to the hotel lobby, where it became apparent to his sodden teammates that he was severely injured. 'I was feeling lousy', Paul said. 'I had a mouth like a badger's arse, but my heart sank when I saw Trauty. He looked like he'd gone 15 rounds with [Rocky] Marciano and his eyes were like owl pellets'.

Shockingly, another day passed – during which Trautmann joined his teammates for an open-top bus parade, attended a victory reception at Manchester Town Hall, and met with an osteopath in St. Ann's Square – before the goalkeeper was correctly diagnosed with a broken neck. Professor David Lloyd Griffiths, an orthopaedic surgeon at Manchester Royal Infirmary, delivered the grim news. 'Considering what you've been through these last few days', Griffiths declared, 'you should be dead'.

If Griffith was familiar with Trautmann's background – as a combat veteran, a prisoner of war, and a football trailblazer – he would have known the German goalkeeper was a true survivor.

Bert Trautmann's impact is immeasurable. A profoundly transformative figure, he exhibited bravery in the face of extreme hostility and hatred, carrying himself with tremendous dignity amid unimaginable pressure. The barriers he broke down and the legacy he left behind makes him one of the most important players in post-war English football.

With the current international nature of the Premier League, it is difficult to consider a time when the signing and debut of a foreign footballer created the controversy associated with Trautmann's. But 1949, the year the German goalkeeper inked a deal with Manchester City, was only four years removed from the end of World War II and many decades away from February 2005, when for the first time an entire squad contained no English players – Arsene Wenger and Arsenal welcomed Crystal Palace to Highbury with a lineup that featured six players from France, three from Spain, and two from the Netherlands.

On the bench were players from Brazil, Cameroon, Germany, the Ivory Coast and Switzerland. Chelsea manager Gianluca Vialli named the first non-British starting XI for a Boxing Day trip to Southampton in 1999. However, Jon Harley and Jody Morris appeared towards the end of the match, as the Blues – unlike the Gunners – were carrying English players on the bench.

Trautmann was not the first European-born foreigner to play in England (that was German Max Seeburg, who made limited appearances with Chelsea, Tottenham Hotspur, Burnley, Grimsby Town, and Reading between 1906 and 1912) but he was the first to become a domestic superstar. The German goalkeeper was virtually without flaw: Naturally athletic, physically imposing, supremely confident, he was renowned for his sharp reflexes, incomparable skill for starting attacks with his deep throws, and keen ability to read the game – opponents said he possessed an uncanny knack for knowing where the ball was going to be.

Named the 1955-56 Football Writers' Association Footballer of the Year and lauded as one of the greatest goalkeepers to ever play in England, Trautmann was similarly celebrated for his strength of character as he stoically endured countless incidents of appalling bigotry. A model of unselfish team play, the German earned the respect of his teammates and, eventually, opposing clubs and football supporters from across the country.

'People have asked me who was the best goalkeeper and only two come into the reckoning, both from Manchester City: Frank Swift and Bert Trautmann', said team-mate Don Revie. 'Swifty had a knack of winning over a crowd by his antics. Trauty had to win their approval by his daring and courage in the face of adverse criticism about his nationality. I have no doubt in my mind that Trautmann was the greatest goalkeeper I have seen'.

Bernhard Carl Trautmann was born on October 22, 1923, in Bremen, Germany, the son of Frieda and Carl, who was a veteran of the First World War and a labourer at a manufacturing plant. Even as a child he excelled in athletics, holding his own against or even bettering boys years older than him. He thrived as a footballer and was an avid player of handball and völkerball, a German game akin to dodgeball that honed his celebrated throwing abilities.

In August 1933, Trautmann joined the Deutsches Jungvolk in der Hitlerjugend, a group that prepared boys ages ten to 13 for the Hitler Youth movement. Standing before a swastika banner, his hand held high in the Nazi salute, he swore an oath of allegiance to 'the saviour of our country, Adolf Hitler'. Jungvolk members were taught basic marching drills with broom handles and organised into self-disciplined teams.

Trautmann's embrace of Nazism, which later motivated him to volunteer for and join the German Luftwaffe in March 1941, is what makes his legacy a complicated one. He revered Hitler for rebuilding his country's war-torn economy and his bravery during the war earned him five medals, including the Iron Cross (First Class) and two commendations for exemplary conduct. In one notable incident, Trautmann, then a prisoner of war, could not understand why a Jewish officer treated him poorly, even going as far as striking the officer following a moment of abuse. Tall, blonde, and blue-eyed, he even looked like the model Aryan.

All of this – the football and Nazism, the unflinching public strength and the ugly private ideology, the good and the bad – is part of who Trautmann was. To ignore this or criticise those who do not, puts the German in a neat little box in which he does not fit.

Less complicated are the legacies of the other major characters in Trautmann's narrative. Such as City director Walter Smith, the club board member most involved with new signings, who had the courage to sign the goalkeeper during a time when anti-German sentiment remained high. Johnny Hart mentioned to the Manchester City training staff that one of his local sides, St. Helens Town, had a goalkeeper with quite the reputation. City manager Jock Thompson dispatched his scouts to watch Trautmann play, and they left significantly impressed. Thompson then informed the City board of the need to sign the German.

Or Rabbi Alexander Altmann, Manchester's communal rabbi. In the lead up to Trautmann's debut with City in November 1949, there was talk of a match boycott by the British Legion as well as Jewish ex-servicemen. Letters poured into the city's newspapers with the most infamous and most quoted exclaiming, 'When I think of all those millions of Jews who were tortured and murdered, I can only marvel at Manchester City's crass stupidity'. Hundreds of supporters even threatened to return their season tickets. Altmann, whose parents were killed in the Holocaust, penned a letter to *The Manchester Evening Chronicle* strongly supporting Trautmann. Of the boycotts, he wrote, 'There is no concerted action inside the community in favour of this proposal'. 'If this footballer is a decent fellow', he continued, 'I would say there is no harm in it. Each case must be judged on its own merits'.

'That did something', wrote Trautmann in an article for *The People* on the eve of the 1956 FA Cup final. 'I was given my chance, and today many of City's Jewish supporters are among my closest acquaintances'.

City captain Eric Westwood was another important character in the Trautmann story. A sergeant in the 1st Battalion, Manchester Regiment, Westwood fought in the war, landing in Normandy three weeks after D-Day. Privately, he expressed misgivings about Trautmann's signing, but, ever the consummate professional, did not share them with teammates. His warm welcome to the German was quoted in newspapers across England: 'There's no war in this dressing room. We welcome you as any other member of the staff. Just make yourself at home and good luck'.

And then there's the English people themselves, perhaps the most meaningful characters in this oft-told football tale. Captured by a British telephone unit in March 1945, Trautmann was classified as a category 'C' prisoner due to his indoctrination from a young age – meaning he was regarded as a Nazi. He joined 3,300 other Germans at a prisoner-of-war camp at Marbury Hall near Northwich, Cheshire. Later, he was given driver duties for the officers' pool at Camp 50 in Ashton-in-Makerfield, 16 miles west of Manchester. Time and again, Trautmann and his fellow German prisoners were astonished by the kindness and generosity of their English captors.

'It was difficult for us to understand', Trautmann recalled. 'Here we were, prisoners of war in a country that was still under severe rationing, and yet every man received the same amount of rations as the civilian population. We had the same amount of meat, eggs, and other basics. Our treatment by the British was to our mind unbelievable'.

In England, the horrors of the war were still fresh, the pain of loss still raw, the destruction wrought still evident. Yet the country's response to watching a man who was once her enemy ascend the steps at her national football stadium to shake hands with her queen – ascend to the pinnacle of the national game – was one of compassion and mercy. Trautmann's story is not merely about football and FA Cup medals and man-of-the-match performances or overcoming adversity on the pitch. Trautmann's story is also about grace and forgiveness and reconciliation.

By the 1962-63 season, it was apparent the strapping, flaxen-haired German goalkeeper was breaking down physically, battered from the 500-plus matches in goal, perpetually tormented by his 'neck problem'. As frequently talked about as this malady was, there was another condition that likely afflicted Trautmann, one that was never discussed: the psychological trauma he endured during his years in combat and its lasting physical impact. Mental health, of course, was an extremely taboo topic at the time.

Trautmann was a central participant in against-all-odds stories of survival as well as a witness to moments of unspeakable horror. Early during his service, he stumbled upon an SS massacre of Jews in Ukraine. 'Of course, it touched me seeing this', he told *The London Evening Standard*. 'If I'd been a bit older, I'd probably have committed suicide'.

Later in the war, the German was found guilty of sabotaging a military vehicle and served three months at Zhitomir, Ukraine, a bleak penal complex that housed political prisoners during the Russian Revolution. His cell, which he shared with two others, was six metres long by two metres wide; his bed was three planks set against a wall complete with a foul-smelling, damp blanket.

While a member of the 35th Infantry Division, Trautmann and seven members of his division were captured by Russian soldiers. Under constant fear of execution, he spent three days in captivity before crawling to freedom under cover of darkness. Back with his division, he traded one hell for another: a torturous two weeks on a freight train being transferred to Smolensk, where morale was low, rations scarce, and the winter cold bitter.

Spring 1944 brought a second capture – this time by French troops – and a second escape. The final chapter in Trautmann's harrowing war story was his survival of the Allied bombing of the French town of Kleve. As the air raid sirens sounded, he took refuge in the cellar of a school. The building suffered a direct hit while the German was sheltering inside a broom closet. A rescue team dug him out of the rubble.

Trautmann's epilogue for the war was written in his autobiography. Taken in by the British and transported to a prisoner-of-war camp in the German town of Weeze, he wrote about his last evening before being shipped to Ostend, Belgium, and later, to English shores. Like countless others, he was a soldier too fatigued to dream of escape, too shattered to yearn for home, too defeated to rejoice in the war's impending end.

> *There were about three thousand of us sitting in groups inside a ring of tanks. A campfire was burning brightly, and as we sat there, I suppose there was not a man among us who did not wonder how long it would be before he again sat at his own fireside. Some of the prisoners began singing softly and suddenly above them all rose the fine tenor voice of one who had been a famous opera star in Germany. I cannot recall his name, but he never had a more appreciative audience than he had that night when, standing on some disused biscuit tins, he sang 'Heimat, deine Sterne', one of the loveliest songs of the Fatherland. And I for one wept unashamedly.*

Physically damaged, emotionally drained, his first-choice goalkeeper position slipping from his grasp, Bert Trautmann's typical composure disintegrated in spectacular fashion in a home match against West Ham United on September 8, 1962. Tied at 1-1 around 30 minutes in, the Hammers exposed Manchester City's weak defensive marking and scored three late first-half goals.

The match's controversial moment came in the 70th minute when West Ham's Malcolm Musgrove fired a shot into the penalty area that looked to have been cleared off the line by a City defender – only for referee Ken Stokes to award the visitors their fifth goal. An incensed Trautmann chased down Stokes and argued that the goal must be disallowed due to Musgrove being offside. Irate with himself for his poor play, and furious at being victimised by referee incompetence, the German's anger was boiling over. Stokes' reaction to his protests blew the lid off the pot: after casually dismissing the keeper with a wave of his hand, Trautmann hoofed the ball into Stokes' back with all the force of a booming free kick.

Given his marching orders for the first time in his career, the German delivered one final act of indignation: he tore off his jersey and tossed it on the ground. Alan Oakes replaced him and promptly let in a sixth and final goal.

Regrettably, Trautmann's on-the-pitch fury spread to the supporters in the Maine Road terraces. After the match, police were summoned to disperse a stone-throwing crowd of several hundred people protesting the keeper's dismissal. Trautmann was later fined £10 by the FA and handed a seven-day suspension. 'It was a stupid thing to do', he admitted. 'I know I'm guilty – there are no two ways about it'.

In an August story in *The Guardian*, City were referred to as 'The Unpredictables', a light-hearted nickname that found traction in the sports pages during the early 1960s. As the Trautmann incident proved, it was especially accurate during this 1962-63 campaign.

City began the season in dreadful form, losing 8-1 on the road to Wolverhampton Wanderers. The loss was followed by a point in the home opener against Liverpool and three successive defeats: 2-0 vs. Aston Villa, 4-1 at Liverpool, and 4-2 at Tottenham Hotspur. Two points were secured at home against Ipswich Town (half a dozen changes were made to the starting XI) before the 6-1 home drubbing to West Ham. After six matches, City had leaked 27 goals – and manager Les McDowall was officially under the spotlight. The local newspapers reported that City's directors would be paying close attention to the club's form over the coming weeks before making any personnel decisions.

'A manager has to be able to take criticism', McDowall said this season. 'You're always getting lambasted. I tend to take worries home with me, I suppose'.

A 3-2 away win in the Manchester derby on September 15 eased a bit of the pressure on the manager. At Old Trafford, City showed a resilience and a revolve that they had lacked all season. The club took a 1-0 lead in the 17th minute thanks to a Peter Dobing penalty kick. City doubled their lead six minutes later when Joe Hayes scored one of the most breathtaking goals of the early season. Positioned on the right wing, Alex Harley sent a ball inside to Dobing, who zipped a pass to Hayes. With tremendous skill and athleticism, the inside forward brought the shoulder-high ball down with his left foot and easily beat Manchester United keeper David Gaskell from close range.

Ex-City centre forward Denis Law drew United level with a pair of goals. A derby day draw looked certain until Harley produced one final moment of magic. Deep in City territory, Bobby Kennedy sent a long ball into the United half that bounced near the edge of the penalty area. Harley went shoulder-to-shoulder with Bill Foulkes as he chased down possession before deftly gaining control and firing a shot past Gaskell with the last kick of the match.

Back-to-back draws to Blackpool came next, including a goalless stalemate in the second round of the League Cup. City's performance in this fledgling tournament – as well as those in previous seasons – were indicative of a club that appeared uncertain of the new cup's status as a viable competition. During the League Cup's maiden campaign in 1960-61, City lost in the third round to Portsmouth, a club that ended the season relegated to the Third Division. The next year McDowall's men were quietly eliminated after one match.

The club's scepticism was not unique. Supporters, players, and club chairmen alike were in wait-and-see mode with regards to England's newest knockout competition.

In the spring of 1960, the winds of change were disturbing the decades-old cobwebs that had accumulated around the English football establishment. The Professional Footballers Association was calling for the abolishment of the Football League's maximum wage, which was £20 during the playing months and £17 in the summer close season. There were also impassioned criticisms that the League's system of retaining and transferring players was an unjustifiable restraint of trade and that the amounts of talent money divvied up among the players at season's end were insufficient. 'It was an extraordinary anomaly', wrote Arthur Hopcraft in *The Football Man*, 'that although the professional player had for 80 years decided the nature and manner of his sport only now did he cease to be the voiceless chattel of its management'.

Talk centred around raising admission prices to 2s 3d or 3s and reducing the number of clubs in the First and Second Divisions from 22 to 20 and in the Third from 24 to 20. But perhaps the biggest news was the introduction of a secondary domestic cup. Organised by the Football League – unlike the FA Cup, which was run by the Football Association – the competition was open to just the 92 clubs within the country's top four divisions.

The cup's chief proponents were Football League President Joe Richards and Football League Secretary Alan Hardaker. The pair aimed to capitalise on the increase in floodlit grounds, which allowed for mid-week evening fixtures, as well as give clubs a means for making up lost revenue when the top three divisions were reorganised and matches were reduced.

Critics of the League Cup – and Richards and Hardaker – asserted that its real purpose was to prevent revenue going to top continental sides that frequently travelled to England for exhibition matches. ('Real Madrid? "We don't want them here", says Hardaker', screamed the headline in the *London Evening Standard*.) 'Big friendlies take money out of the country and the new competition should keep it here', stated the League secretary. And Richards: 'This could be a godsend to the smaller clubs. It will take the place of a lot of friendlies, and I think we all agree that floodlit friendlies are being played out. We are offering the public something new – something more appealing than friendly matches'.

Richards and Hardaker likely did not expect the negative reaction the League Cup received after its introduction and throughout its first seasons of play. Criticism from supporters and clubs was particularly harsh. Many argued that the additional matches cluttered up the fixture list; others doubted that mid-week football would find a stable audience.

Six clubs refused to join the competition: Arsenal, Luton Town, Sheffield Wednesday, Tottenham Hotspur, West Bromwich Albion, and Wolverhampton Wanderers. The Hatters eventually agreed to participate, but it would be years before the other five did. 'This League Cup competition is a step backwards at a time when we must go forward', declared West Brom Chairman Wilson Keyes. 'If we are going to improve our football, we must have matches with continental opposition'.

Fleet Street was equally harsh in its denunciation. 'For the League's new competition, the Football League Cup, has failed to set this season alight', went an editorial in *The Torquay Herald Express*. 'It has not lured football's missing millions back to the terraces. It is such an untidy competition, with first-round ties, first-round replays, second-round ties, and second-round replays all crowding in together: so hard, indeed, to keep in touch'.

Manchester City fell victim to the League Cup's untidiness and its glut of replays during the autumn of 1962. After a goalless draw in the second round, City and Blackpool faced off again in a replay at Bloomfield Road on October 8. The result was the same, though this time goals were in abundance. Alex Harley scored twice, and 18-year-old Neil Young netted his 15th career goal in a match that ended 3-3.

Young, the local lad from Fallowfield who could hear the thunderous roar of the Maine Road terraces from his childhood home, was embarking on a career that would ultimately make him a club icon.

When Neil Young stepped onto the Maine Road pitch for a home match in 1994, his first time at the ground in roughly 15 years, the tumultuous reception from Manchester City supporters filled him with immense pride. Few on the terraces were likely aware of the battles Young had fought during his post-football life.

His career ended after a 13-match stint with Fourth Division Rochdale, where he played 'in front of one man and his dog and when I went across to take a throw-in, I could hear the bus rattling by on the street outside the ground'. With only a meagre £60 to his name – one week's worth of wages for playing with the Dale – Young was forced to sign on the dole, a decision that brought him much embarrassment and dismay when he queued up for his cheque every Thursday morning. 'From being a professional footballer for sixteen years', he wrote in his autobiography, *Catch a Falling Star,* 'I suddenly found myself on the scrapheap. My self-esteem took a pounding. I was Neil Young: I won medals, trophies, I went in exclusive nightclubs, I drank champagne and hung out with the rich and famous'.

Young competed during an era in which there were no advisors who specialised in addressing the unique financial challenges professional athletes face during their playing careers and retirements. Young had not saved a pound nor made a single investment. 'In those days', he wrote, 'footballers tended to pick up their wages on a Friday and that was that'. Among City players, Colin Bell opened a restaurant and Francis Lee ran a paper business he inherited from his father, but such post-football ventures were exceptions to the rule.

Young hired a van and did removals with his father-in-law, a job that ended after four years when he divorced his wife. He managed a sports shop in Urmston, a position he secured because the owners thought having an ex-professional footballer in the store would attract more shoppers. He acquired a milk round but quit after six weeks, worn down by the grind of getting up at 4 a.m. every day and trudging down dimly lit streets for poor pay. Next was a job at a local supermarket, working from eight in the evening until eight in the morning stocking shelves.

Much like his post-football existence, Young's personal life was a bitter struggle. He became estranged from his three children and had to sell his family home in Cheadle, Greater Manchester, and move in with his mother. Destitute, purposeless, and in constant pain from what would later be diagnosed as a deep vein thrombosis, Young sank into a severe depression. 'To my mind I was in the winter of my life', he wrote. 'Nobody apart from my mum wanted anything to do with me – I felt worthless sitting there in a chair in my mum's flat'.

As Young wrote in his autobiography, he saw no light at the end of the dark tunnel his life had become, no hope of escaping his feelings of defeat and despair. In his mother's kitchen one morning, he opened a box of paracetamols and swallowed its entire contents. 'I didn't want to live anymore', he said. 'I felt I had nothing to live for, nothing to offer anyone'. His mother found him unconscious and phoned the emergency services. At Stockport Infirmary, his stomach was pumped.

Young's path to mental health recovery was long and arduous. He found fulfilment and a sense of purpose through a friendship that began during a hospital stay for colitis. After his discharge, Young arranged for his new mate – a fan of Manchester United of all clubs – to attend a match at Old Trafford ('We had a police escort all the way down Sir Matt Busby Way', he remembered) and organised a fundraiser for the man's wife and family.

He found renewed confidence and a sense of pride thanks to the brotherhood of football. Wishing to relive his winning goal against Leicester City in the 1969 FA Cup final, Young contacted *Granada Television* to obtain a copy of the match but was deterred by the £350 cost. On a whim, he wrote a letter to Gary Lineker, who supported the club as a child and later played there for seven seasons. The former England striker mailed Young a tape of the match televised in colour along with a cordial note: 'I was ten when you beat my team, and I remember crying my eyes out going back home from Wembley with my dad. However, it gives me great pleasure to send you this copy of your game'.

During his 11 years with City, Young displayed a penchant for turning season-defining matches into 'his games'. 'When Youngy plays, City play', was what Peter Gardner, the City reporter, often said. In addition to his FA Cup-winning goal in 1969, he tallied a brace in a 4-3 away win against Newcastle United in the final match of the 1967-68 season, a victory that clinched City their second First Division title. He scored twice against Schalke 04 in the second leg of the semifinals of the 1969-70 European Cup Winners' Cup and nabbed the opening goal in the competition's final two weeks later. The 2-1 win over Polish club Górnik Zabrze gave City their first European trophy.

Tall and lean at six-foot-one-inch, Young was a delightfully graceful winger, celebrated for his galloping runs down the right side – and then later in his career, left side – of the pitch. Gifted, with a powerful left foot and a keen nose for goal, he was City's top scorer during their championship 1967-68 campaign. But the historic goals, the numerous trophies, and the endless praise never changed him. He was still the same old Fallowfield lad, one who forever remembered the short distance

he frequently walked from his home off Platt Lane to Maine Road, one who never forgot the long distance he had travelled from boyhood fan to City first-teamer. When he scored his winner in the 1969 FA Cup final, he immediately thought of his mother, who was attending one of his matches for the first time. 'What a thrill she must have had when that went in', Young wrote.

He was born on February 17, 1944, the second son of Alice Bradshaw. His mother enjoyed telling him that during the last few months of her pregnancy, Young habitually kicked her with his left foot. When he was older, he went from practicing in the womb to kicking a ball at Platt Fields Park in Fallowfield. For a change of scenery, Young and his mates held kickabouts on the tarmac at Platt Field's car park, the hard, unforgiving surface helping him develop his terrific close control. He also credited his growth as a footballer to his brother Chris, five years his senior, who allowed Young to play in his pick-up games, typically against much older competition. 'He'd keep an eye out for me when I'd do cheeky things on the pitch', Young wrote, 'like nutmeg one of his mates and nip round the back of him to pick up the ball'.

The son of an alcoholic and absentee father, Young idolised his older brother. He tagged along with Chris for City matches, entering the ground towards the end of the game, when the club opened the gates for free admission. 'I felt something truly special walking into Maine Road', Young said. 'I felt as if I belonged there. Every other Saturday, Chris and I would do that, go in for the last twenty minutes, and then I would run home and dream about playing for my club'.

Young competed for his school team at age five, typically at centre-back, before later joining, along with his brother, a local club named Parkfield Rovers. He was playing for Manchester Boys when he was spotted by Harry Godwin, the legendary chief scout for City. He signed amateur forms for the club in May 1959, only a few months past his 15th birthday, and joined as an apprentice in July 1960. He continued with a trade, a fall-back plan if his dream of playing football never panned out, toiling away as an electrician in Manchester while training with City and attending to the duties expected of apprentices: reporting at 9 a.m. to place training kits in the Maine Road dressing room, cleaning the first team's boots under the watchful eye of assistant coach Lawrie Barnett, ensuring the dressing room was spotless.

Despite the physically and mentally exhausting days, the meagre weekly pay, and the mind-numbing bus rides between his electrician job, the training grounds in Urmston, Maine Road, and his home, Young remained focused on his goal of making the starting XI for his beloved Blues. 'I would sit in that first team dressing room and dream about playing for City', he wrote. 'Running out to a huge roar, the fans idolising you and chanting your name. Then [inside forward] Johnny Hart would come in, wake you up from your trance, and make you clean up some more'.

The dream became reality on November 25, 1961, when Young made his debut at Aston Villa. Trautman, whose very boots he had once cleaned, presented him with a pair of his own before the match. 'Look after those boots', the German goal-keeper told him. 'Make sure you play well in them'. Young did, while his brother Chris watched from the terraces, and was voted man of the match in City's 2-1 loss. He was a regular in the starting XI for the rest of the season, scoring 11 goals in all competitions.

Young's autobiography includes numerous fascinating anecdotes of what life was like for 1960s English footballers, when the gulf between superstar and supporter was not as massive as it is today, and when long-held club traditions played a more important role in the lives of players. Young wrote of his glowing pride upon receiving his club blazer, complete with a City badge, after playing in a dozen matches with the first team. And he wrote of his walk from Moss Side to his Fallowfield home following the conclusion of a match, mingling with City fans, patiently listening to their criticisms and critiques.

After totaling 26 total appearances during his first season, Young became a permanent fixture in City's starting lineup in 1962-63, playing a total of 38 times – the first of nine consecutive seasons in which he made 30 or more appearances. (Young logged a career-high 52 appearances for City during the 1968-69 season, which would have equalled Mike Summerbee's 1965-66 club record for most appearances if not for Mike Doyle achieving 53 appearances.)

The winger was in the line-up for the October 6 home match against Leyton Orient, a club competing in the top flight for the first time in their history, but who recorded just six wins and 21 points as they finished bottom of the First Division. Harry Dowd was in for Bert Trautmann, who was serving his seven-day suspension for the September 8 meltdown against West Ham United. ('Trautmann will be occupied in judging a beauty contest in Derbyshire', went the match preview in *The Guardian*, 'where the vital statistics unquestionably will be more attractive than Manchester City's'.) The 24-year-old Dowd played admirably between the sticks, and City prevailed 2-0 for only their third clean sheet of the season.

The victory over Orient came in the middle of a nine-match stretch in which City took 11 points out of a possible 18 – not a run of form that would capture a First Division title perhaps, but good enough to ensure a finish in the top half. Alex Harley, who came over from Scottish club Third Lanark in the 1962 close season for £19,500, settled into the No. 9 spot. After a brace against Ipswich Town on September 5 and a match-winner in the Manchester derby, the intelligent and hard-working Scotsman nabbed his first hat-trick in sky blue during a 3-2 victory over Sheffield Wednesday on October 20. He recorded four more braces during the 1962-63 campaign, did all of City's scoring in their three FA Cup matches, and ended the season with 32 goals in the league and cup competitions. Not quite the footballing artist, Harley wrung everything possible out of his limited skills. This and his unfailing enthusiasm made him a massive favourite among the Moss Side faithful.

Versatile forward George Hannah was the mainspring of countless City attacks – a 'master of his feet and the ball' (praised *The Observer*); 'that inscrutable, immaculate schemer' (enthused *The Guardian*) – linking up seamlessly with fellow forward Peter

Dobing, who finished second on the team in scoring with ten goals in all competitions. Nineteen-year-old winger Dave Wagstaffe – later to become the first player to receive a red card in England when they were introduced in the 1976-77 season – utilised his speed and persistence to bully his way through determined tackles. And 26-year-old inside-forward Joe Hayes, playing in his 10th season with City, still fought and harried like he did during the club's FA Cup-seeking years of the mid-1950s.

City's weakness was not up top – the club scored a respectable 58 goals, the same total as Sheffield United in 10th – but instead, its hesitant, wayward, loosely organised (at best), completely chaotic (at worst) defence. The 102 goals conceded in the league is a club record that may never be broken. City managed only five clean sheets during their 42-match First Division campaign while letting in three goals or more in an astonishing 17 games.

Match reports from the 1962-63 season reveal manager Les McDowall's tactical desperation as he attempted to save City from the abyss of relegation. Less than a year after becoming the youngest player to participate in a league match for the club, Glyn Pardoe was shuffled from one position to another: the No. 9 in a match at Wolverhampton Wanderers, the No. 10 versus Liverpool, the No. 7 against Blackburn Rovers. Pardoe's cousin on the squad, Alan Oakes, was frequently expected to supplement his defensive midfielder duties with attacking runs into opposing territory. But this was simple tinkering compared to the newest formation devised by McDowall. Lacking the name recognition of his Cup-winning Revie Plan, or the disastrous Marsden Plan, McDowall's unimaginatively titled The Plan was a 2-5-3 formation that deployed a seven-man defensive barrier behind the ball and three forwards spaced widely apart, allowing for considerable freedom of movement.

In a 2-1 home win over Birmingham City on March 2, these spaces were deftly exploited by City's front three with Harley and Matt Gray making the scoresheet. *The Guardian's* James Holland praised McDowall for bringing such boldness and invention to the pitch but also did not hesitate to label The Plan 'a negative one', to criticise the 'flat, uninspiring play' that occurred between the two goals, and to declare that The Plan was a stark departure from City's tradition of attack-minded football. Of course, if McDowall's newest formation produced points and spared City from playing the next season in the Second Division, the unconventional approach was worth alienating journalists and supporters alike.

The Plan helped deliver consecutive 1-0 wins over Walsall and Bury in the third and fourth rounds of the FA Cup, but alarms were raised when the decisiveness and speed necessary for the formation's success were frequently lacking – weaknesses that came to the fore in a disastrous fifth-round FA Cup tie against Norwich City on March 16. Halfway through the 2-1 defeat, McDowall sent The Plan to the ash heap of football history. 'That 2-5-3 formation', wrote *The Observer's* Arthur Hopcraft, 'which was intended to provide a midfield shuttle service but which only created a back-pedaling muddle'.

During the first half, City's players – particularly Oakes, Wagstaffe, and right-back John Benson – ran themselves ragged attempting to make the formation work. Meanwhile, the three-forward approach to creating space failed time and again when Wagstaffe and Hayes were pulled into City's own half to help defend and top-scorer Harley was triple-marked, leaving Dobing isolated and ineffective. Hopcraft's eulogy for The Plan was harsh but fair: 'The monster they created got out of hand and one hopes it will now be confined to the corridors beneath the stand'.

One positive that emerged from The Plan was the glittering play and positive attitudes exhibited by two of City's brightest young prospects, Pardoe and Oakes, who were models of adaptability, industriousness, and commitment during the club's arduous second half of the season.

A right-footed left-back, Pardoe developed into an outstanding footballer – one of the best English players to never win a cap. Born in Winsford, Cheshire, on June 1, 1946, Pardoe was utilised in a variety of positions as a schoolboy, leading him to develop his trademark happy-to-play-anywhere attitude. Under McDowall and his successor, George Poyser, Pardoe was used primarily as a striker, a position at which he thrived due to his confidence levels and natural touch. For Joe Mercer and Malcolm Allison, he assumed the same role – netting a career-best 12 goals during the promotion season of 1965-66 – with the occasional stint in midfield. Back in the First Division, an injury crisis forced Pardoe, having already been deployed at half-back and centre forward this season, to move to left-back. In this position he flourished thanks to his deceptiveness quickness, strong tackling abilities, and outstanding passing skills. By the time his career wrapped up in 1976, he had played every position for City except centre-back and goalkeeper. Perhaps Pardoe's finest moment was the 1970 League Cup final when he tapped in a Colin Bell back-header in extra time to clinch a 2-1 victory. It was his only goal of the 1969-70 campaign.

Beloved by his teammates for his humble attitude, admirable work ethic, and inherent calmness both on and off the pitch, it was no surprise that Pardoe found success as a member of City's coaching staff when his playing career concluded. Tony Book, a teammate from the great City sides of the late 1960s and early 1970s and a manager who employed Pardoe as an assistant, had perhaps the best assessment of a player celebrated for his flexibility: 'He wasn't just a great full-back – he was a great full-back who played most of his career out of position'.

Unlike Pardoe, Oakes held down one position during his 17-year career with City: holding midfielder. He was a pillar of dependability during City's trophy campaigns under Mercer and Allison, making 40 appearances or more in nine consecutive seasons, including a staggering 59 in 1969-70. His record 680 appearances for the club are 74 more – nearly two seasons' worth of matches – than the man second on the list, goalkeeper Joe Corrigan. For City supporters in the post-war era, there were few more familiar sights than that of Oakes trotting onto the Maine Road pitch with his oversized shin pads, wearing the No. 6 shirt. But this impressive longevity only tells half the tale of a player who personified all that is great about City.

Born in Winsford, Cheshire, on September 7, 1942, Oakes signed amateur terms in 1958 at age 15. He turned professional one year later and became a key contributor for McDowall during the 1959-60 campaign, making 19 appearances. Content to let his more celebrated teammates grab the headlines, Oakes impacted matches in ways that did not show up on a scoresheet. As the heart of City's engine room, his ability to read a match, fantastic work rate, and dressing room leadership made him one of the top midfielders of his era. 'He was a lovely lad off the field', Bell said of Oakes, 'but he became utterly committed on the field. No footballer ever covered his shirt in more honest sweat.

Known for the great service he provided his more attack-minded teammates ('He could ping a 50-yard ball to your feet from one wing to the other', said Mike Summerbee'), Oakes did possess a scoring touch as evidenced by goals against Athletic Bilbao

in the first round of the 1969-70 Cup Winners' Cup and Middlesbrough in the League Cup semi-final six years later. He never won a cap for his country, but this was largely due to the abundance of stand-out midfielders England possessed in the 1960s.

With Oakes, Pardoe, and company eliminated from the FA Cup and League Cup – including a run to the sixth round of the new competition, their best run yet – City could focus solely on First Division survival and navigating a bloated spring fixture list. The winter of 1962-63, later dubbed the Big Freeze of 1963, was one of the coldest on record in the United Kingdom. The freezing temperatures and accumulating snow meant City played in only three matches in December and one in February. So desperate was the club for minutes on a pitch that they flew out to Dublin in mid-February to take on Burnley in a friendly.

The Big Freeze's impact on City even went beyond football. During a January blizzard in the Northwest, Dobing's father-in-law, John Peter Yates, abandoned his vehicle when snow made roads impassable. He was overcome by the elements attempting to walk home.

Five matches in March yielded just two points. Additional losses to Sheffield United and Leicester in early April meant City headed into Easter weekend in 21st with 21 points. A dozen fixtures over five weeks remained. A dozen fixtures to save themselves.

Boardrooms, managers, coaching staffs, and players will never acknowledge a specific match or even a singular moment during a relegation season in which suffering the drop seemed unavoidable, inevitable – fated even. Football supporters, on the other hand, have made a tradition of it.

During the 1962-63 campaign, City drew Wolverhampton Wanderers at home after being up 3-0 inside a half hour – the equaliser being a wind-assisted header that appeared destined to sail over the crossbar only for it to strike its underside and bounce over the goal line – but that shock result was in mid-December, when McDowall still had time to adapt and tactically innovate, when months of football on less heavy pitches remained, when talk of relegation was only whispered.

No, City supporters likely pointed to their club's relegation being foreordained after a disastrous May 2 away loss to Blackburn Rovers. Clinging to a 1-0 lead courtesy of an Alan Oakes goal, McDowall's men collapsed utterly and entirely during the match's final 15 minutes. After Rovers equalised, a long throw-in that goalkeeper Bert Trautmann half-hit with his fist saw Rovers go ahead; the third arrived when Blackburn's John Byrom poked in the ball with his knee after a botched shot attempt. A Mike Harrison header two minutes from time made the score line 4-1.

City's vulnerable defence – now reaching comical levels with their persistent wayward covering, poor tackling, and general disorganisation – leaked six goals in back-to-back defeats to Blackpool and Aston Villa before turning in one of their finest performances of the season: a 1-0 win over a free-scoring Tottenham Hotspur side that had amassed 111 league goals and finished runners-up to champions Everton.

The stage was set for possibly the biggest Manchester Derby of the post-war era. City entered the May 15 showdown with two matches left to play and 30 points. Manchester United were in an equally precarious position: three matches remaining and 31 points. Win and you possibly consigned a bitter rival to the Second Division; lose and you likely spent a miserable close season knowing your relegation ticket was punched by an all-too-familiar enemy. The stakes could not have been higher.

More than 52,000 packed into Maine Road for the Wednesday night match, far and away City's largest draw of the season. 'It was quite like old times', wrote Eric Todd in his match report for *The Guardian*, 'very old times – to see such a big crowd at Moss Side'. The home side quickly gave the raucous gathering something to cheer about. In the eighth minute, Peter Dobing sent a superb pass into the penalty area. Alex Harley ran onto the ball and turned it past United goalkeeper David Gaskell to hand City a 1-0 lead.

Bolstered by their clean sheet versus Spurs, City's defence was again in outstanding form. Bill Leivers, Matt Gray, and Cliff Sear turned in stand-out matches as the hosts shut down United's famous attacking talent of Bobby Charlton, Denis Law, and David Herd. City appeared to have doubled their lead later in the first half, but Harley was ruled offside.

The home side continued to have most of the play after the break. Harley again nearly put City ahead by two goals – this time getting his head on a Neil Young free kick – but his attempt was saved brilliantly by Gaskell. Meanwhile, United's attack remained unresponsive with most of their shots coming from long range. Victory and a season-saving two points appeared certain.

But then, nothing is ever a certainty in football, or in relegation circumstances, involving City. With six minutes to play, Dave Wagstaffe inexplicably sent a 30-yard pass back to keeper Harry Dowd. Law closed in, and during the ensuring tussle for possession, Dowd wrapped his arms around the United centre-forward's legs. The referee awarded the away side a penalty and Albert Quixall converted. United escaped with a 1-1 draw.

Three days later at West Ham United, City's defence had one final opportunity to display to the English football world their sheer ineptitude. Geoff Hurst netted two goals during the opening eight minutes. Alan Sealey made it three on the half-hour mark before Ron Boyce, during one last moment of total farce for City, scored from a cross while sitting on the ground. When the final whistle sounded, McDowall's men had lost 6-1, ensuring the club's relegation. 'There was worth mentioning', Albert

Barham wrote in his match report for *The Guardian*, 'only one shot from Gray, one from [Alan] Oakes, one from Harley, and two by [Joe] Hayes in retaliation. Sad facts to record. A sad match to watch and a sad day for City'.

On May 29, *The Guardian* reported that McDowall's resignation was accepted by the club's board. As a footballer and a manager, the Scotsman spent 25 years with the club. 'As a player and as man', Todd wrote, 'Mr. McDowall was in the above average class'.

For the manager and Colin Barlow, Trautmann, and Hayes, a golden era was concluding. For Glyn Pardoe, Oakes, and Young, a new one was dawning.

1982-83:

'They've Done It! Raddy Antic! Four Minutes from the End!'

If Manchester City had earned a reputation for comical incompetence, it must be noted, in the interest of fairness, that the club also demonstrated a remarkable resiliency. In 1902, 1909, and 1950, City suffered the drop but immediately secured a spot back in the First Division the next season. Relegation in 1926 was followed by a finish of third and then a Second Division title the next year. Yes, City were proving to be frustratingly adept at being sent down, but their flair for earning promotion was just as impressive.

So, when the club was relegated at the end of the 1962-63 campaign, there was legitimate reason to believe another swift return would occur, a hope shared by supporters and players alike. Players such as local lad Roy Cheetham.

Though a midfielder of impressive skill, Cheetham, who holds the distinction of being the club's first-ever substitute, coming on for Mike Summerbee in a 4-2 away victory over Wolverhampton Wanderers in August 1965, never appeared in more than 30 matches in a season during his 12-year tenure with City. Born and bred in Eccles, Greater Manchester, he debuted on March 8, 1958, wearing the No. 4 shirt in a 2-1 win at Luton Town. Cheetham was in the starting XI on one more occasion that spring, which meant he was only a partial witness to City's historic – and utterly mad – 100 goals scored/100 goals conceded season. He was a regular (29 appearances) during the 1963-64 campaign, the club's first in the second tier in over a decade, and an occasional contributor (12 appearances) in 1964-65, when City slumped to 11th – the (then) second-worst finish in club history, only topped by a showing of 13th in 1893-94, when City were known as Ardwick AFC.

By that point, City – both competitively and structurally – were closer to a Third Division club than a First, a sad truth even the players accepted. In James Lawton's *Forever Boys: The Days of Citizens and Heroes*, Cheetham spoke candidly about the rot that had set. 'It was a dead club', the midfielder said. 'There were loads of talented players, like Glyn [Pardoe] here, but they weren't being used, or nurtured, as they should have been'.

The 1964-65 season's nadir occurred after a 2-1 loss to Swindon Town on January 16, when the supporters' simmering frustration with the club's performances exploded into fury. Demonstrations took place outside Maine Road's Main Stand; bricks were hurled at windows. Wing-half/full-back Bobby Kennedy recalled how a chance Saturday afternoon produced moments of sheer absurdity and unbridled aggression:

> *Our groundsman Stan Gibson would put grass seed out at the start of spring to try and get the pitch going for the next season. Growing a pitch then was much more difficult ... Stan had sown seeds prior to the Swindon game, and during the match the atmosphere was very poor. Pigeons came on to the turf and sat eating the seed in the middle of the pitch. We had to play around them ... After the game there was a bit of a demonstration and one or two bricks were thrown – that was a major disturbance at the time because general disorder was not known – and our chairman, little Albert Alexander, went out to face the fans. It was a brave thing to do, but Albert was an absolute Blue and felt the pain of the day himself.*

Alexander's desperate pleas for calm quelled the mob of supporters. City's squad was not so easily mollified. Kennedy described a post-match dressing room in which players expressed their exasperation with the club's direction. Several even stated a desire to leave.

City went winless in the league in January and then picked up only one victory in February and March. A humiliating 4-0 loss to Bolton Wanderers on April 10 was followed by a 2-0 defeat to Crystal Palace on Good Friday – the final two games of manager George Poyser's career. He resigned over the Easter weekend. Former City star Fred Tilson took over for the last four matches. When the curtain fell on the 1964-65 season, it was in front of only 8,409 fans at Maine Road. Goals by Jimmy Murray and Neil Young gave the hosts a meaningless 2-1 win.

Alexander and the City board had one objective during the close season: hire a manager with the experience, acumen, and mettle necessary to lead the team out of the Second Division. Rumours abounded that the board were pursuing former club star and successful Northern Ireland manager Peter Doherty as well as Bill Shankly, who led Liverpool to the First Division title the previous season. Instead, City ended up with a former FWA Footballer of the Year winner who stepped away from the sport because of an illness and a former West Ham United centre-back who spent the previous year managing Plymouth Argyle in the second tier. Both of their personal records left supporters sceptical. Even the most optimistic fans would not have predicted the coming decade of domestic and European success.

Swedish car manufacturers Saab became Manchester City's first shirt sponsor in 1982

'Football could live without Joe Mercer', City's new manager declared soon after his arrival, 'but I found out that I couldn't live without football'.

A star for Everton then, later, Arsenal, Mercer spent a year away from the game after a stint at Aston Villa. In five-and-a-half seasons, he delivered a Second Division title and a League Cup trophy, but after a minor stroke, Villa fired him in July 1964. 'I sweated blood for the club for more than five years', Mercer told one of his former players. 'I battled back to full health, but my reward for all the effort I had put in was the sack. I should have taken note of how directors can pull the rug from under managers'.

Announced as City boss on July 13, 1965, Mercer immediately unveiled his coaching staff, adding Dave Ewing and Johnny Hart, members of City's back-to-back FA Cup finalist teams in 1955 and 1956. He also retained the services of chief scout Harry Godwin, who had discovered current club players like Neil Young. 'I've heard you're good at nicking one or two youngsters', the new manager said to the chief scout. 'Nick a few for me, will you?'

But the signing that had the biggest, most enduring impact on the club was the appointment of a player considered a pioneer of modern football techniques while at West Ham United, a 37-year-old whose playing career was cut short when he had a lung removed after a bout with tuberculosis, a manager who had been, much like Mercer, out of work.

Malcolm Allison, a tall, broad-shouldered, handsome man whose passion for debating and discussing tactics, developing unique training sessions, and working with footballers one-on-one was matched by his love of quaffing champagne and chasing glamorous women. He was defined by his excesses: intense to a fault about the game he worshipped, troubled off the pitch by his addiction to the extravagant.

Allison possessed an unduly high opinion of his own importance yet was overly preoccupied with what others thought of him, a contradiction brilliantly articulated in Colin Schindler's *The Worst of Friends: Malcolm Allison, Joe Mercer, and Manchester City:* 'They saw the pictures in the paper of the cigars and the clothes and the birds, and they thought that was all he was: Big Mal, a bigmouth, a big-time Charlie. They'd be amazed to learn that he spent as many nights in the living room of his flat in Sale reading books as he did drinking champagne in the Cabaret Club. They might be flattered that he spent the time he did thinking about them, perhaps even by how much he resented the power they held over him'.

Whether in the boot room at Maine Road or the backroom of a London night club, Allison believed that to truly reject the ordinary one must embrace the extraordinary. 'Look big, think big, be big' was his mantra. His most bizarre tactical scheme was dubbed 'the wheel' and it involved keeping possession of the ball within a circle comprised of all ten outfield players. The wheel was to gradually advance downfield towards the opponent's goal until a player fired a shot. In his domestic life, Allison was just as impulsive and unpredictable. His son David shared a story in which his father went out for fish and chips on a Friday evening and did not return until the following week.

Allison's enthusiasm for managing was evident during his playing days at Upton Park. In *The Essential History of West Ham United*, authors Kirk Blows and Tony Hogg describe Allison as a 'visionary who in six short years would revolutionise the club's archaic regime and transform training, coaching techniques, and tactics to secure promotion'.

Perhaps worried that effusive praise for Allison would tarnish his legacy, West Ham United manager Ted Fenton downplayed his role. 'Apart from being a good player', he stated, 'Malcolm was fantastically keen and enthusiastic. He was a fitness fanatic and inspired the others. Because of that I made him club skipper'.

He was also alleged to have influenced the Hammers' radical decision to ditch traditional heavy, buttoned shirts for tight-fitting, short-sleeved V-necks and continental-style short-shorts and to have introduced heavy weight-lifting to the squad's training sessions.

In terms of tactics and formations, Allison was heavily influenced by the adaptive and inventive Hungarian sides of the 1950s. The tiny Eastern European nation modernised the well-established W-M formation by eliminating one of its key positions: the classic English No. 9, that strong, fearless, one-dimensional centre forward situated at the top of the W – that 'brainless bull at the gate' in the words of renowned football writer Brian Glanville. Under manager Gusztáv Sebes, the Hungarian national team transformed the W-M into an M-M with the centre forward dropping deep to become an auxiliary midfielder and the two wingers pushing up to create a fluid front four. The formation worked to devastating effect in famous wins over England in November 1953 and May 1954.

Allison took note and was determined to bring his own unique ideas and inspirations to West Ham. For example, he emphasised the need to play out from the back rather than embrace the popular route-one philosophy utilised by managers like Stan Cullis, who guided Wolverhampton Wanderers to three First Division titles in the 1950s. Why hoof it up field, possibly resulting in a 50/50 ball and a loss of possession, when one can scan the pitch, find an unmarked teammate, and play a smart pass – Allison's preferred approach during his days as a centre-back for the Hammers.

Hiring the perpetually enthusiastic and ever-magnetic Allison as coach allowed Mercer to step back and assume a reduced role with the club, one that focused on, as Gary James wrote in *Joe Mercer: Football With a Smile*, delivering 'warmth, wisdom, and wisecracks' to his players. Mercer's decision to absolve himself from much of the day-to-day management of City was also the result of much self-reflecting after his stroke. Villa players witnessed the not-so-endearing aspects of his volatile personality – the anger, the edginess, the high-handedness. Many speculated he was privately resentful that his playing career did not end on his terms, but instead, abruptly concluded when he broke his leg during a collision with teammate Joe Wade during a match against Liverpool on April 10, 1954. 'I was near the halfway line, about 20 yards from the trainers' box', Mercer remembered, 'and I dummied to head a cross, then stepped back and was going to trap it and turn it aside, but Joe Wade came in thinking I wasn't going for it, and we collided. "It's broken, Bill," I said to [Liverpool's] Billy Liddell'.

What pushed Mercer to constrain his worst impulses at City's training ground or in the Maine Road dressing room was the suspicion that his stroke was caused by the extraordinary stress associated with managing a professional football club.

With his staff in place, training began in earnest with all eyes on the August 21 season opener at Middlesbrough. What Mercer and Allison quickly discovered was that City's 21-man squad was inexperienced, directionless, and sorely lacking in confidence. 'Our first job was to get team spirit', Mercer explained. 'We did not seek it by pandering nor by rules. We worked and we talked. We told the players: "You might think this is a new broom come to sweep clean. It is! And it is going to get harder and tougher". And it did'.

The Mercer-Allison partnership's first move was a controversial one: selling Derek Kevan to Crystal Palace. The inside forward led the club in scoring the previous two seasons, including an impressive 36 goals in all competitions during the 1963-64 campaign, but Allison was displeased with his lack of effort in training sessions. However, excluding wartime leagues and cups, since statistics from these competitions are not considered official, Kevan's 36 goals is the third-highest total for a City player, only bettered by Tommy Johnson's 38 during the 1928-29 season and Erling Haaland's off-the-scale 2022-23 campaign total. Supporters were unhappy with the move – and even more so when City lost a pre-season friendly to Scottish First Division side Dundee.

After another lacklustre outing – this time a 1-1 draw with Walsall – Mercer and Allison finally brought in reinforcements. The first signing was £25,000 Scotsman Ralph Brand, an established striker from Rangers. The second was winger/forward Mike Summerbee for £35,000 from Swindon Town. Mercer was a guest player at Aldershot during the Second World War and was a teammate of Summerbee's father. Brand's signing was an example of poor scouting and decision making; Summerbee's was a lesson in how to evaluate talent smartly and spend wisely.

City started the 1965-66 campaign with four draws in their first seven matches, including a pair of six-goal thrillers at Coventry City and Norwich City. The club first tasted defeat on September 18, away to Cardiff City, then grabbed three away points out of four in consecutive matches against promotion contenders Southampton and Huddersfield Town. City then saw out October with successive clean sheets against Preston North End, Norwich, and Charlton Athletic, sending them to the top of the Second Division table. Mercer and Allison also dipped into the transfer market, signing Everton centre-back George Heslop, who made 198 total appearances over the next seven seasons, and Aston Villa wing-half Stan Horne, the club's first Black player.

Throughout November and December, City maintained a top-three position in the league. Glyn Pardoe, Summerbee, and Neil Young shouldered the goal-scoring load. Pardoe recorded three braces; Young nabbed a brace of his own against Preston and a hat trick in a 5-0 drubbing of Leyton Orient on December 11.

The New Year's Day match was the most anticipated one in years at Maine Road: a showdown with top-of-the-table Huddersfield. The biggest crowd of the season (47,171) – as well as the most spectators for a league match since May 1963 – cheered goals by Johnny Crossan and Mike Doyle. The 2-0 victory positioned City as one of the top challengers for the Second Division's two promotion spots. Go-for-broke Allison felt the squad was one more influential signing away from becoming the clear favourites; the more pragmatic Mercer fretted about the club's finances and the monetary impact of such a signing.

In the end, Allison won, and the coach attended a Bury match to scout a 20-year-old midfielder considered to be one of the hottest prospects in the Second Division. Sitting among rival managers and scouts, many from top-flight clubs, Allison devised a clever ruse – and one that allowed him to be his big-talking, bombastic self: he loudly disparaged the midfielder throughout the match, focusing on his mistakes and miscues, when he was actually impressed with his performance. Having thrown the competition off the scent, Allison signed the Bury playmaker – with Mercer okaying the funds – for approximately £42,000. On March 19, the young midfielder, Colin Bell, made his debut at Derby County and scored the match's only goal. Like Summerbee, Bell became a Maine Road legend, a star among stars, the centre-piece of sides that delivered the club the greatest five-season stretch in their history.

After elimination from the FA Cup in the sixth round, then a defeat at home to Bury one week later, City closed the season with a flourish, picking up 11 points out of a possible 14. Bell scored again, this time during a 1-0 win at Rotherham United that secured promotion. 'Afterwards I tasted champagne for the first time', the midfielder remembered years later. 'I couldn't believe how quickly I was part of a winning side'. Nine days later, City clinched their sixth Second Division title with a 3-2 victory at Charlton.

The 'dead club' in desperate need of leadership and guidance was now blessed with not one but two coaches of true quality and commitment. In Mercer, City had a quiet, supportive leader, a genuine calming influence, a manager who had a remarkable way of making his squad feel deeply appreciated. 'Mercer seemed like a man who had embraced, for all its buffetings, the warmest aspects of life', wrote James Lawton in *Forever Boys: The Days of Citizens and Heroes*, his book on the trophy-winning sides of the late 1960s and early 1970s. 'He knew its cruelty but also he knew, and was clearly rediscovering, its joys'.

While Allison was brash and excitable, prone to episodes of unchecked arrogance, such as when he sauntered in front of Old Trafford's Stretford End before a Manchester Derby match and gestured to indicate City would brush aside United like they were pieces of dirt, Mercer was the soft-spoken, respected club diplomat, satisfied with having the trophies do the talking. He was also willing to step aside and let Allison indulge his wildly creative side. 'I had all these new training methods and fancy ideas', Allison recalled, 'and I used to say to him, "Look, Joe, I fancy doing this", and he'd say, "Yeah, okay Malcolm, you do it". He always gave me great encouragement. He was like a father figure to me'.

Allison was comparable to Mercer in that he similarly developed a genuine admiration for his players and an unwavering dedication to helping them reach their full potentials. 'Malcolm goads you, persuades you, using any means possible to simply get it through that you are the best player in the Football League', Young explained. 'His psychology is simple – it gives you confidence'. Mercer even admitted that his coach's connection with the squad ran deeper and stronger than his.

Allison's impact also went beyond throwing an arm around a player's shoulders and sharing words of honest encouragement. He was maniacally obsessed with finding every possible edge to make his footballers perform better on match days. 'Malcolm was into eating the right things ... drinking the right drinks', remembered Bell. Allison organised training sessions during which players donned gas masks to assist them in breathing more economically or strapped on boxes that measured their pulses, heart rates, and recovery times. He understood that the daily grind of training left even the most resolute players mentally exhausted. Monday running was the only certainty; other training days brought an air of mystery. 'After I had been there a couple of weeks', remembered Tony Book, 'he took us up into the mountains for a couple of days, just to break the routine. We lived in log cabins and did a bit of fishing'. Bell had similar memories: 'We might come in one day and find a bus there, and Malcolm would say we were going to Blackpool for a sauna and lunch'.

Having been involved with their partnership since its earliest stages, Bell understood what made this unique, versatile collaboration work:

> *If there was one person Malcolm would listen to it was Joe. He let him do his own thing most of the time but if Malcolm went off the straight and narrow, Joe was there. It was a father-son combination. Joe would get up and say a few words before matches then Malcolm would take over on the tactics and formation.*

Having secured promotion in May 1966, the duo bolstered their squad in the summer with the £17,000 signing of Book, who Allison developed a strong affection for while coaching him overseas at Toronto City as well as at Bath City and Plymouth. 'He was one of the best and quickest defenders I had seen in any class of football', the manager gushed. During the 1966-67 season, Book was tasked with playing sweeper – a position that was still a rarity in England; during a televised match, *BBC* commentator Kenneth Wolstenholme referred to Book as a 'sweeper-up'. This adjustment, along with having the remainder of City's defence man-mark opposing players, pulled City out of the bottom three and propelled them to the sixth round of the FA Cup. The club finished 15th, 21 points behind champions Manchester United.

City avoided the first-year relegation fate that befalls many promoted clubs. But Mercer and Allison were not content with mere survival. Like the dazzling and daring style of play they embraced – 'We always went out to win and never contemplated holding out for a point', said Alan Oakes – the two managers went for broke with their transfer dealings and their tactics. Challenging Manchester United, Liverpool, and Leeds United for the coming season's First Division crown was the number one goal.

The 1967-68 campaign opened with City taking one out of a possible six points. The club followed that up with a six-match winning streak, four of which were clean sheets. Allison fine-tuned City's formation once again, shifting Young inside from his position on the wing and, identifying Doyle's talents in the air and Pardoe's versatility, moved the pair into midfield and defence respectively. The reshuffling meant Mercer and Allison were now tasked with reorganising City's attack-minded players to find the most effective combination. Tony Coleman, in only his second season with the club, impressed with a goal against Southampton and another in a notable 2-0 victory over Nottingham Forest on September 2. Local lad Paul Hince scored in consecutive wins over Newcastle United and Coventry. Despite these encouraging performances, Mercer and Allison believed the squad required additional offensive firepower.

Fortuitously for City, a 23-year-old forward who was averaging one goal every two matches was embroiled in a contract dispute only 15 miles away. On September 29, Francis Lee of Bolton Wanderers informed his manager, Bill Ridding, that his time with the club had come to an end. Ten days later, Mercer signed him for a club record transfer fee of £60,000. City's fabled five-forward line was now complete.

A passage from David Tossell's *Big Mal: The High Life and Hard Times of Malcolm Allison, Football Legend* captured how this otherworldly quintet perpetually moved, swapped roles, exploited space, and, more than anything else, scored goals that accounted for 75 of City's 105 goals that season:

> *Summerbee and Lee would interchange positions effortlessly; Coleman could be mercurial on the left; Young's free role and powerful left foot provided any number of crucial goals; Bell's renowned dynamic running, while providing the pulse of the team, often served to overshadow his own qualities as a thoughtful, skilful player.*

Successfully executing this energetic and fluid style of football was only possible with proper coverage from the five outfield players positioned behind the forwards – a group that was as flexible and efficient as the teammates they supported: Doyle slipped into an attacking wing-half role or dropped deep to provide cover; Oakes, a midfielder by trade, filled in at centre-back alongside Heslop; full-backs Pardoe and Book bombed forward or provided defensive support depending on the circumstances.

Summerbee made the bold claim that the Dutch learned their tactical system of Total Football – which emphasised all-around skill, versatility, and creativity so that players could perform both attacking and defensive duties – from Mercer and Allison. He also boasted that City would often shoot at goal after only three passes. But it was Summerbee's summation of the club's aesthetic that was most accurate: 'We played simple football at a fast pace'.

'It was all one-touch or two-touch', Bell remembered. 'That's what we worked on in training and it all became natural, with people moving players all over the field. The beauty of that side was that we didn't have any individuals. Nobody would keep the ball and do his own thing to be eye-catching. Nobody was better than anyone else'.

And no club was better than City. From December 1967 to April 1970, Mercer and Allison's squad produced a string of unforgettable victories – in the league, in domestic cup competitions, and in Europe. A club that delivered only sporadic triumphs during its nine decades of existence made up for lost time with five trophies in under two years. Older City supporters can recite the victories, like a litany, the names of the clubs vanquished like beads on a rosary.

A 4-1 win over Tottenham Hotspur on a snow-covered Maine Road pitch – 'The Ballet on Ice', as the match came to be known, forever a part of club folklore on account of Book's dressing room advice to his teammates to remove the top layer of leather from their boot studs for a better grip. The 4-3 triumph at Newcastle, clinched by a Lee goal in the 63rd minute, which secured the First Division title, leaving City's 20,000 travelling supporters with tears in their eyes and lumps in their throats. The 1-0 victory over Leicester City at Wembley Stadium in the FA Cup final, a spectacle of eye-catching fashion – Mercer's men took to the pitch in their now iconic red-and-black kit – as much as it was a showcase of stalwart defending. The 2-1 nailbiter in the League Cup final, City outhustling and outlasting West Bromwich Albion in extra time largely due to Allison's pre-season workouts, which gave his squad the speed of sprinters and the stamina of milers. And finally, the European Cup Winners' Cup final: on a drenched, blustery Wednesday night in a largely empty Prater Stadium in Vienna, City nipped Górnik Zabrze of Poland, 2-1, to become the first English club to win domestic and European trophies in the same season.

Even today, after 15 years of overwhelming success under Sheikh Mansour, these sides still rank among the greatest in club history. Mercer and Allison were blessed with a group of gifted, coachable players who exceeded expectations – Book: a defender of the highest quality and greatly valued for his leadership; Pardoe: a versatile mainstay in the starting XI, adored for his modesty and work rate; Doyle: a confident, formidable battler on the pitch, possessor of a caustic tongue off it; Tommy Booth: a model of consistency, a player who embodied the spirit of the team; Oakes: a midfielder of unwavering commitment and the heart of City's engine room; Young: a graceful striker with exceptional timing and technique; Lee: a forward of astonishing football ability, possessor of a self-assuredness that never wavered; Summerbee: a sublime blend of pace and power, said by Book to be 'as strong as an ox – you knew he could run past people all day long'; and Bell: the superstar who had everything – power, skill, control – the player supporters dubbed 'King' for both his extraordinary talents and professional integrity.

Lauded for their individual excellence, it was their team unity and common purpose that made this exemplary three-season run possible. 'As Alan [Oakes] always says', Pardoe declared, 'it was as though we were more like a family than a football team'.

So, when disfunction unavoidably took hold and stagnation regrettably set in, the players were largely blameless. The decline was a natural outcome of placing two single-minded, strong-willed individuals in charge of a football club. 'Together Joe Mercer and Malcolm Allison forged a friendship and a working relationship that was the most rewarding of their professional lives', wrote Colin Schindler in *The Worst of Friends: Malcolm Allison, Joe Mercer, and Manchester City*, a fictionalised account of the pair's partnership. 'Individually neither of them achieved anything as great as their joint accomplishments. The best of friends became the worst of friends. It was the tragedy of success'.

And the seeds for their acrimonious breakup were planted before the pair ever managed a match together.

Perhaps Joe Mercer felt it was a throwaway remark, one of a thousand that occur during the countless exchanges between managers, coaches, and players during the long road trips to away matches, a comment he expected to be immediately forgotten once the whistle sounded. Or maybe Mercer was truly being forthright, the newly paired mentor and his protégé sharing a true moment of candour. Whatever the case may be, on the afternoon of August 21, 1965, during the bus trip to Middlebrough's Ayresome Park, their first match in charge only hours away, Mercer turned to Malcolm Allison and said, 'Son, if you do well with City there will be great rewards. Two years will do me'.

Mercer, likely intoxicated by the club's continuing success, certainly reluctant to end his lifelong relationship with football, refused to step down. The two years became four and then five, and with each trophy won, Allison felt less inclined to manage in his boss' shadow. The resulting power struggle was unpleasant, prolonged, and enormously damaging to City. Angry and desperate, Allison arranged a takeover to grant him the power he desired. 'How do you hijack a football club in full flight?' Mercer was said to have asked.

Allison's ploy failed – he backed Oldham-based windows tycoon Joe Smith, who wished to purchase £100,000 worth of vice-chairman Frank Johnson's shares, a deal that would put him close to taking control of the club – but it only delayed the inevitable. Allison's desire for full control was finally granted in October 1971. After a 3-0 loss to Bolton Wanderers in the League Cup, he was appointed team manager and Mercer was named general manager. In his first season in charge, Allison steered City to fourth in the table, one point behind title-winners Derby County.

In the coming years, Mercer's question took on greater significance, for City were indeed hijacked: by profligate spending, by misguided managerial appointments, and by continuing boardroom turmoil. Grey, gloomy days lie ahead.

⚽⚽⚽

Football media coverage from the 1960s and 1970s was startlingly sanitised as television commentators and newspaper correspondents ignored the horrifying abuse Black players received from the terraces, in dressing rooms, and on training grounds. For this reason, it is difficult to know what Stan Horne – the first Black footballer for Manchester City as well as Fulham – endured throughout his playing career. But within the pages of books like Emy Onuora's *Pitch Black: The Story of Black British Footballers* are accounts of appalling racial hatred told by the footballers themselves, moments of grotesque intolerance that Horne no doubt also experienced.

Such as when 20-year-old Paul Canoville came on as a substitute for Chelsea on April 12, 1982, officially breaking the club's colour barrier, and was met with racial slurs, monkey chants, and cries of 'Sieg Heil' from his own supporters. Or when Leyton Orient's Laurie Cunningham and Bobby Fisher ran onto the pitch for a December 7, 1974, match at Millwall's home ground, the Den – one of the most hostile venues for Black footballers – and in addition to being targeted with the usual racial venom, were pelted with bananas and a carving knife.

The repulsive, hateful occurrences were endless. What Wolverhampton Wanderers' George Berry and Bob Hazell – a hard-tackling, physically imposing centre-back pair – suffered at Leeds United's Elland Road in the late 1970s was painfully retold in Onuora's book: 'Men, women, and children, with their twisted, contorted, furious faces, spitting, gesturing, throwing bananas, threatening death, urging their own players to maim, hurt and kill'. 'The most racist set of fans I've ever come across in my life,' George Berry concurred.

Today, in an era of Show Racism the Red Card and Kick It Out, when numerous initiatives have been launched to attempt to stamp out bigotry in football, it is difficult for supporters to fully comprehend the racism that permeated the English game in the 1960s, 1970s, and 1980s. Blame for allowing the problem to become so deeply rooted must be shared. And supporters, teammates, and coaches were not the only parties complicit in the racism that poisoned the sport. Uncertain of how to respond to match day displays of bigotry, the Football Association remained silent. Clubs ignored the far-right groups that used weekly football matches as a vehicle for espousing racial hatred and selling racist literature – shockingly, both outside and inside football grounds. *Bulldog*, the youth paper of the National Front, even featured a league table of the most bigoted fans. Meanwhile, the details of racial incidents involving players and fans were conspicuously absent in newspaper reports and television coverage. Media outlets also frequently used racially charged language when discussing Black footballers. Wingers like Cunningham were 'Black gold' or a 'Black pearl'; a centre-back such as Berry worked his 'Black magic' against an opposing forward. More subtle prejudice was just as scarring. Horne was criticised as being 'off-colour in midfield' in a *Fulham Chronicle* match report from April 1972.

Horne's career began when Black players in English football were a rarity. Following a month-long trial as an inside-right with Aston Villa, the 17-year-old signed as an apprentice. After two years, the versatile Horne, who had appeared in every outfield position for Villa's reserves and youth team, made his first-team debut under manager Joe Mercer on December 7, 1963 – the second Black player to take the pitch for the Villains. Unknown at the time, it was the highlight of his tenure with the club. Eight months after his debut, Horne was treated at Queen Elizabeth Hospital Birmingham for severe hypertension and advised by medical staff to permanently quit the game. His Villa contract cancelled, he returned to his home in Witney, Oxfordshire.

Yet Horne's football tale did not conclude here – there were new barriers to be broken, additional doors to be opened for English Black players. Much like Horne, Mercer spent time away from the game due to an illness. He understood that the loss of football in your life felt like the death of a loved one. Months after he was appointed City manager in July 1965, Mercer made the flexible outfield player one of his first signings. Unlike his stint at Villa, Horne was quickly given an opportunity with the first team. In a September 22 home win over Leicester City in the League Cup, he made his debut wearing the No. 4 shirt and became City's first Black player. Three days later, he started in the league, performing gallantly in a 1-0 victory over Derby County at Maine Road.

Horne [pictured] made 21 total appearances during the Second Division title-winning campaign and another 38 in 1966-67. Hampered by an Achilles injury, this total dwindled to six the next season when City were crowned First Division champions. Initially denied a winner's medal due to a lack of appearances, Horne was presented with a nine-carat gold replica – along with former teammates Harry Dowd, Paul Hince, and Bobby Kennedy – during halftime of an October 2021 home match against Burnley.

As satisfying as this honour was, Horne understood that his impact went beyond standout match performances and championship medals. Shattering City's colour barrier was a groundbreaking moment that forever changed the club – a landmark event that galvanised a group of young, aspiring Black footballers from City's very own backyard.

'The sign "Denmark Road" is newly painted in black and white, symbolic colours for an area which is as interracial as any in the world'. So begins a story in the June 12, 1957, edition of *The Manchester Guardian* on Moss Side, an inner-city area that was Manchester City's home patch for eight decades. During the early 20th century, Moss Side was a destination for Irish and Polish immigrants; after the Second World War, the area became a hub for migrants from the Caribbean. The new arrivals were known as the Windrush Generation after the ship the *Empire Windrush*, which brought workers from Jamaica, Trinidad and Tobago, and other islands to help fill post-war labour shortages.

The Windrush Generation was joined by immigrants from the Indian subcontinent and these groups, along with the existing Irish and Polish communities, made Moss Side one of the most ethnically diverse areas in England. Multi-cultural rooming houses, like the one described in *The Manchester Guardian* story, were sprinkled throughout the area: 'A tall African pays £2 for a similar room on the next floor. His

neighbours include an Indian family, a Chinese, a Nigerian, and an Irishman, who is his friend, "except when he drink"'. Moss Side's public spaces were similar tapestries of various races and ethnicities, as depicted in this passage from *The Manchester Guardian*: 'It is early evening, almost dusk, and Denmark Road, seems "quiet", not ominously quiet, but relaxed like any residential district. Children are skipping in a small playground, watched by a line of indulgent mothers, some of them English, some African, some West Indian'.

Alex Williams was born into this brilliantly diverse environment on November 13, 1961, the son of Caribbean immigrants who arrived in Moss Side during the 1950s. He moved to nearby Levenshulme when he was four; by his recollection, his was the first Black family to settle there. Williams attended matches at Maine Road one Saturday and then Old Trafford the next – until Neil Young's FA Cup-winning goal in 1969 cemented his City fandom.

Aged 14, he was playing for local Sunday league clubs when he caught the eye of Steve Fleet, former City keeper and youth team coach. He began travelling to Maine Road two nights a week after school to participate in training sessions with City's youngsters. He was offered an apprenticeship in July 1978 and, after several seasons of playing with the youth and reserve sides, made his debut with the first team on March 14, 1981. City notched a 2-1 home win over West Bromwich Albion with Williams making a key save when the match was scoreless. But the bigger, more important story was the milestone the 19-year-old achieved: his appearance made him the first Black goalkeeper of the modern era to play top-flight football in England. Preston North End goalkeeper Arthur Wharton is considered the world's first Black professional footballer.

'The ironic thing about the game was West Brom's away strip was green-and-yellow-striped tops', Williams told *ITV News* in 2020. 'Because they had green in their shirts, I couldn't wear my green goalkeeper's top. The top I had to wear was our away goalkeeper's top, which was bright red. I was the first modern-day Black goalkeeper running out wearing a bright red goalkeeper's top. You couldn't get more colourful than that'.

Williams' genial personality and infectious enthusiasm – qualities that make him the perfect fit for the executive manager position of City's community programme – are evident when discussing the racially fuelled hostility he encountered on the pitch. Shockingly, he found a modicum of humour in these poisonous atmospheres and used the supporters' racism as a personal motivator:

> *I remember one game where I ran out and someone said, 'Look, there's a Black!' I wasn't even worthy of having a name. And in those days, you could actually take your alcohol into the stands and people were like looking at the pints of alcohol thinking, has this been laced with something? What's going on? The reactions ... You could hear people laughing and things ... But it made me play even harder than I probably normally would.*

Many of the Black footballers from this era spoke of the additional stress that came with playing on the wing. Positioned near the touchlines, one was closer to the hateful invective coming from the terraces. As a goalkeeper, Williams was even more isolated, particularly when play was in the opposing team's end. Standing alone in his green goalie top, he was an easy target for racial abuse. Additionally, he was battling the ugly stereotype that Black footballers lacked the mental acuity to play in important decision-making positions, such as goalkeeper.

While on the pitch, Williams' thoughts often turned to his father standing in the terraces and the mix of emotions he surely felt: pure joy from watching his trail-blazing son play First Division football, simmering anger over the racist behaviour of supporters. 'My father was so proud', the goalkeeper remembered. 'Remember his life had been hard at times. He'd come over from Jamaica and had to take on all sorts of jobs to feed the family. So, me playing for City was a great time for him ... Although, I have to admit I sometimes worried about how he felt about the abuse and the bananas'.

Williams cut a solitary figure on the field of play, but in the dressing room and on the training ground, he was well supported by teammates, particularly the club's other Black players. Over the years, City earned an excellent reputation for signing local talent. Joining Williams at City were Clive Wilson, Roger Palmer, Gary Bennett, and his older brother, Dave – all were from in and around Moss Side, local lads who grew up within the club's catchment area and would have been aware of the tremendous impact Stan Horne made a decade earlier.

Signed from the highly regarded local Manchester team Moss Side Amateurs, Wilson became a Maine Road favourite due to his levelheaded play and superb technical ability. He made his debut on December 28, 1981, when he started at left-back against Wolverhampton Wanderers.

Williams and Wilson forged a strong bond: they were classmates, had back-to-back places on the school register, and played together at Manchester Boys. They even shared a birthday: November 13, 1961. 'City always had Black players in the team', Williams said. 'I think it just made me feel a little bit more at home'. Dave Bennett and Palmer formed their own partnership, two central strikers with pace and muscle who quickly established themselves as the youth team's primary goal scorers.

The Bennett brothers were born in Longsight, an inner-city Manchester area three miles south of the city centre. 'I played football anywhere', Dave remembered, 'on the street, in the park, or in our backyard and did well with my primary school side'. The Bennetts teamed together during their school days, such as Bur-

nage Grammar School, before later joining City.

Gary never made a first-team appearance with the club; older brother Dave did and achieved a pair of important milestones during his City career. On May 9, 1981, Dave was in the starting XI for the FA Cup final against Tottenham Hotspur, making him City's first Black player to take the pitch at Wembley Stadium – then started in the replay five days later, which Manchester City lost 3-2. Two years earlier, in an April 1979 home clash with Everton, Dave came on as a substitute for Tommy Booth. With Palmer also on the pitch, this marked the first time the club had two Black players in action at the same time. But the elation over making his first-team debut quickly turned to fury due to a moment of ugly racism.

> *I'll not name him here, but I was running around bright and full of energy and tried to knock it past an Everton player when I got dumped on my backside. As he put his hand down to help me up, he said, 'If you do that again, I'll break your legs you Black bastard'. I'd felt six-foot-four when I came on, but he made me feel about five-feet-two. And to this day, I don't know whether he did me the biggest favour of my career or if I should have jumped up and taken matters into my own hands. What he did was made me realise that this is what I was now up against and that I'd have to face that kind of abuse on a weekly basis.*

The ceaseless racial vitriol at away grounds brought Dave and Palmer closer, the pair emotionally supporting one another on the pitch and in the dressing room after matches. At home, the atmosphere could not have been more different – and more welcoming. 'Playing at Maine Road was brilliant', Dave said. 'Because I was one of their own, it helped me. I was a local lad, went to local schools and came through the ranks. I can honestly say I never witnessed any racial abuse while I was a City player at Maine Road. The fans could see I would give a 110% every time I played, and I loved playing at home because it was where my heart was'.

The supportive environment no doubt contributed to the players' stellar performances. With Williams between the sticks and Wilson playing on the left side of midfield, City advanced to the 1979 FA Youth Cup final, where it lost 2-0 to Millwall on aggregate. The next season, Gary Bennett joined them as the team returned to the final, only to fall again, 3-2 to Aston Villa.

Youth side glory paved the way for first-team success. Williams and Wilson each made over 100 appearances for City. Wilson totalled another 350 during the next 13 years of his career, later playing for Chelsea, Queens Park Rangers, Spurs, and Cambridge United. Palmer became a fan favourite at Oldham Athletic and was the club's all-time scorer. Gary Bennett spent 11 seasons at Sunderland, competed in two cup finals, and was twice voted the club's player of the season. Dave made 65 appearances for City and enjoyed one of the most memorable League Cup runs in club history (five goals in four matches in 1980-81).

As Emy Onuora wrote in *Pitch Black: The Story of Black British Footballers*, what City's Black footballers experienced during their playing days was truly unique. 'There was none of the isolation', Onuora wrote, 'the sense of otherness, the feeling of being an outsider that had so characterised the experiences of many of Williams's contemporaries'.

In the years after his retirement, Williams commended City for their colour blindness, even stating that their record in giving opportunities to Black players was comparable with that of West Bromwich Albion, who during the 1977-78 campaign became the first English club to regularly include three Black players in its starting XIs – Brendon Batson, Laurie Cunningham, and Cyrille Regis – with manager Ron Atkinson nicknaming them 'the Three Degrees' after the eponymous American female soul group. Although, West Ham United had become the first top-flight club to field three Black players at the same time when Clyde Best, Ade Coker, and Clive Charles took the pitch for the Hammers in April 1972.

'The club were great', Williams praised. 'They never looked at you like that. I never thought of myself as a Black player or Black goalkeeper. I just thought of myself as a player ... It was just a great place to be'.

And what a player Williams was. Not only did he possess the physical characteristics of a standout goalkeeper – strength, quickness, height (he was six-foot-four), large hands – he also displayed a poise and maturity beyond his years. However, despite the natural talent and mental sharpness, he totalled only five appearances during his first two seasons. He seemed destined to scrape around for minutes once more when the 1982-83 campaign kicked off in late August.

Then, in the third match of the season, Williams' opportunity arrived. Longtime custodian Joe Corrigan went off with a dislocated shoulder after three minutes. Williams started three days later at Notts County, played admirably in a 1-0 defeat, and notched his first win on September 11 at Spurs. The match report in *The Guardian* was effusive in its praise for his performance: 'The 20-year-old Moss Sider Williams enhanced his claim to be first-choice goalkeeper with half-a-dozen excellent saves worthy of the injured Corrigan'.

Williams made 16 more appearances for City this season, none more memorable than the final one, a May afternoon match that decided the club's top-flight future and produced one of the most unforgettable television moments in English football history.

If you were a Manchester City supporter born during the early 1970s – too young to remember the unbridled success of the Joe Mercer-Malcolm Allison reign – your adolescent and young adult years were dominated by negligence, frustration, and despair. Yes, there were moments to celebrate, even cherish – the 1981 FA Cup final, the consecutive finishes in fifth during the final two seasons of the old First Division – but such moments were outweighed by abject failure. Over a 19-season stretch from 1982-1983 to 2000-01, City suffered relegation five times. Prior to 1982, during nine decades of play dating back to the club's entrance into the Football Alliance in 1891, there were only six relegations from the top flight.

For much of the 20th century, City were a First Division mainstay, a quote-unquote big club with an admirable amount of hardware in their trophy cabinet, a rich history that stretched back to the Football League's origins in the Northwest, and a roll call of forward-thinking managers, transcendent players, and sporting trailblazers. For the century's final two decades, City fell victim to years of calamitous financial mismanagement: exorbitant transfer fees paid out for new footballers who were later sold for a fraction of what the club paid; managers suffered the axe before their contracts expired, leaving City on the hook for their remaining salary; high turnover expanded the playing and coaching staffs, creating a bloated wage bill; renovation projects at Maine Road cost significantly more than originally estimated. Dazzled by a decade of domestic and European success, intoxicated by their own self-importance and lofty status as a club with a ferociously devoted fanbase, reality became distorted by grandiose dreams. City, a top-flight fixture, were transformed into a bottom-feeding failure. 'It was around this time that "Blue Moon", City's anthem for the era, first emerged mournfully from the heart of the Kippax', wrote David Conn in *Richer Than God: Manchester City, Modern Football and Growing Up*. Football historian Dr. Gary James identified the first match during which the anthem was belted out by supporters: an August 19, 1989, defeat to Liverpool at Anfield. 'Why they chose that song is a mystery', wrote James in *Manchester: The City Years,* 'but it seemed to dovetail neatly with the atmosphere that day. Gradually it was heard more often, and by the end of the season was an important factor behind City's campaign of consolidation'.

The song neatly embodied the atmosphere of the 1980s. Heading into the 1989-90 season, City had played four of their previous six seasons in the Second Division. The club's supporters were disillusioned, cynical, shattered – the sharp emotions captured in the song's poignant lyrics. Domestic and continental dreams had been crushed; the unconditional love of the colours had soured. The great irony of 'Blue Moon' as the club's anthem – and what also gives it a unique status among club anthems – is that its most heartbreaking line, 'You saw me standing alone', is sung full-throated by supporters packed into grounds that hold tens of thousands. Perhaps there is no loneliness worse than being alone in a crowd.

City's two decades in the wilderness did not result from the sins of one person but from a variety of individuals. The first joined the club in April 1971, a year after a squad of standout footballers propelled City to domestic and European glory. When he resigned as chairman in November 1993, the club was an estimated £4 million in debt and had secured just one trophy in the previous two decades. That autumn, 'Blue Moon' cascaded down from the Kippax with more than the usual significance.

If Peter Swales had one deficiency of character, one fatal flaw that triggered his downfall, it was that, as chairman of Manchester City, he led from the heart and not the head. His affection for the colours was genuine and undeniable, even if many at the club whispered that it bordered on fanatical. Inside his home in the affluent Manchester suburb of Bowdon he created a shrine to City – sky blue walls, shelves filled with memorabilia – in which he would play videotapes of milestone victories. He had nothing but reverence for the position of club chairman, praising it as 'the greatest job in the world'. Many of his player signings were acts of staggering recklessness, but they were completed with the sincere belief that he was making City better on the pitch while ensuring the club made headlines in the national broadsheets and tabloids. 'Whatever you say about Peter Swales', remarked Raymond Donn, City vice-president under Swales and a fervent backer, 'you could never claim that he didn't love the club like a supporter'.

Born on Christmas Day, 1932, Swales spent his childhood in Ardwick, a Manchester district that was home to Hyde Road, City's grounds prior to Maine Road. His father's occupation as a fishmonger provided the family with little income, circumstances that instilled in him an intense drive to rise above his family's working-class background. While a National Serviceman, Swales ran a freelance uniform pressing service out of his barracks. He also hired radios at the cost of 10 shillings each and charged fellow conscripted men a shilling a piece for listening privileges.

Swales partnered with Noel White to launch a company that sold sheet music, instruments, records, and music-related accessories. Later, the pair moved into the rapidly growing market of television rentals with the Northwest as their target market area. They leapt into professional football in February 1961, taking over Altrincham.

Accounts differ as to how Swales landed with City – an unsurprising development when one considers the egos involved. Swales claimed he encountered club directors John Humphreys and Sidney Rose at a Hale Barns pub, and coolly and confidently told the pair, 'You know all this trouble you're having – I could sort that out for you'. Eric Alexander, chairman at the time, and several other directors insisted Swales was not the white knight he made himself out to be and that it was Humphreys and Rose who made overtures to the businessman.

What is indisputable is that Swales' rise to chairman was swift. He became a director in April 1971 and then took over for Alexander after City's annual general meeting on October 5, 1973. Just 40 years old, he had assumed control of a club with a national presence, an ardent following, cash to spend, and a squad of experienced first-teamers – Colin Bell, Mike Doyle, Francis Lee, Mike Summerbee – and promising newcomers – Colin Barrett, Willie Donachie, Rodney Marsh. City were primed for a sustained run of excellence.

Swales was bursting with confidence, but this was understandably overlooked in the excitement with his appointment. 'I will give my best for City', he wrote in a match programme that autumn, 'and my best has stood me in reasonable stead before. I will work harder than anyone else. And I cannot promise any more than that'.

Swales was assiduous in his duties as chairman, never tiring in his quest to have City return to the summit of English football. But his industriousness hid a tendency to focus too stubbornly on a specific goal, to become too enraptured with a particular idea. Whether it was handling the everyday operations of the club, appointing new managers, or completing transfer deals, Swales the overambitious all too frequently undermined Swales the diligent.

Ron Saunders was his first managerial hire. 'I know for sure that he is the right one', the chairman wrote in a match programme. 'If he goes down, I go with him. It's as blunt as that'. Saunders was on the job less than five months when he was sacked in April 1974. Swales, of course, remained as chairman.

Club legend Tony Book was hired as manager and while his four-and-a-half-season tenure delivered consistency (finishes under Book: eighth, eighth, runners-up, and fourth) and capacity crowds (at one point, City claimed 23,000 season-ticket holders, more than any other club in England), it was defined by failing to produce what Swales craved so desperately: trophies. With just one to his name – the 1976 League Cup – Book was ushered out the door.

Now demonstrating that he was just as adept with rash hirings as he was with rash firings, Swales brought back Malcolm Allison as manager in January 1979. Asked if he was happy to return as coach, Allison replied, 'I am not just a coach, I am a scientist'. If there was a table for unconstrained arrogance, Swales and Allison would have sent City top.

But the events that truly sent the club on a path to fiscal ruin occurred one month later: Finance director John Humphreys passed away and the decision was made to leave his position vacant. With no level-headed individual at Maine Road to offer guidance and advise caution, Allison was essentially given a blank cheque for player signings – a blank cheque that Swales was more than delighted to sign.

Two massive egos in conflict can be damaging to a football club; two working in tandem can be cataclysmic. Swales and Allison's financial profligacy was astonishing, farcical, and devastating in the long term. The disastrous 1982-83 relegation campaign can trace its roots to the ruinous summer of 1979, when the club announced one head-scratching signing after another: £250,000 for Crystal Palace midfielder Steve Mackenzie, a precocious 17-year-old who never played a first-team match for the London club; £750,000 for Michael Robinson, a striker with just 48 matches of experience – all with Second Division Preston North End; £140,000 for Yugoslavian defender Dragoslav Stepanović, bought from a German club with a name that would have been at home in a C.S. Lewis book – Wormatia Worms! – and a long history of second-tier football; £300,000 for winger Bobby Shinton, who spent most of his career in the Third and Fourth Divisions; and the club's first-ever one-million-pound transfer: a Wolverhampton Wanders midfielder who became synonymous with the outrageous ineptitude of the short-lived Swales-Allison partnership.

'The club you're leaving obviously want the most they can get', said Steve Daley years after his £1.45 million signing. 'The club you're moving to want to pay whatever they have to if they really want you. No one regrets more than me that it didn't work'.

Swales and Allison's recruitment approach appeared to be focused on generating flashy headlines rather than procuring players who fit into the club's system. Daley's signing broke the English transfer record; the £250,000 for Mackenzie was the most ever paid for a teenager.

Importing so many new players in one close season inevitably brought concerns about playing time and positioning. Allison dodged such issues by cutting out the heart of the 1978-79 squad. Dependable forward Brian Kidd (57 goals in three seasons) was sold to Everton in March 1979; Gary Owen moved to West Bromwich Albion that May. Peter Barnes, son of City legend Ken Barnes, and 1979 club Player of the Year Asa Hartford were jettisoned that summer. Allison's indiscriminate purge even included a veteran international (Dave Watson), the club's top scorer in 1978-79 (Mike Channon), and a footballer who had spent his entire career at City (Kenny Clements).

During the 1978-79 campaign, these seven players accounted for a staggering 295 total appearances. The punk movement's 'year zero' ethos – a scorched-earth philosophy that said music before punk was irrelevant and must be eradicated – had officially come to Moss Side. By the summer of '79, punk was gasping for breath; Allison's squad was on the verge of doing the same, the manager's total break with the past having the unintended consequence of sabotaging its present.

City opened the 1979-80 campaign by picking up four out of a possible 12 points. Their form improved in September and October – a six-match unbeaten run included a 1-0 win over title contenders Nottingham Forest – before dipping again in late autumn. Defeats to eventual champion Liverpool and Crystal Palace were followed by a 2-0 derby win over Manchester United on November 10 (Robinson and Tony Henry provided the goals) and a 1-0 road victory against Bolton Wanderers one week later during which Daley netted his first. Three successive losses sent City down the table; wins over Derby County and Everton propelled them to 12th heading into the Christmas period. Certainly not a position that guaranteed safety, but in a 22-club First Division, one that left Allison and his squad feeling confident they would avoid a relegation battle.

The collapse that ensued was shocking in its absurdity. After the win over the Toffees on December 22, City did not register another victory until April 12. The club-record 18-match winless run included a stunning 1-0 upset to Fourth Division Halifax Town in the third round of the FA Cup as well as seven other games in which the team failed to find the back of the net.

Desperate to turn around City's season, Allison worked the transfer market. He offloaded Shinton to Newcastle United for slightly more than half of what he paid (£175,000) and then completed his second one-million-pound transfer: Norwich City forward Kevin Reeves (£1.25 million). 'I'll tell you what we have obtained for our money', Allison said, 'a player who has shown the ability to hit the target nine times out of ten when striking at goal'.

Reeves scoring touch was greatly needed during the desperate final three weeks of the season. He registered his first goal for the club in a 2-1 victory at Wolves on April 12, the two points sending City up to 17th. A victory over Bristol City one week later all but assured their safety. Allison's men were defeated at Derby County on April 26, then wrapped up the season with a 2-1 home win over Ipswich Town with Reeves scoring again.

For the one-million-pound-plus signing, it was an auspicious start. For the returning Allison, not so much. The manager had the full confidence of his chairman, but after disappointing maiden campaigns from many of his new signings, a pair of third-round cup exits, and a finish of 17th in the table, he did not enjoy the same support from the City faithful.

From a June 23, 1982, blurb in *The Guardian*: 'Fancy seeing you here. Malcolm Allison, the former manager of Manchester City, joins ITV's soccer panel today alongside John Bond, who succeeded him at Maine Road. They will be commentating on the Brazil v New Zealand match, although if they will allow a shot in edgeways remains to be seen'.

By the time of the 1982 World Cup, Allison was 20 months removed from the City job after a calamitous season-plus in charge. On October 9, 1980, Peter Swales asked for his resignation as well as assistant manager Tony Book's, one week after the chairman assured the pair that barring a disaster, their jobs were safe. Losses at home to Liverpool and away to Leeds United left City as the only First Division side without a victory. The historically abysmal form – wins in only three of their previous 31 league matches, good for a paltry 20 points out of a possible 62 – poor player scouting, and foolhardy transfer spending – according to an article in *The Guardian*, Allison shelled out £4,515,000 on new talent – left Swales with no choice but to finally give his managerial duo the sack.

Unsurprisingly, Allison remained as brash and abrasive as ever. In a television interview on November 29, he was asked if he 'may have blown it as a manager'. The ex-City manager angrily deflected the question by launching into a biting criticism of his successor: 'It's an amazing game – football. You know, all of a sudden John Bond's a genius. He bought three players and made Manchester City play. I wonder why he never could do it before in the previous 12 years of management'. Then, as mentioned in the press piece regarding Allison's World Cup punditry, he did not allow the television correspondent a shot in edgeways.

> *Interviewer: 'He had some success with Norwich in fairness to John Bond'.*
>
> *Allison: 'What success?'*
>
> *Interviewer: 'Well, I mean, he got them to League Cup finals and – '.*
>
> *Allison: 'One League Cup final'.*

Bond may not have been a football genius, but he quickly recognised after arriving at Maine Road on October 17 that he needed to restore discipline, boost confidence levels, and eliminate the air of arrogance associated with the club due to his predecessor. *Granada Television's 'City!'* documentary – made at the urging of Swales, who wanted more exposure for the club and understood that television was emerging as a powerful tool for accomplishing this – aired a few months after Bond's appointment, and it revealed Allison at his most narcissistic: Strutting shirtless around the dressing room, showing off his chiselled physique; puffing away arrogantly on a post-match cigar while arguing with journalists; speaking condescendingly to Swales when discussing the current squad.

Bond saved City's 1980-81 season – and it only took him a little more than two months to do so. After being blanked by Birmingham City at Maine Road on October 18, the club won nine of its next 13 matches, taking 20 out of a possible 26 points. After New Year's Day, City picked up eight points over their next seven games, all but securing their First Division safety. The club finished 12th in the table, a remarkable achievement for Bond considering where City stood when Allison was sacked. But perhaps his best work was done in the domestic cups, as he guided the squad to the semifinals of the League Cup (Liverpool won on aggregate, 2-1) and the 100th FA Cup Final. City lost a thrilling 3-2 replay to Tottenham Hotspur, but the run produced one of the most memorable moments in the club's history: Paul Power's extra-time free-kick goal from nearly 25 yards out that beat Ipswich Town in the semis.

The club's coffers now stuffed with cup money, Swales unveiled major redevelopment plans for Maine Road. His £6 million, five-year proposal would replace the Kippax and Main Stand roofs, add 36 private executive boxes, install a new floodlighting system and television gantry, and boost capacity to approximately 54,000.

Meanwhile, Bond redeveloped the squad, signing Norwich City midfielder Martin O'Neill for £275,000 and Nottingham Forest striker Trevor Francis for £1.2 million – the club's third million-pound transfer in two years. Bond later added his son, Kevin, a centre-back who was playing for the North American Soccer League's Seattle Sounders, and midfielder Asa Hartford, the player of the year Allison jettisoned two years earlier.

Francis was an instant hit. He tallied a brace in his first match, a 3-1 away win over Stoke City, and scored four more times before 1981's end. With Dennis Tueart also providing scoring punch, Bond's men picked up 21 out of a possible 27 points in November and December – the 1981-82 season was the first during which three points were awarded for a victory. 'After winning the last game of 1981 against Wolverhampton Wanderers', Francis wrote in his autobiography, *One in a Million*, 'we went to the top of Division One. It is my belief that if the club had strengthened with two or three players in the following January then we could have challenged for the championship'.

Bond pursued Manchester United's Joe Jordan and Norwich City's Justin Fashanu, only to see the former sign for Milan and the latter with Nottingham Forest. City's deteriorating financial state meant neither transfer was feasible – a fact that was unknown to both supporters and journalists. There was also a growing suspicion among the club's hierarchy that signing high-profile footballers – or in this case, merely chasing them – was driven by Swales' maniacal obsession with passing United as the city's preeminent club on the pitch and in the sports pages.

Both goals were unfulfilled during the 1981-82 campaign. Tueart was felled by a major ankle injury, Gerry Gow, Tommy Hutchison, and O'Neill were sold, and the club managed three wins after February 13 to finish in 10th – 20 points behind rival United.

That close season, rumours first emerged about the club's worsening fiscal situation. A shirt sponsorship deal was signed with Saab, worth £400,000 over two years, but Swales stated that the cash was not available to Bond for signing players. The previous year's optimism slowly gave way to disillusionment. The era of 'typical City' was dawning.

⚽⚽⚽

As far as debuts go, this one was anything but grand. At 3:40 p.m. on September 16, 1937, association football made its first appearance on television. Titled *'Football at the Arsenal'*, the 15-minute BBC broadcast was watched by the few thousand north Londoners wealthy enough to afford sets.

The programme featured a kickabout between the Gunners' first XI and their reserves as well as a demonstration of basic football techniques. At the historic broadcast's conclusion, Arsenal manager and BBC sports commentator, George Allison, teased the Mickey Mouse cartoon that was airing after the broadcast, prompting one of his players to quip, 'Here's something really worth watching'.

While *'Football at the Arsenal'* was light on substance, it did whet the appetites of sport-loving television viewers. Portions of the 1938 FA Cup final between Preston North End and Huddersfield Town aired on April 30, 1938. That spring, the BBC also televised the first football match in full: the final game of the 1937-1938 British Home Championship tournament between England and Scotland.

Though decades passed before television's true impact was felt, it can be argued that no other influence on the English game has been as transformative. Stated simply, television revolutionised football, and not just how the sport was watched, marketed and understood, but also how it was played, managed, and officiated.

Today, the Premier League holds the much-coveted distinction of being the most-watched sports league in the world. Matches are broadcast in 212 territories to 643 million homes for a potential television audience of 4.7 billion people. Nearly one billion viewer hours are totalled across live and highlights programming on *Sky Sports, BT Sport, Amazon Prime Video,* and *BBC Sport*. And as further evidence of English football's ever-growing popularity on television, eight of the top ten most-watched Premier League matches of all time have taken place since 2019.

As equally astounding as the viewership numbers is the television money. In February 2022, *The Athletic* reported that the Premier League's overseas broadcasting rights topped domestic rights for the first time ever. During the 2022-23, 2023-24, and 2024-25 seasons, foreign TV deal will bring in $5.05 billion to England's top flight. UK broadcast rights will be worth another £5 billion over this same time span.

The eye-watering amount of incoming revenue means that television directly impacts club revenue, stadium improvements, transfer fees, player wages, manager and coaching staff salaries, youth player development, and agents' fees. It also means the bulk of a football club's revenue no longer comes via the turnstiles.

For supporters, television's impact cannot be measured in pounds and pence. When the Football League negotiated its first deal – £5,000 from the BBC for the *Match of the Day* highlights programme; the money was shared equally between clubs – it opened up the sport to new and bigger audiences, a path that reached its inevitable conclusion during the 2020-21 campaign when for the first time all 380 top-flight matches were broadcast live in the United Kingdom.

Prior to television coverage, only the lucky supporters with match tickets watched their favourite stars and clubs. *Match of the Day,* and the programming that followed in the ensuing decades, became windows to the football world, transforming sitting rooms into terraces. Just as crucial was how the medium created a visual record of the game's most extraordinary moments. With every significant English football goal captured by TV cameras, it meant television powered supporters' collective memories.

'Where were you when [fill-in-the-blank] happened?' was not a question fans asked one another in the pre-television age – but now it can be, and it is done by Manchester City supporters with startling frequency. 'Where were you for 'the Ballet on Ice', that exhilarating 4-2 victory over Tottenham Hotspur at a snowy Maine Road in December 1967?' 'Where were you for Denis Law's backheeled goal against his former club, Manchester United, on the last day of the season in April 1974?' 'Where were you for Dennis Tueart's brilliant overhead kick in the 1976 League Cup final – or Paul Power's stupendous blast from nearly 25 yards out in April 1981?' Whether it was grainy black and white or soft, watery colours, the club's greatest moments are preserved on television for future generations of City supporters to cherish.

As were, of course, the instances of disaster and despair. Such as the final day of the 1982-83 First Division season, when City and Luton Town delivered an ending so intensely dramatic, so astonishingly cruel, so spontaneously wild, that it felt lifted from the pages of a sports pulp magazine. And with television cameras present, the moment became immediately iconic.

Like countless other squads facing the spectre of relegation before ultimately suffering the drop, City entered the 1982-83 campaign fraught with uncertainty. Trevor Francis, the club's leading scorer the previous season, was sold to Sampdoria in early August, primarily because his wages were close to £100,000 a year. 'Francis is one of the greatest players in the game', manager John Bond told *The Guardian*, 'but I couldn't go home any longer each night with a noose around my neck and feeling it getting tighter'. Francis provided shocking details on this ever-constricting financial noose in his first autobiography, *The World to Play For*: The club failed to pay his wages for two months; at a Christmas party for the players' children, Joe Corrigan was instructed to collect £10 pounds a head; physio Roy Bailey reused elastic bandages for ankle tappings; chief scout Ken Barnes was not permitted to make phone calls until 1 p.m. – when cheaper rates applied.

The club's perilous finances meant the top signings were solid footballers but not difference-making, match-changing talent: West Ham United striker David Cross, Southampton midfielder Graham Baker, and left-back Ian Davies, a free transfer from Newcastle United. In what was perhaps the most damning pre-season assessment of any First Division club, *The Guardian* described City as 'the footballing equivalent of the British motorway system – in a perpetual state of repair and partial function'.

What made the financial rot especially maddening was the serious money that was coming into the game, particularly to the bigger clubs. In 1983, the Football League embraced sponsorships and announced that it would be known as the Canon League. That October, Spurs became the first football club to float their shares on the London Stock Exchange. Additionally, the distribution of gate money in league matches changed significantly. The rule stating that a share of receipts went to visiting teams was amended to allow the home club to keep the entire proceeds.

All of this was pushed to the back of supporters' minds when the 1982-83 campaign started off promisingly. Bond and company won at Norwich City and then in the home opener against Stoke City; new arrival Cross found the back of the net in both matches. A bizarre victory over Watford – left-back Bobby McDonald filled in as emergency goalkeeper for 87 minutes after Corrigan went off with a dislocated shoulder (to which fans chanted 'Scotland's number one' to McDonald); Tueart, making his first appearance in nearly nine months, scored the winner 15 minutes from time – sent City top of the table.

Unknown at the time, this gutsy, uplifting victory at Maine Road was the high point of the season. With Corrigan expected to be out for six weeks, 20-year-old Alex Williams donned the green shirt. The goalkeeper played admirably in a 1-0 loss to Notts County and even better in a 2-1 victory over FA Cup holders Tottenham four days later, during which he made half-a-dozen excellent saves. Standout performances were also turned in by 19-year-old Tommy Caton, the sweeper providing superb cover for Williams, and Baker, who scored twice: the first after a deflection off a Spurs wall, the second one a cheeky lob over keeper Ray Clemence. Two defeats followed – including a 4-1 clubbing at West Ham during which Kevin Bond and Asa Hartford were sent off in the second half; the heroics of Williams, who saved a penalty, prevented an even uglier scoreline and earned him an ovation from the Upton Park crowd – dropping City to ninth.

With the season seemingly headed for oblivion, Bond and his men in sky blue turned in a stellar October. Home wins over Coventry City and Swansea City, and draws with Sunderland and Manchester United, sent City shooting up the table. On November 6, a 2-0 victory at Maine Road over Southampton took the club to second. The football press lauded City for suffocating opponents with their effective sweeper system, a tactical approach typically utilised by Continental sides.

Aiming to bolster his squad and build on October's momentum, Bond aspired to sign former Blue Peter Barnes, Ipswich Town forward Eric Gates, Birmingham City midfielder Archie Gemmill, and Southampton full-back Ivan Golac. Unfortunately, all four deals fell apart due to insufficient funds. The transfer market that City helped inflate with their trio of million-pound signings had collapsed, impacting all the top clubs in the First Division.

Supporters were made aware of City's precarious financial state at the end of October when it was revealed that the club lost £960,000 in the previous year. Peter Swales terminated the contract of first team coach John Sainty, a cost-cutting move that angered Bond, and trimmed the squad to 24 professionals and nine apprentices. Assistant manager John Benson even admitted that the club was scouring the lower divisions and non-league football for cheap talent. Peter Barnes shared how the budget-slashing impacted his father, Ken, the club's chief scout.

> *He built up a really good team of scouts, who all seemed to think the world of him and his office at the ground was the stuff of legend. You never knew who you'd meet in there. Talk about open all hours – and there was always a cup of tea to be had. I can recall Bernard Halford telling dad*

to keep an eye on the milk bill. Can you believe it? This was the club that'd paid a million and a half for Steve Daley and dad gets pulled up for using too much milk. Incredible.

Two points behind leaders, and reigning champions, Liverpool, the credibility of City's title challenge was now questioned by the football press. Once the boardroom malaise spread to the coaching staff and players, the doubters were proven correct. The club sleepwalked through November (four points out of 12; a third-round exit from the League Cup) and December (seven points out of 15, including a dreary 5-2 loss to Liverpool). Wrote esteemed football correspondent David Lacey: 'Manchester City looked as poverty-stricken on the field as they are reported to be off it'.

Individually, City's footballers endeavoured to prove Lacey wrong. Aged 32, Tueart still possessed the pace to stretch a defence and the vision to deliver a pin-point pass. Corrigan returned to form after injury; Kevin Bond was ever dependable at sweeper. Cross was the squad's only consistent goal-scorer, and Hartford was the superb creative influence he had been during his previous stint with the club. Bond's pursuit of new (and discounted) footballers became so determined, so desperate, that he worked out a deal in which United loaned out reserve winger Peter Bodak for a month. Even City's rivals took pity on them.

New Year opened with a 2-2 draw at Birmingham City (loanee Bodak had his only goal for the club) and a 2-0 loss at Watford. Lauded only three months earlier, Bond's sweeper system was now criticised for weakening the midfield and neutering the squad's attack. After a Cross brace powered the home side to a 4-2 win over Norwich City on January 15, the club did not taste victory again until the beginning of April – 11 matches in all. Supporters were forgiven for confusing the winless 1983 with the winless 1980.

Surrendering four goals became an all-too-common occurrence: 4-0 to Brighton & Hove Albion in the fourth round of the FA Cup, 4-0 to Coventry, 4-1 to Swansea, 4-1 to Southampton. The unexpected Cup exit was what finally convinced Bond he was captaining a rapidly sinking ship. On February 3, he resigned, only one-third of the way through a four-year contract worth more than £200,000.

A February report in *The Guardian* wrote of an 'obsessed individual' who stood outside Maine Road after every match, screaming for Bond's dismissal. After the manager's resignation, the 'obsessed individual' said his nephew asked, 'What's Uncle David going to shout this week?'

John Benson assumed the role of manager, yet the poor results continued with some supporters claiming, amusingly, that the club had only put Benson in charge so it would not have to change the initials on the managerial tracksuit. During a 2-2 home draw with Spurs on February 5, a banner was unfurled at Maine Road that read 'Swales must go too'. The new gaffer did succeed where his predecessor failed, bringing in the much-sought-after Golac on a free transfer. He also delivered on his promise to sign non-league footballers. On April 22, the club announced that striker Ian Thompson of Southern League Salisbury City was moving to Maine Road at the end of the season. Eighteen months after splashing out £1.2 million for Trevor Francis, City paid £7,500 for a schoolteacher competing in a semi-professional league several tiers below the First Division. The staggering disparity was another indicator of how far the club had fallen financially.

Kevin Reeves and Cross each scored in a 2-0 win over West Bromwich Albion at the Hawthorns on April 2, handing Benson his first win. City failed to find the back of the net in consecutive losses to Liverpool and Stoke before relieving a bit of relegation anxiety with a victory over West Ham at Maine Road. But the club was back in the thick of a bottom-three battle after failing to pick up a point against Arsenal and Nottingham Forest.

April turned to May, and like any squad battling to avoid the drop, City's safety was no longer dependent on their results, but the potential points accumulated by other bottom-of-the-table sides. When Birmingham drew at home to Brighton on May 2, their points pulled them out of the relegation zone for the first time all season and sent City to 20th.

The club's final two fixtures were now must-win encounters. Ahead of the Brighton match at the Goldstone Ground, a preview in *The Guardian* captured the trademark humour-tinged cynicism of City followers: '"I see no reason why we can't stay in the First Division", said John Benson, the Manchester City manager yesterday. The most reasonable among their supporters might disagree, pointing out that for the last three months or so they have been watching 11 or 12 reasons to the contrary'.

With the Seagulls also fighting for survival, the May 7 match became the tight, turgid shambles that football fans are familiar with through endless late-season relegation battles. Players clattered into one another, fouls were assessed, warnings and cautions were given. The game's only goal was in the 74th minute. A Brighton clearance from the penalty area found its way to Power on the left wing. He one-touched a pass to McDonald, unmarked outside the left corner of the penalty area, who crossed the ball toward the six-yard box and a waiting Reeves. The forward rose above a Seagull defender to flick a header into the top left corner for the biggest goal of his City career.

One match remained, and for the first time in 20 years, the club faced final day uncertainty. Benson and his squad clung to 19th in the table, tied on points (47) with Birmingham but one spot behind the Blues on account of goal differential. City's upcoming opponent, Luton Town, sat on 46 points, one spot behind in 20th, setting up an epic do-or-die cup final – with survival in the First Division as the prize. City possessed the advantage: A win or a draw ensured safety. Meanwhile, the Hatters needed all three points to avoid the drop.

The previous two seasons had seen strong, mid-table finishes, a trip to the League Cup semifinals, a run to the 100th FA Cup Final, headline-grabbing signings, extraordinary goals and unforgettable moments, a £6 million plan to redevelop Maine Road, and, above all else, an unprecedented ambition to not only be the foremost club in Manchester but the entire country. Yet here were City, their hopes in a perilous state, teetering on the edge of ruin, 90 minutes from a relegation plunge.

Saturday, May 14, was a warm day in the northwest of England. In that morning's *Daily Express*, Power was quoted as saying, 'This is my vital game of my career'. Strong words coming from a footballer who had – along with six of his teammates in the starting XI for City – appeared in the FA Cup final replay two years ago to the day. 'A lot of careers are riding on this one game', the captain added, 'but the future of the club is the most important thing of all'.

If past results were anything to go by, City could expect a tricky tie. On December 11, they fell 3-1 to Luton at Kenilworth Road. In the aftermath of the defeat, Bond was quoted as saying that he would rather lose than draw if it meant his team had tried. If he was still in charge for the rematch, he would have thought differently since a draw on that December day would have helped ensure City's survival.

At 1:45 p.m., the gates to Maine Road opened, and supporters milling about the Claremont Road and Lloyd Street stalls hawking badges and scarves and vans selling burgers and hot dogs began to fill the terraces. Unsurprisingly, City crowds were down, but the enormity of this afternoon's match compelled more fans than usual to make the trek to Moss Side. The announced attendance, 42,843, was the second largest of the season behind the March Manchester derby.

Benson named the same side that nipped Brighton the previous Saturday: 1 Alex Williams, 2 Ray Ranson, 3 Bobby McDonald, 4 Nicky Reid, 5 Kevin Bond, 6 Tommy Caton, 7 Dennis Tueart, 8 Kevin Reeves, 9 Graham Baker, 10 Asa Hartford, 11 Paul Power (captain). As for shape, City employed a 4-4-2 with Bond anchoring the midfield in front of Reid and Caton, and Tueart and Reeves pushing forward with Hartford in support. For Tueart and Hartford, this was familiar territory: The pair were in City's lineup during the final match of the 1974-75 season when a 1-1 draw with Luton consigned the Hatters to the Second Division. They were yearning for a repeat of history.

Power, making his 250th appearance for the club, led his team onto the pitch, and at 3 p.m. referee Arnold Challinor blew his whistle to start the match. City took to the attack immediately: A surging run from Hartford delivered a ball to Ranson; his cross from the right touchline dropped into the six-yard box where Luton keeper Tony Godden snagged it away from a leaping Tueart.

The Hatters' first attack came in the ninth minute. Brian Stein rounded Power, crossed from the touchline, and Mal Donaghy headed on goal – but his attempt was right at Williams. Nine minutes later, the goalkeeper was tested again when he made a leaping, tipped, save off a Trevor Aylott shot, only for play to be pulled back because of a Luton foul. Right before the halftime whistle, City had their best scoring chance of the match. Positioned in his own half, Reid picked out Reeves bursting into the right channel. The forward superbly controlled the pass before firing a shot that skipped past the far post.

The clubs conceded a combined 153 goals that season, but neither managed a breakthrough during the first 45 minutes. 'Well, we're no further forward in a sense than we were at the start', said BBC television commentator John Motson.

In the 57th minute, Luton nearly broke the deadlock: Donaghy won a header from a corner; the ball fell to teammate Paul Walsh, and his quick shot was reflexively stopped by a falling Williams. Eight minutes later, Luton manager David Pleat made his only substitution, bringing on attacking midfielder Raddy Antic for Wayne Turner.

City continued the trend of near-misses. A Hartford free kick delivered the ball to Caton, who headed toward a waiting McDonald, but he failed to connect.

The attempt did have the effect of galvanizing the Maine Road crowd. Less than a minute afterward, with supporters cheering wildly, a second free kick led to a Tueart shot that was smothered by Godden.

The match entered its final 15 minutes with Benson and his men sensing First Division safety. Another terrific save from Williams ricocheted off Reid's leg and hit the bar in the 76th minute. Four minutes later, a nifty Hartford run ended with a backheel into the path of Power, who sent the ball to Tueart. His header sailed over the woodwork. The match hung on a knife-edge. Anticipating the sound of the final whistle, the Maine Road faithful could barely contain themselves. Seconds felt like hours. For longtime supporters, the final minutes were eerily akin to the closing moments during the title-decider in May 1968, when City clung to a one-goal lead at Newcastle United.

Only this match ended differently – and quite disastrously. With the conclusion of full-time approaching, Stein sent a high, arching cross into the penalty area that Williams pushed to the edge of the 18-yard box – right to a waiting and unmarked Antic. The substitute's low, first-time, shot arrowed through a mass of bodies and into the back of the net. 'They've done it!' screamed Motson to football fans across England watching in parlours and pubs. 'Raddy Antic! Four minutes from the end!'

After his desperate clearance, Williams was left lying on the floor near the penalty spot. From this position, he miraculously managed to get his right hand on Antic's shot, but the kick was delivered with too much power. Motson dubbed it 'the cleanest shot of the afternoon'. Years later, Williams was still haunted by that May afternoon and his involvement in the match's decisive goal. 'Could I have stopped the goal?' he said. 'I've asked myself this dozens of times over the years, and I can honestly say I could not have done any better. I dived and did actually touch the ball, but I couldn't do anything more than that'.

Immediately after the shock goal, Benson brought on Steve Kinsey for Baker. In the Maine Road crowd, the cameras found a distraught Swales, cigar between his fingers, head in hand. As stoppage time loomed, the Kippax belted out a wholehearted rendition of 'We'll Support You Evermore'. City needed a last-minute miracle, but in a season of never-ending underachievement and disappointment, expecting the miraculous to occur was foolish. The team threatened just one more time: Hartford's corner found McDonald, who cannoned a close-range shot, but Challinor stopped play for a City foul.

The final whistle sounded, and the Hatters celebrated wildly on the pitch. And this is when English football was gifted an iconic moment that signalled a new age in the sport, one in which the images that flashed across the nation's television screens were as crucial as match results and photographs in newspapers: Captured by BBC cameras, Pleat skipped across the Maine Road pitch in an unsightly beige suit and matching shoes, arms waving, hands clapping, seeking out Hatters to embrace.

A true 'where were you when [fill-in-the-blank] happened?' moment if there ever was one. Even as City supporters yearned to forget that it ever happened. In *The Guardian's* match write-up by Julie Welch, the season's epitaph was simple yet fitting: 'You felt like crying for City, and a lot of people did'.

1995-96:

'What is the Difference Between Manchester City and a Lift?'

Sam Barkas' popularity among Manchester City supporters received a boost when he passionately defended his struggling teammates in a much-publicised letter to *The Manchester Evening Chronicle*. Sam Cowan etched his name in the club's history books when he represented City in three FA Cup finals. Eric Westwood's heartfelt words of acceptance to newly signed German goalkeeper Bert Trautmann were quoted in newspapers across England: 'There's no war in this dressing room. We welcome you as any other member of the staff'. Roy Paul led his teammates out at Wembley in two consecutive FA Cup finals, the second ending with a long, proud trek to the Royal Box to receive the trophy. Les McDowall's stint as captain shaped his character and prepared him for his successful 13-year stint as manager. Whether he was experiencing Wembley highs or relegation lows, Paul Power was deeply committed to the badge and departed Maine Road ninth on the career appearances list. Tony Book skippered City to four major trophies during his distinguished career – the most by anyone prior to the Sheikh Mansour era.

They were all captains, seven of the club's most notable. Tirelessly supportive of teammates, maniacal about winning, master communicators, endlessly industrious on the training ground and pitch, wholly confident while remaining genuinely humble, they exemplified the role of football captain. And they were all natural descendants of William Sumner, who served as the club's very first.

Born four days before Christmas in 1860, Sumner was an engineering student living in Gorton when he started playing for a cricket team organised by nearby St. Mark's Church. In later years, he donned a football kit for Manchester Association, a club based in Eccles, Greater Manchester, and competed in an FA Cup tie against Stoke in November 1883. His swapping of cricket for football was a harbinger of St. Mark's sporting future.

Consecrated on November 30, 1865, the church was the centre of a rapidly growing West Gorton community. Rector Arthur Connell encouraged parishioners to establish community programmes that gave the neighbourhood's male inhabitants an alternative to the antisocial activities that occupied their free time: for the men, chronic drinking in pubs and beer houses; for the adolescent boys, 'scuttling', which were pitched battles between gangs armed with belts, sticks, and stones; for both groups, bare knuckle boxing matches. Connell's mission was rooted in spirituality, but the true goal of St. Mark's community programmes was improving the health of minds and bodies.

One of the more popular was the church's cricket club, chaired by a man named William Henry Beastow. A resident of Hyde Road in West Gorton and then later Clowes Street, Beastow witnessed firsthand the desperation and hopelessness wrought by the neighbourhood's poverty, crime, and addiction. Motivated to improve his community's well-being, he became a member of Gorton's board of health, a councillor for West Gorton, and a sidesman at St. Mark's. As his relationship with the church deepened, so too did Beastow's involvement with sporting activities.

In his book, *Manchester: The City Years*, Dr. Gary James provided details on match reports for St. Mark's cricket club in 1867 and 1868. He also wrote that the first actual cricket match likely occurred during the new church's first summer in 1866. Under Beastow's guidance, the club steadily grew in popularity. Throughout the 1870s, match reports in area newspapers detailed the exploits of both a first team and a junior team. Even Beastow's family were caught up in the cricket fervour: His son and stepson played with the junior side during the summer of 1879.

The sport gave West Gorton's male adults and adolescents viable alternatives to pub and street life, but unbeknown to Beastow, cricket's popularity was on the wane. Sumner's arrival in the area in 1879 coincided with St. Mark's switch from cricket to football.

In November 1880, the cricketers – specifically, the junior cricketers – took to a football pitch for the first reported occasion. As James stated in his book, cricket only kept the males of West Gorton occupied during the summer months. A long, dragged-out cricket match also did not deliver much of an intoxicating rush. 'Someone clearly saw football as an activity that could prove a more attractive proposition', James wrote.

Just who – whether it was one individual or numerous – suggested and spearheaded the transition to football is lost to history. What is known is that St. Mark's first match kicked off at 3.15 p.m. on Saturday, November 13, 1880. Sumner and his teammates lost 2-1 to a Baptist church from nearby Macclesfield. James Collinge netted St. Mark's only goal.

The setting and conditions for this historic match were stunningly unlike any facet of modern football. No glittering multi-tiered stadiums, luxury dressing rooms, world-class training facilities, and sensationalised media coverage. The players changed inside the church or its schoolroom before taking the short walk down William Street to the scrap of urban land that served as the team's playing field. The pitch was located adjacent to a factory and was part of Brooks & Doxey's Union Ironworks complex – 'nothing more than wasteland', James wrote. Maps from the period show that it was located north of St. Mark's Church on Thomas Street, which is presently Wenlock Way.

Line markings on the pitch were likely non-existent. The goal was formed by driving two posts into the ground and running a strand of tape from one to the other – a common practice at the time. Each team had 12 players. St. Mark's dozen footballers were local West Gorton lads – much like Sumner – no different from a modern Sunday league team. For Collinge, the match delivered a much-needed respite from the everyday grind of life in industrial Manchester. Both of his parents had passed away, and the 19-year-old was raising three younger siblings with his elder sister, Martha. A brief match report, likely submitted by Beastow or a player, appeared in *The Gorton Reporter* the next day.

At its essence, this was football in late 19th century England: simple and pure, local, amateur, not driven by results, nourishing for both soul and body. Everything the sport's harshest critics would contend that it was not more than 100 years later.

As David Goldblatt details in his comprehensive and engrossing tome, *The Ball is Round: A Global History of Football*, the sport's rapid growth among the working class – especially within the dense network of small but growing towns scattered across Lancashire – was spurred by England's transition from a largely rural and agricultural society to a highly industrialised and urbanised nation. During the last quarter of the 19th century, family incomes jumped by approximately 30%, giving the males in a household the extra money to attend football matches. Industrialism also brought widespread literacy to the working class, delivered through self-help movements and compulsory junior schooling funded by local governments. This further boosted the sport's popularity by creating a market around the game for football-related newspapers, magazines, and advertising.

Equally as crucial was the growth in working-class leisure time, during which a family's extra disposable income could be spent. The 1850 Factories Act created the five-and-a-half-day week, stating that all work must cease on Saturday at 2 p.m. When the steam whistle blew and the factories and mills emptied, the crowds walked en masse to the football ground for the start of a match. The traditional 3 p.m. kickoff was born. 'Like the railway companies that insist on standard time to anchor their timetables', wrote Goldblatt of the Football League's inaugural Saturday on September 8, 1888, 'like the stockbrokers and shipping companies who deal in global time, simultaneous coordination needs standard time. Three o'clock in Bolton, is three o'clock in Liverpool, is three o'clock in Preston, Stoke, and Wolverhampton. The first five games of the Football League kick-off together'.

Three o'clock, Saturday afternoon became ingrained in the football supporter's psyche, an hour to hungrily anticipate, a rewarding conclusion to a punishing work-week, a time to later celebrate or lament when the final whistle sounded. More than a century later, during the summer of 1991, the final whistle was blowing on the old order – with its Saturday afternoon kickoffs, limited television coverage, and equitable distribution of wealth. The Football League was on the brink of the biggest upheaval in its 103-year history.

On July 31, an English super league – whispered about in 1950 as a means for the Three Lions to recapture their international prestige; predicted in 1961 when the maximum wage was abolished; an inevitable certainty after the summer of 1988 when ten clubs (the 'Big Five' at the time – Arsenal, Everton, Liverpool, Manchester United and Tottenham Hotspur – as well as Aston Villa, Newcastle United, Nottingham Forest, Sheffield Wednesday, and West Ham United) threatened a breakaway competition that had the financial backing of ITV – took a giant step towards becoming a reality when the High Court threw out the Football League's objection to a separate competition for the country's top clubs organised and run by the Football Association. The summer-long debate sharply divided supporters. Those championing the FA's plan criticised the other side's sentimentality for a creaky league structure in desperate need of modernising. Backers of the Football League condemned the break-up as nothing more than club greed run amok.

Opponents of this new Premier League were given ammunition for their argument when the fledgling competition announced in May 1992 that it agreed to sell 60 live matches a season to *British Sky Broadcasting* for £304 million. The five-year deal was unprecedented in English football both for the eye-watering cash amount and how it would be dispersed. No longer would television money be evenly divided among the 92 clubs in the country's top four divisions. This treasure trove – which included an initial payment of £850,000 as well as an added £450,000 in sponsorship money – would be gobbled up by only the Premier League's 22 participants.

Having remade football's television landscape, Sky Sports set about doing the same to the sport itself. The simple tradition of the 3 p.m. kickoff was ignored for the sake of TV scheduling. Weekly fixtures were set for Sundays and even Monday evenings, Premier League chief executive Rick Parry citing the unbridled success of Monday night American football games in the United States. On-the-pitch entertainment was provided by cheerleaders known as the Sky Strikers, another marketing strategy influenced by the ever-growing behemoth across the Atlantic known as the National Football League. Determining which of these revolutionary changes was the most unpopular among traditionalists was hopeless – both were equally loathed.

To the chagrin of many Manchester City supporters, the Sky Sports pomp and pageantry arrived at Maine Road on August 17, 1992, for the first-ever 'Monday Night Football' programme – or 'Ford Monday Night Football', to be precise, the American automobile manufacturer having inked a deal to be the exclusive broadcast sponsor for coverage. 'Mondays are changing!' host Richard Keys enthused as the pre-match coverage kicked off. 'No longer that start-of-the-week depression. We're into a whole new ball game on Sky Sports. Mondays are now officially part of the weekend'. Deep in the bowels of the old stadium, reporter David Livingstone interviewed the match official for the night, Martin Bodenham, who tediously detailed the travel challenges he overcame while driving to the match from his home in Cornwall.

The surreal pre-match programme then descended into the absurd. The cheekily dressed Sky Strikers leapt and twirled in the centre circle, teenage dancers carrying balloons flooded the pitch, a giant banner was unfurled that carried Sky's football marketing slogan ('It's a whole new ball game'), and oversized sparklers shot flames 20 feet into the air. As the Sky Sports anthem echoed through Maine Road – Simple Minds' 'Alive and Kicking' – City supporters could be heard singing emphatically in the terraces, as if to remind viewers that after this ostentatious display there was a football match to be played. The festivities' final act, one that was simple coincidence or cruel teasing from Sky's marketing folks, was the delivery of the match ball by the Parachute Regiment's display team. Its nickname? The Red Devils.

As for the match, despite the unusually late kickoff (7.45 p.m.), both sides were energised for their Monday night football debuts. A fast, wide-open game ended 1-1 with David White scoring for the home team. The most noteworthy storyline for City was Paul Lake's inclusion in the starting XI, his first league appearance after a two-year absence due to a lengthy knee injury.

While Lake and his teammates lingered on the pitch, applauding fans in the terraces, savouring a historic night for English football, they were likely unaware of the journey their club had undertaken since its first match in the autumn of 1880. Less than two miles separated that West Gorton 'wasteland' from the club's home in Moss Side, but the distance travelled felt like one-thousand light years. New destinations awaited: some familiar, some unexpected, some never visited.

'I think Man City's a club for successful supporters – people who are successful in life but need bringing down a peg or two at some point', opined *Key 103* DJ and *Imagine FM* breakfast presenter Spence McDonald, a lifelong supporter of the club. 'You couldn't support United because all your life would be full of success. But City, it reminds you that life is fickle. If you were a manic depressive and you supported City, I think you'd throw yourself off Barton Bridge'.

After relegation in May 1983, the club continued to teach fans season-long lessons in hardship and humility. The next spring, City appeared headed for a quick return to the First Division before three consecutive losses in April derailed their chances. Manager Billy McNeill guided the club to a promotion spot the next season only for City to be sent down again – their eighth drop – in May 1987. The season was a particularly wretched one. McNeill stepped down in September with the team in the middle of a 12-match winless streak. Jimmy Frizzell took the helm and fared even worse: City went three months and 14 games without a victory. The eight top-flight wins equalled the 1949-50 squad for the least in club history.

Under the stewardship of Mel Machin, City secured automatic promotion in May 1989. Peter Reid took over as player-manager in November 1990 and during the final two seasons of the First Division, guided the club to its best stretch in nearly 15 years: consecutive finishes in fifth. However, the positive results on the pitch duped supporters into believing the club's financial and boardroom situations were sound. Relegation killed plans for a purpose-built training ground in Cheadle that was projected to cost £400,000. The club continued training on council-owned facilities at Platt Lane, where supporters turned up to cheer – or heckle – the players and coaching staff. Suffering the drop also delayed the installation of 32 corporate boxes at Maine Road, a revenue game-changer in the days before lucrative television money. In 1965, Manchester United installed hospitality boxes that offered supporters a meal, a bottle of wine, and the opportunity to meet a former player. City finished above their rivals six times during one seven-season stretch in the 1970s; due in part to the long-term financial advantage their ground provided, United emerged as the more successful club.

This superiority was never more evident than during the 1992-93 season, the inaugural campaign of the Premier League. United cruised to their first title in 26

years, topping runners-up Aston Villa by ten points. City finished a respectable ninth in the table, but the season was an endless source of frustration and embarrassment. Reid's unimaginative, route-one football alienated supporters; his direct approach was at its most dreadful in September when the team lost three consecutive matches 1-0. The next month, Peter Swales declared that since the most recent signing – Terry Phelan for an outlandish £2.5 million – had drained the club's coffers, Reid would have to make do with the current squad. As the Maine Road faithful witnessed each Saturday, it was one in desperate need of updating: City managed only 30 goals in 21 home league matches.

The supporters' long-simmering anger boiled over near the conclusion of an FA Cup loss to Tottenham Hotspur on March 7. For Swales and the club's board, the day started full of optimism. City unveiled their all-seater Umbro Stand, complete with long-overdue executive boxes. While not a particularly impressive structure, it did offer supporters the best sightlines of all the seated sections at Maine Road as well as substantially more leg room than in the North or Main Stands. With a partially modernised stadium to marvel at and City only one victory from the semifinals, the largest crowd of the season (34,050) was in attendance. A Mike Shelton goal gave the home side the lead, inspiring the raucous crowd to sing of faraway trips to Wembley. Maybe this most tepid of seasons would produce a trophy after all.

But those voices were quickly silenced. A Nayim goal brought the match level before Steve Sedgley put Spurs ahead. Two more from Nayim booked Tottenham a spot in the semifinals. A late consolation goal by Terry Phelan delivered a glimmer of hope to City supporters – except for the several hundred in the brand-new, unfenced Umbro Stand who angrily poured onto the pitch before the match restarted. The act emboldened supporters from all corners of the ground to do the same, with many charging towards Spurs fans in the North Stand. Police on horseback dispersed the crowd. The match official took both sides off the pitch, but the unnecessary disturbance merely delayed the inevitable: an FA Cup exit and a 17th consecutive trophyless season for City.

There would be one final moment of peculiar significance. In a much-publicised incident after City's end-of-season home loss to Everton, an egg was thrown in the direction of Swales, hit a steward, and splattered on the City chairman. Egg-on-the-face puns filled newspapers in the days afterward. Ian Niven, a member of the club's board for 20 years, pleaded with supporters to swap projectiles for pen and paper: 'We are an open club. Any fans with complaints can write a letter or come into the club and talk to someone'. Nearly lost in the madness of the moment was the genuine, seething hatred for Swales. Protests had occurred in past seasons, most notably after the relegations in 1983 and 1987, but the egg-tossing incident and anti-Swales demonstrations at Maine Road the afternoon of the Everton match had an end-of-days feel to them.

During the summer close season, Reid pursued six players, all of which either rejected City or the club refused to rustle up the necessary transfer funds. With the manager and board increasingly at odds over the assessment and value of football talent, Swales made perhaps his most bizarre hire. On August 19, he announced the appointment of John Maddock, a former newspaper sports editor and current public relations consultant, as the club's general manager, a position that came with responsibility for buying new players. At the press conference announcing the arrival, Swales stated, without a trace of irony, 'The club is in very good shape, apart from winning matches'.

If Maddock's lack of a footballing CV did not draw the fans' ire, his behaviour during the first week on the job certainly did. He dubbed himself the club 'supremo', took to the papers to cite a shortage of team spirit after a 2-0 home loss to Blackburn Rovers, and recommended to the board that Reid, who signed a three-year contract in June, be sacked. Reid ultimately was on August 26.

Maddock promised supporters he would bring on 'a true professional who is going to help put Manchester City back on the football map'. His landmark appointment was Brian Horton, then the manager of tiny Oxford United, a club that was relegated from the second tier later that season. Keen-eyed City supporters remembered Horton from the infamous final-day defeat to Luton Town in 1983. After manager David Pleat made his celebratory jig across the Maine Road pitch, the first player he embraced was Horton, his captain.

The former Hatter was the 12th and final man appointed to manage City under Swales' chairmanship. His arrival was also the most unexpected and perhaps a symptom of the board's desperation. 'We just couldn't believe Brian Horton had been given the job', said longtime forward David White. 'When we were told, there was uproar in the dressing room. Some of the players literally hadn't heard of him'.

City opened September with their first two victories of the season, against Swindon Town and Queens Park Rangers, but by then, results on the pitch took a backseat to a rapidly escalating struggle for ownership of the club. Emboldened by the public animosity for the chairman – 'Swales out' chants became a fixture at matches after the first week – Francis Lee attempted to force his way onto the board. Flush with cash following the multi-million-pound sale of his paper recycling business, the former City star insisted he was not launching a takeover attempt and that he was only remedying the club's problems with a much-needed money investment. On September 6, Swales rejected the offer, stating that he and retired businessman Stephen Boler, who each owned approximately one-third of the club, had a watertight agreement not to sell to a third party.

Over the next two weeks, the dramatic battle for the future of the club played out in the nation's sports sections. Four days after rebuffing Lee, Swales declared he was now ready to sell, placing the valuation of his shares at £15 million. On September 11, Lee sat in the director's box for the QPR match, the guest of his takeover partner, businessman and former City player Colin Barlow. Seated just four rows in front of Swales, Lee received a second-half standing ovation from supporters, who were increasingly enthused about his takeover bid. The photograph of Lee standing triumphantly, one arm raised to acknowledge the crowd, Swales a faceless figure in the background, remains one of the most iconic associated with the club. An hour after the match's conclusion, Swales, no doubt wounded by Lee's reception at Maine Road, reversed course again. 'Let's get one thing right', he stated emphatically. 'We don't want to sell Manchester City'.

Fans who backed Lee, now organised under the name 'Forward With Franny', called for a boycott of the September 22 League Cup match against Reading and asked those who did to donate their match ticket money to their campaign. The group predicted up to 7,000 supporters would stay away, costing the club £50,000 in revenue. Much like City, who drew 1-1, the boycotters did not secure the result they desired. The official attendance of 9,280 was only 687 less than the same home round of this tie the previous year.

As the 20th anniversary of Swales' appointment approached, October 5, his dogged determination to remain in charge grew stronger – having made it known that he wished to become the first chairman at a major club to serve two decades. Under City's takeover rules, Lee's consortium was permitted one uninvited takeover bid a year and would not prepare an offer until reviewing the club's accounts. Swales denied him access. And when Lee and company did place a £10-million bid at the end of October – £2 million for one-third of the club's shares, £8 million for signing players – Swales was behind its rejection for being 'well short of reflecting the full value of City'.

In an October 1 story in *The Guardian*, Swales announced that before player transfers were considered, City had a surplus of £2.3 million on a turnover of £10.1 million for the 1992-93 season. Transfer dealings cost £1.2 million, so the club was left with an overall profit of £1.1 million.

Incensed over the refusal to accept Lee's offer, supporters emulated the dirty tactics of their chairman. Prior to the QPR match, an anti-Swales demonstration was held outside Maine Road during which the chairman's address was distributed along with photocopies of the local A-Z. Swales was mailed razor blades in the post and received death threats over his home phone. His wife, Brenda, spoke of returning from a match and encountering a police cordon outside their residence in Bowdon. 'I didn't know what was happening, so I went inside and looked out of the bedroom window', she remembered. 'It was hard to believe, but there were police all round the back garden. Apparently, pubs had received maps to our house, asking people to come round and sort Peter out'.

But it was not the supporters who eventually forced out Swales – it was the club's shareholders. At City's annual meeting on October 28, they voted 79-52 not to re-elect him as club chairman. 'We are a corner-shop ground in a world of supermarkets', said one of the frustrated shareholders. Swales used his majority shareholding to overrule the decision on a card vote and remained in charge for one more month. Fittingly, City did not record a victory during that time-span and even lost to United, the rival Swales was infatuated with supplanting as Manchester's preeminent club. When he finally resigned on November 29, he cited the negative impact of the hate campaign against him. 'I felt that staying on was creating an additional burden for the players', Swales claimed, 'and the manager, who had conducted himself admirably in the most difficult circumstances'.

By the end of his tenure, Swales' passion for the club and his confidence in transforming its fortunes had turned to pure arrogance. He became the dreaded football chairman who believed that his club could, and would, not go on without him. Noel Bayley, who founded *Bert Trautmann's Helmet*, which joined *Blueprint* and *King of the Kippax* as the most popular fanzines sold outside Maine Road, summed up Swales best: 'He was a politician with no policies, whose only mantra was "give me another year and I'll get it right". And a year became another year and another'.

With both sides haggling over shares, the takeover drama extended into 1994. Swales' hesitancy was also rooted in a fervent desire to oversee one last run to Wembley, one final opportunity to add to his meagre trophy haul. City were knocked out of the FA Cup on January 29, losing 1-0 to Cardiff City. A takeover deal was finalised in the days after the defeat. In the end, Lee and his business partners – Barlow, John Dunkerley, and D.A. Holt – only pooled together enough funds to purchase a 15% stake in the club. Any disappointment over Lee coming up short financially – as well as any bitterness over the shambolic, protracted takeover – was forgotten the day of City's next match: at home to Ipswich Town on February 5. 'It was like one big party', said David Wallace, editor of *King of the Kippax*. 'I think that because the waiting between the start of the FWF ['Forward With Franny'] campaign and Lee taking over was so long, we all felt a sense of relief that it was all over. We could finally turn the club around'. David Conn described the scene in his book, *Richer Than God: Manchester City, Modern Football, and Growing Up:*

> *The match that day, against Ipswich Town, was a carnival of celebration. There was a banner, specially made for the occasion, welcoming the saviour, then a festoon of blue-and-white balloons was released to the Moss Side sky. Franny took Swales's seat in the directors' box and, with that familiar blonde hair and trademark dimple smile, arms splayed in a blue-suited businessman's echo of his stance at St. James' Park, he accepted the acclaim, the love and the yearning, of his old worshippers at Maine Road.*

City's performance on the pitch that day only enhanced the sense of optimism. Garry Flitcroft and Carl Griffiths scored as the home side recorded just its fifth league victory of the season. The party atmosphere surrounding the club continued in the weeks after the takeover. 'This will be the happiest club in the land', Lee declared. 'The players will be the best paid, and we'll drink plenty of champagne and sing until we're hoarse'.

But when it comes to football, reality has a way of asserting itself – and often, quickly and rudely. Even with Lee on board and Barlow serving as the club's first full-time managing director, City managed only four more wins the rest of the way, tallied a paltry 38 goals (third lowest in the club's history for a 42-match season), and finished 16th. Niall Quinn and Michael Sheron were joint top scorers with six goals each – the lowest in the club's history.

During the close season, Lee made headlines when a practical joke gone awry resulted in an exploding cigar blowing up in his face. The cigar was meant for sports agent Eric Hall and had been placed in his jacket by the wife of England manager

Terry Venables. Unaware that it was a cigar of the exploding variety, Hall gave it to Francis Lee with whom he was negotiating a deal.

The scene was all too prophetic. City improved on their win, goal, and point totals during the 1994-95 campaign yet managed to finish one spot lower in the table. Horton, the most peculiar of Swales' numerous managment hires, was given the sack on May 16. In true City fashion, he learned about his dismissal in the morning papers. Lee needed little time to find Horton's replacement – and his choice proved that Swales was not the only City chairman who was skilled at making head-scratching managerial appoinments.

As a man, Alan Ball possessed a remarkable gift for winding up others: fellow players, opponents, referees, supporters. 'He could start a fight in a phone box', said Tottenham Hotspur captain Alan Mullery. After a hat trick against Fulham, he refused to sign autographs because he felt the Craven Cottage crowd had considered him to be just another footballer before the match. He perpetually needled England teammate Jack Charlton for his fashion sensibilities. And in what was perhaps his most controversial incident, Ball incited a rabid Hampden Park during the 1971-72 Home Internationals when he celebrated the winning goal by flashing a V-sign at the terraces and wiping his nose on the corner flag. Manager Alf Ramsey said to Alan Ball after the match, 'You really are a naughty boy'.

As a footballer, Ball was a wind-up toy that never wound down. When his father first saw the newborn Ball and his shock of bright red hair, he immediately knew his son's sporting future: a perpetual-motion footballer. 'His energy observed no natural law', wrote the famed sports journalist Hugh McIlvanney. 'The more he expended, the more he appeared to have'. Years of building his stamina through swimming and cross country paid off when the 1966 World Cup final entered extra time and England needed an energising individual performance to carry them through the final 30 minutes. 'He was awesome', said teammate Norman Hunter, who watched from the Wembley Stadium stands. 'He was all over the place, and he just ran and ran'.

So, it is savagely ironic that for a perpetual-motion athlete, a footballer who could run himself mad, a player who prompted BBC commentator Kenneth Wolstenholme to exclaim 'He'll be running half an hour after the finish!' during extra time of the World Cup final, the most well-known moment during his managerial stint with Manchester City involved a member of his squad standing motionless with the ball, positioned in one of the pitch's four corners, frozen like a commemorative statue outside a football ground.

Of course, when Ball accepted the City job on July 3, 1995, becoming the 13th man to manage the club since 1971, there was no indication that his tenure would deliver an episode of such inertia and ineptitude. His was a familiar footballing name: Ball won a World Cup medal, assisted on Geoff Hurst's goal to put England ahead in extra time, joined Howard Kendell and Colin Harvey in Everton's 'Holy Trinity', and starred at Blackpool and Arsenal. Still, his appointment was met with harsh criticism, as more appealing candidates were rumoured in the lead-up to his appointment – Arsenal's highly successful George Graham was Francis Lee's first choice; Franz Beckenbauer, one of Ball's opponents in the 1966 final, was even mentioned as a possibility.

Plus, Ball's managerial CV was hardly sparkling, the top complaint among supporters who inundated Manchester radio stations with their objections that summer. The former England star had overseen relegations at three separate clubs – Portsmouth, Stoke City, and Exeter City – and was on Graham Taylor's staff during the Three Lions' disastrous 1992 European Football Championship. However, in the position that landed him the City job, Ball was wildly successful: In 18 months at Southampton, he rescued the club from relegation, guided them to tenth in the Premier League, and turned attacking midfielder Matthew Le Tissier into a genuine star.

During his playing career, supporters were wowed by his pace and movement, by his ever-willingness to fight and scrap, by the skills that made him arguably the best one-touch passer of his generation. Equally extraordinary were his subtle strengths: the way he read a game, dictated the pace of play, bent a match to his will. Attributes that logically meant a post-playing career in management. 'He was one of those guys you could count on because he knew the game', said England teammate George Cohen of Ball's football acumen. 'He had the brain of a real professional. An old head on young shoulders'.

Ball's biographer, David Tossell, wrote that watching his best matches at Everton were like spying on the most perfectly executed one and two-touch sessions on the training ground: 'His sharp mind, innate sense of his surroundings, and his snooker player's eye for angles allowing him to decide on his delivery before the ball arrives'. One touch, a pass, then a move into space for a return ball, Ball advancing his teammates forward a few yards at a time, relentlessly attacking the opposing side's defence, never playing it backward, never slowing down for a respite. 'I preached the need to play the ball through me, through the middle, from where I could prompt more initiatives' was how Ball summarised his approach.

His football brain was sharpened by his father, (James) Alan, a wing-half/inside forward who played reserve team games for Birmingham City as well as a handful of matches for Oldham Athletic, Rochdale, and Southport. 'I never met anyone as fanatical about football as my dad', Ball stated. As a child, he was brought to Southport matches, plopped on the bench with the reserves, and instructed to watch the action on the pitch. Years later, when Ball transitioned from spectator to player, post-match rides to the family home in Farnsworth were dominated by Alan senior's honest appraisals of his performances.

Theirs was a father-son relationship shaped by the sport. They found a strange comfort in the practice rituals, Alan senior kicking his son's shins to ready him for tough midfield play or tying his right leg to a drainpipe to improve the kicking ability of his weaker left foot. They shared in the pure joy that followed a performance in which it was apparent that their endless training together was worth the sweat and pain, Alan senior having determined that what Ball lacked in strength and height would be compensated by heart and skill. And they collectively endured and learned from football's inevitable disappointments and defeats. Ball called Alan senior his 'mentor, coach, advisor, critic, psychologist, disciplinarian, and caring father' – intentionally leaving the most important title for last.

The advisor was consulted when Ball joined Everton several weeks after the World Cup triumph. The unrestrained confidence, unmistakably present in front of the packed terraces, was absent in the dressing room, as Ball anxiously sought the acceptance of new teammates. Help your colleagues pick up their win

bonuses, Alan senior counselled, and they will welcome you as one of their own. Nearly three decades later, now in Manchester, a similar unease took hold when Ball the manager stood in front of his new squad for the first time. His training ground speech – perhaps the defining off-the-pitch moment of City's wilderness years in the 1990s – was a staggering mix of braggadocio, aloofness, and poor humour. Ball reminded his players that he possessed a World Cup winner's medal before boasting that he was not just a champion in football but also in the field of alcohol consumption.

'When you have achieved so much', said forward Uwe Rösler, 'and Alan Ball achieved so much, you don't need to speak about it. You know what you have done. You let other people speak about it. Franz Beckenbauer doesn't talk about himself. People talk about him. Your history should do the talking for you'. 'The players already knew he was a World Cup winner', said Tony Book, who was also at the Manchester University training ground for Ball's introduction, 'and I think they just wanted to hear about how they themselves could improve or what he had in mind for the coming season'.

What the new manager did have in mind was making an immediate splash in the transfer market. On July 14, Ball completed his first deal: £2 million for Georgian midfielder Georgi Kinkladze, a well-known name to British football fans thanks to an exquisite chip over Welsh goalkeeper Neville Southall in a Euro 1996 qualifying match. City pursued the young footballer for six months. Lee scouted him three times; Ball was enamoured with the Georgian after watching five minutes of video highlights.

A month later, on the eve of the season opener, the manager strengthened his squad at the back with deals for Portsmouth defender Kit Symons and German international goalkeeper Eike Immel. When asked about his re-building efforts, Ball's words must have certainly stung his predecessor, Brian Horton: 'It is a bit like cleaning out the drains'. Aside from the signings (and the drain cleaning), City's biggest pre-season story was the release of a new line of official T-shirts marketed by Manchester rock band Oasis. Sporting a trendy lowercase version of the club's name, the tees paid homage to the city's rich musical heritage. 'For us, football and music have always gone together', said local drummer Tony Meehan. 'Maybe we're into the music so much because we haven't won anything in ages'.

The pundits expected 1995-96 to deliver more of the same. In his Premier League preview that ran in the August 19 edition of *The Guardian*, renowned football correspondent David Lacey had City slotted at 19th. In the three previous Premier League campaigns, this finish guaranteed safety. But with the competition having trimmed from 22 to 20 clubs, 19th meant the dreaded drop. 'All the major ingredients for another Maine Road crisis are there', Lacey wrote. 'The boardroom murmurs, a patchwork quilt of a team containing overpriced under-achievers, especially at the back, and a new manager with, Southampton apart, no great record of keeping his sides up'. His words would prove to be stunningly prescient.

August 19 was a brilliant day in Moss Side, the type of clear, bright first Saturday of the season that instils optimism in even the most cold-hearted cynic, nourishes the spirit of the most ardent fan, and compels the longtime supporter to contemplate how they survived three months of football dormancy. Then the opening whistle sounded, and cruel, ugly reality scored from the spot. Apart from Rösler, who tied the match in the 51st minute, and Kinkladze, a constant menace to the Tottenham Hotspur defence and already christened the Kink of the Kippax, City were dreary and unimaginative. They even managed to work in a moment of farce: Spurs' only goal resulted from a communication breakdown due to the language barrier between Immel and his English-speaking back four. One positive note, as reported by Jeremy Alexander in his match report for *The Guardian*, was that no chants of 'Swales in' emanated from the terraces.

By August's end, supporters were queuing up 'Ball out'. On the 23rd, Rösler scored City's only goal in a 2-1 away loss to Coventry City. Three days later, a 1-0 defeat at Queens Park Rangers was punctuated by 18-year-old midfielder Michael Brown being sent off ten minutes into his first-team debut. A 2-0 home loss to Everton on August 30 sent City bottom of the table.

Only four matches into the season and reinforcements were already needed. After the loss to the Toffees, City signed Portsmouth striker Gerry Creaney to bolster the squad's unproductive front line. Despite the move, no attacking improvement was evident in a 1-0 home defeat to Arsenal on September 10. City's scoreless drought now stood at three matches.

Six days later, the chasm between the league's nobility and peasantry was made clear to Ball and his squad. Title favourites Newcastle United romped to a 3-1 victory in a contest that was not as close as the score indicated. Richard Edghill was sent off after 25 minutes, a call that left the manager seething. 'This is what's happening to the game these days', Ball said afterwards. 'You can't tackle anymore'.

In truth, the red card did little to change the complexion of the match – City were already playing like they were a man down. Peter Beardsley showcased his knack for creating or finding space. Les Ferdinand scored twice – the second arriving in the 59th minute, putting the game out of reach – and David Ginola turned in a virtuosic performance in midfield. Ferdinand and Ginola arrived during the close season when Newcastle splashed £16 million on new talent. Creaney, who cost a microscopic fraction of this sum, was City's lone bright spot on the day; his goal was the club's first in nearly a month.

'I played with some great players and against some great players, but the best I ever played with was Alan', Kevin Keegan once praised. 'The greatest thing was his football brain. He could see things that other players just wouldn't see'. So, what was Ball seeing that his struggling squad did not see? And what ideas in that sharp football brain of his did he plan on implementing to save City's rapidly worsening season? Not a soul knew, for Ball had gone silent. 'You'll turn it into a story, so I'll say nowt', the manager told assembled media after a scoreless draw in the League Cup against Division Two side Wycombe Wanderers on September 19. Maine Road supporters did the talking for him. The anthem 'Blue Moon' was changed to 'One shot / We only had one shot'. When the final whistle sounded, a cascade of boos rained down from the stands.

The match put Ball and his squad in the record books – but it was an ignominy, not an honour. The seven matches without a win to open the season was the longest such streak in club history, topping the six-match skeins put up by the 1911-12 and 1980-81 sides. City closed September with a 1-0 home defeat to Middlesbrough and a 3-0 setback to Nottingham Forest on the road, stretching their remarkably bad run to nine games. In the aftermath of the defeat, Ball ducked out of his post-match press conference.

Two months into his tenure with City, the World Cup winner's tactical limitations were coming to the fore. He could infuse his players with confidence and passion, inspire them to find that extra bit of motivation and perseverance in tight matches, but if his squad needed an innovative gameplan or inventive adjustments at halftime, Ball could not deliver. Just as concerning was Ball's ever-growing Kinkladze crisis.

At Southampton, he recognised Le Tissier's supreme talents and made the midfielder the fulcrum of the Saints' attack. Le Tissier estimated he played 64 times for Ball and tallied 45 goals. 'It was the happiest time of my career', he said. Le Tissier recalled a players' meeting during which Ball placed a hand on his shoulder and instructed the team on how they were to attack. 'This is your best player', Ball said. 'This is your best chance of getting out of relegation. Every time you get the ball, look for him. That is your first thought'. Ball ordered his squad to make Kinkladze their first thought, only to see this tactical approach slowly fail week after week for two reasons: The Georgian was not the goal-scorer Le Tissier was, and City did not field a lineup of players that were accustomed to supporting an improvising attacking midfielder with an abysmal work rate off the ball.

Teammates grumbled that Kinkladze was pampered away from the pitch. His mother was settled in Manchester to cook and care for the homesick midfielder. Teammates similarly objected to how the Georgian was indulged on the pitch, how Ball endlessly tinkered with starting XIs to find one that accentuated his strengths. 'The problem with Georgi', said teammate Nicky Summerbee, son of club legend Mike Summerbee, 'was that you couldn't play 4-4-2 because to get the best out of him you didn't wouldn't want him playing a conventional running midfield game. [Ball] changed the formation all the time, a sure sign you don't know what you are doing'.

Having combined for 37 goals during the 1995-95 season, Rösler was frustrated by the departure of his strike partner, Paul Walsh, who went to Portsmouth in the deal for Creaney, then grew more embittered when his manager repeatedly altered the squad's shape. 'Alan Ball tried everything', Rösler remembered. 'Two up front, played Kinkladze on the wing. Then he played him in a diamond as a ten. Then he played split strikers when Niall Quinn played on the right wing, and I played on the left wing and Kinkladze played through the middle. Niall had played for Ireland in the World Cup and now he was being asked to play right wing. I felt there was too much focus on trying to find the right position for Georgi – who was our most talented player – rather than what was best for the team'.

Midfielder Steve Lomas experienced firsthand the strain Kinkladze's idleness and spontaneity placed on players. 'I have the utmost respect for Alan', Lomas said, 'and he was a terrific coach, but I always felt we would have been better playing

3-5-2, keeping two up front and Georgi in behind. There was a big demand on the midfielders when you tried to give Georgi that freedom'.

Ball's long-awaited first win as City manager finally came on October 4 in a League Cup replay with Wycombe. Rösler netted two goals in two minutes, Quinn added a third, and Keith Curle converted from the spot to round off the scoring. It was the club's first victory since April 17.

In what was perhaps an indication that the winless streak was loosening his grip on reality, Ball complained in the match programme that poor officiating – not poor managing or a negative dressing room environment – was to blame for his squad's staggering 25 bookings and three dismissals. He also crudely declared that 'the game is being made into one for fairies'. The manager conveniently abstained from mentioning the recent Middlesbrough match and the season's most glaring example of his squad's lack of discipline: Frustrated at having his jersey pulled and no foul called, Rösler tore off his shirt and waived it in a linesman's face. Shockingly, referee Gary Willard only gave him a yellow card.

The victory over Wycombe relieved a bit of the pressure on Ball. But there was still the matter of securing his first Premier League win with the club, a pursuit that was about to become more arduous: Manchester United, Leeds United, and Liverpool – all top-five clubs the previous season – were up next on the fixture list.

The October 14 derby match proved you can indeed 'win something with kids', as Fergie's Fledglings squeaked out a 1-0 victory. Twenty-year-old Paul Scholes scored from a corner kick in the fourth minute. Quinn, having recently found favour with his manager, wasted two excellent scoring opportunities. In his post-match press conference, Ball was eager to dole out blame. 'You give people responsibility to mark in dead-ball situations', he said. 'And they virtually hand a free header to a lad who is five feet, seven inches'. Ball was at least spared another round of jeers and name calling; ongoing renovations at Old Trafford meant City supporters watched the game on a video screen at Maine Road.

A scoreless home draw with Leeds on October 21 ended City's eight-match losing streak in the league. Four days later, the club was eliminated from the League Cup courtesy of a 4-0 hammering at Liverpool. Ball said he became an 'angry little sod' in his efforts to motivate his lackluster squad. One ponders what the manager transformed into three days later when City were thrashed once again at Anfield – this time by a 6-0 score. Halftime adjustments were nonexistent; only a superb performance from Immel kept this from being historically humiliating. Visiting supporters, with nothing left other than their senses of humour, regaled their beleaguered manager with the chant 'Alan Ball's a football genius'.

Nearly one-third of the way through the season and City had taken an astonishing two points out of a possible 33. 'What is the difference between Manchester City and a lift', went an oft-heard local joke that season. Answer: 'A lift does not take seven months to go down'. The club's seven goals in 14 league and cup matches earned Ball's team the nickname 'the Blank of England'.

But then, there are no hopeless situations in football – only football supporters who have grown hopeless about them. Just when City's fans were at their most despondent, their most pessimistic, Ball and his men turned in a sparkling November. There was a 1-0 home win over fellow relegation favourite Bolton Wanderers on November 4, the lone breakthrough a goal-of-the-month candidate: a bit

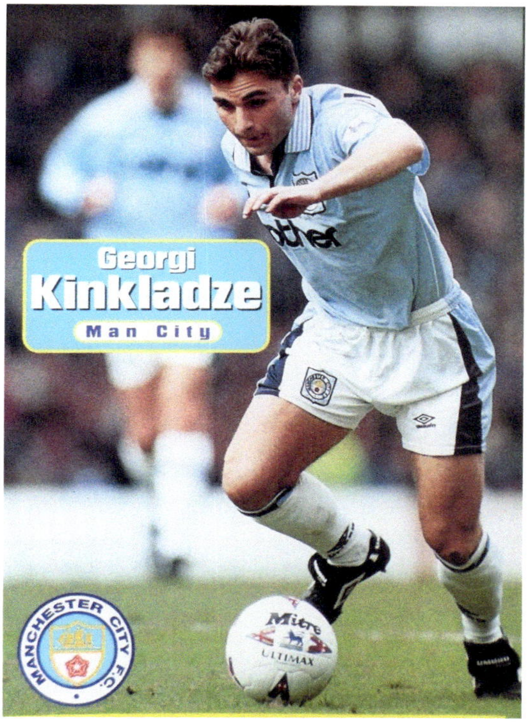

of intricate footwork from Quinn was followed by a clever run down the left wing, a nifty touch and cross from Kinkladze, and a clinical finish by Summerbee. A 1-1 draw at Sheffield Wednesday came next on November 18.

Four days later, a 1-0 victory over Wimbledon at Maine Road lifted City off the bottom of the table for the first time in three months. The solitary goal was the result of more magic from Kinkladze and Quinn. With seconds remaining before the full-time whistle, the Georgian sent a sleek through-pass to the Irishman in the penalty area. Quinn dashed toward goal, deftly turned two defenders, and struck a low left-footed drive past the goalkeeper.

November 25 produced a similar result: a 1-0 win at home – this time over Aston Villa, a club in third – with Kinkladze and Quinn dazzling supporters yet again. The midfielder played a lovely one-two with the striker, collected the back-heel return, and left-footed the ball into the net from a narrow angle. The victory was especially sweet for the club as goalkeeping legend Bert Trautmann was in attendance to open the towering new Kippax stand.

City's stellar run of form continued with a 1-0 away victory over Leeds, the club's third successive clean sheet. Ball, named Carling Manager of the Month for November, was now being lauded for his decision-making, his swap of Creaney for Edghill paying dividends when the former netted the match's only goal. Mired in 20th at the end of October, City were now 16th.

The end of the year also saw activity in the transfer market. Poland's Kazimierz Deyna was signed from Legia Warsaw. Defender Terry Phelan was sold to Chelsea for £750,000. Ball used £500,000 of these funds to sign 19-year-old Martin Phillips, a midfielder he managed during his tenure at Exeter City. Ball was so enamoured with the youngster he once declared that he would be Britain's first £10 million player.

City were dealt a harsh reality check on December 9, when a 4-1 loss to Boro ended their five-match unbeaten streak. Kinkladze – *The Observer* match report noting that fans had branded him with his now-famous nickname: Kinky – put his team ahead in the 16th minute. But in another sign of City's ineptitude, Middlesbrough played rather poorly in the second half yet still put three past Immel in the span of ten minutes.

A rematch with Forest on December 18 ended in a 1-1 draw, City tallying only their 10th league goal of the season. Rösler ended a scoring drought that stretched back to August 23, Immel was his typical resolute self between the posts, and solid midfield performances were turned in by Lomas and Curle, who moved up from his usual centre-back position. 'Watching Manchester City is like having your heart on the end of a yo-yo string', wrote *The Guardian's* Cynthia Bateman in her match report. 'How do their supporters stand it?' As City's play went from brilliant to blundering, and back again, versus Forest, so too did their season. The club closed 1995 with a 1-0 loss to Chelsea at Maine Road and a 2-0 defeat to Blackburn Rovers. The latter setback was notable only for City making history when it became the first team to play four foreigners: Immel, Kinkladze, Rösler, and Denmark's Ronnie Ekelund, who arrived on loan December 15 from Barcelona.

On December 22, 1995, the Premier League scrapped the limit on the number of European Union players a team could field. Manchester City threatened a legal challenge to the Bosman ruling, faxed the European Commission for the clarification of the foreigner rule, and were given the green light to play as many EU players as they liked. The Bosman ruling was named after Belgian midfielder Jean-Marc Bosman, who challenged the UEFA rules that said a player could not depart their club even though their contract had expired. On December 15, 1995, the European Court of Justice ruled that footballers should be free to move when their contracts had expired and that European Union clubs could hire any amount of EU players.

Back in the relegation zone, Ball had five months to elicit more consistent play from his squad and secure Premier League safety. More than enough of the season to incorporate Kinkladze into a formation that maximised his talismanic and at the same time, self-indulgent style of play. Plenty of time to put that lauded football brain to work and justify his position.

Before any of this could occur, a surprising, but not completely unexpected, retirement pushed match results to the background.

Paul Lake can recall the day with perfect clarity. Saturday, September 23, 1989. The morning of the 111th league Manchester derby. The 20-year-old midfielder was driving to Moss Side, mentally preparing to pull on the No. 11 shirt that afternoon, too young to comprehend the enormity of the moment, green enough to be, as he put it, 'wobbly-legged' on account of the nerves. Lake stopped at the traffic lights at Stockport Road and Dickenson Road and caught the eyes of a father and son standing on the sidewalk, both decked out in replica Manchester City kits, blue-and-white scarves draped on their shoulders. 'Having clocked me sitting there in my car', Lake remembered, 'this bloke nudged his lad and then did something that will stay with me forever. Pressing his palms together as if in prayer, he looked at me beseechingly and mouthed three simple words: 'Please! Please! Please!'.

Lake and City answered this father's entreaties – and those of countless other diehard supporters – when they thrashed their biggest rivals in a historic 5-1 victory. There is an iconic photograph from that match, snapped after Ian Bishop's goal made it 3-0, a photo that was blown up to emblazon an entire wall at Maine Road's souvenir shop: Lake embracing Bishop, Bishop's legs wrapped around Lake, his fist in the air. Lake's face is a mix of emotions: pride, joy, disbelief. His is also the face of a player with his whole career in front of him, a career that promised further derby day victories, winners' medals, moments of individual brilliance. A career that would have his name spoken about in reverential tones, that would be mentioned with the club's all-time greats. Swift, Doherty, Trautmann, Bell, Doyle ... Lake.

What Lake's career ended up being was a testament to the power of resilience and hope, a demonstration of how the human spirit can triumph over the most terrible adversity. Lake retired after nearly six years of repeated knee injuries and endless surgeries, but his relentless and gruelling battle to return to the pitch, to pull on that sky-blue jersey one final time was an inspiration to injured footballers everywhere. He officially stepped away from the game on January 4, 1996, days away from undergoing his 15th knee operation in five years. Lake announced his retirement to assembled media at an empty Platt Lane, City's squad having already completed their training session. 'A good job, really', he wrote in his autobiography, *I'm Not Really Here,* 'because I don't think I could have faced being confronted by a troupe of fighting-fit, smiley-faced lads on this day of all days'.

After the requisite interviews and photographs, Lake departed his old training ground one final time, anxious about this next chapter in his life, unsure of how to carry his new title of ex-footballer. In his book, he brilliantly captures the moment he departed:

> *It was at this precise spot in the middle of the car park that my dad had dropped me off for my first training session with Tony Book. On a wet and windy Thursday evening in 1982 he'd wished me luck, waved me off and driven away in his Hillman van, leaving me standing there alone, eyes wide and knees knocking, not quite knowing which way to turn or what lay ahead. Nearly 15 years later, that same doubt and uncertainty prevailed.*

A total of five appearances in the previous five seasons, a veritable stranger to the City squad and the coaching staff, done with the game at age 27 – it was not supposed to happen this way. Lake, a Manchester area lad, childhood City supporter, and product of the club's youth system, was expected to be a fixture in starting XIs for years as well as a mainstay for the national team. 'It's a tragedy not just for Manchester City, but for England as well', said Howard Kendall, who managed Lake during parts of two seasons. 'I've seen a lot of brilliant young players in my career, with many of them going on to become household names. But believe me, Paul Lake was as good as anything I've ever seen'.

For Lake, having a ball at his feet seemed like the most natural thing in the world. He said his ability to control it, dribble it, and pass it was wholly instinctive and that his sense of awareness when on the pitch – regarding his positioning, his teammates, the ball – stemmed from pure intuition. It was not bombast or arrogance, just the words of the rare athlete blessed with both the physical and mental gifts to supremely master their sport. 'I didn't quite know how, or why, I found football so easy', he said. 'I just did, and that was that. "You've got a gift, son", Dad would often tell me'.

Lake was born on October 28, 1968, to parents from Ardwick, home of City's former Hyde Road ground. He grew up on Bowker Avenue in Haughton Green, a predominantly working-class area in east Manchester six miles from the city centre. Lake remembered the day that divided his adolescence into two distinct parts: before football and after football. Christmas, 1974, he received a snow-white Mitre match ball for a gift – 'with its porcelain-smooth skin and brand-new leathery smell' – and from that day forth, a ball never left his foot. He spent his free time playing in Haughton Green Park, typically with his older brother Mike and his friends, staging imaginary international matches and Manchester derbies. (Lake was converted to the blue side by his milkman, Albert Gains, who owned a pair of season tickets at Maine Road.) At midday, the Lakes and their mates dashed home for lunch – ham butties, a bag of salt 'n' vinegar Chipsticks, a mug of tea – then hurried back to the park to take advantage of the remaining hours of daylight.

Lake was making appearances for the Denton Boys under-13 team when he caught the eye of City scout Ted Davies. Within a week, he joined Cheadle-based Blue Star, one of the numerous City feeder clubs in Greater Manchester. He was one of a small group of promising young players for the satellite team, some local, some not. Scouser Steve Redmond 'oozed confidence and cockiness but commanded everyone's respect because he had the footballing talent to justify the swagger', Lake praised. Sale native Andy Hinchliffe possessed 'a sweet left foot that could have rewired the back of a television'. Ian Brightwell, who hailed from the West Midlands, was 'a supreme athlete who could play effortlessly in any right-hand-side position'. And David White, another lad from Manchester, who developed an extraordinary rapport with Lake, 'complementing each other's strengths and covering for each other's flaws'.

Competition for places was fierce, primarily due to the wealth of talent at Blue Star, but Lake's gifts were evident from the moment he joined the club. He was taken on as an associated schoolboy with City in July 1983. Life became mornings training sessions at Platt Lane – always under the watchful eye of youth team coach and City legend Tony Book, who was known affectionately as 'Skip' by everyone at the club – and boot-boy duties at Maine Road, including scrubbing the studs of standout goalkeeper Alex Williams. Lake relished the tutelage he received from Book and in his autobiography, detailed his straightforward coaching ethos:

> *By doing the simple things well and nailing the fundamentals, you created a solid basis upon which to showcase your skill and flair. He advocated a brand of pared-down football in which a simple ten-yard pass dispatched at the right moment could be more effective and efficient than a flamboyant nutmeg or a showboating step-over. Those who ignored Skip's doctrine, those played lazily, casually, or just downright badly, would be in danger of being fast-tracked to the top of his football scrap heap.*

Under his guidance and support, Book's side cruised to the two-leg final of the 1985-86 FA Youth Cup. Brightwell, Hinchliffe, Lake, and Redmond started in both matches. Lake equalised with a penalty rebound to secure a 1-1 draw at Old Trafford; David Boyd and Paul Moulden scored at Maine Road to clinch the trophy for City. Lake remembered how thoroughly charged up him and White, a fellow Mancunian, were for the second leg: 'With sky blue blood coursing through our veins, just the mere mention of United got us wound up like coils. We were desperate to get one over on our cross-town rivals and the prospect of losing to them was inconceivable'.

Longtime City supporters could not recall a more talented and exciting group of young players. Pundits had them pegged for future trophies and future medals. Ownership was desperate for such results due to the club's dire financial situation: The transfer coffers were empty; young talent additionally meant cheaper wages.

Lake signed his professional forms during the autumn of 1986 and made his first-team debut on January 24, 1987, at Wimbledon, replacing the injured White and playing central midfield. The next season, the core of that trophy-winning youth side became regular fixtures in Mel Machin's starting XIs. Hinchcliffe, Redmond, and White recorded more than 50 appearances each while Lake and Brightwell tallied 40 and 39 respectively. Even Moulden and Ian Scott saw minutes. The squad finished a respectable ninth in the Second Division in 1987-88 before rising to second the next seasons, earning a return trip to the top flight.

Dubbed the Barnes Babes, after chief scout and former City star Ken Barnes, Lake and his fledgling teammates garnered national attention with rumours circulating that Liverpool manager Kenny Dalglish and his Tottenham Hotspur colleague, Terry Venables, wished to poach them. A popular article on the Barnes Babes featured photographs with price tags slapped onto their foreheads. Lake was valued highest at £600,000.

Yet this lifelong City supporter and budding club star had no intention of departing Maine Road. 'I was blue to the core', Lake said. He was the most indispensable footballer on that promotion-winning squad, playing in every outfield position and wearing eight different shirt numbers. And he was regularly exhibiting the flair and poise that his brother and his mates witnessed in Haughton Green Park all those years ago: nutmegging and streaking past opponents towards goal, skipping over or swerving past outstretched legs, anticipating and avoiding tackles. Lake made his international under-21 debut in September 1988 before eventually graduating up to the 'B' squad.

He was one of the last players cut by Bobby Robson for his 1990 World Cup squad but was touted as a certain international. His future was not bright – it was fluorescent.

Much like his Christmas morning in 1968 forever split his adolescence into two distinct parts, the September 5, 1990, match at home to Aston Villa did the equivalent for his football career. There was before the knee injury, and then there was after the knee injury. During the close season, manager Howard Kendall gave Lake the captaincy and a new contract. That afternoon he wore the armband for only the third time. Adding to the sense of drama, recently appointed England manager Graham Taylor was in attendance to scout both Lake and Villa's David Platt. In the 65th minute, Lake leapt with an outstretched leg to intercept a ball to Tony Cascarino, an innocuous play he had made countless times throughout his life. 'As I did so', Lake remembered, 'my right boot got stuck in the turf, my body twisted awkwardly, and, with an almighty crunch, I landed in a heap on the ground. As I hit the deck, I felt a weird clunk in my knee, followed by a sharp, searing pain'. 'Sometimes the most innocuous incidents in football are the most damaging', said television commentator Clive Tyldesley as Lake lay on the pitch, unaware of the painful accuracy of his words.

Lake's injury diagnosis, treatment, and rehabilitation became a case study in how *not* to manage a major knee injury. After two days of icing and compression, an X-ray revealed no bone damage. Lake was told that an MRI scan of his ligaments and tendons was not necessary. He was given a rehab programme of gentle, stress-limiting exercises and light weight training to strengthen his hamstrings and quads. Then came training at Maine Road: jogging around the perimeter of the pitch and hopping up and down the concrete steps on the Kippax terracing. His return to on-the-pitch training ended abruptly when his right knee gave way while attempting cone drills. The next day, Lake learned he had ruptured his anterior cruciate ligament.

And thus began five years of endless progress and setbacks, episodes of hope and moments of agony, extended rehabilitation stints at the FA's Centre of Excellence and Medical Education Centre at Lilleshall, sleepless nights tortured by self-blame and guilt, worries over personal finances in the absence of appearance money and win bonuses, and, most shockingly, two further ruptures of his ACL. Lake's journey was a reminder that footballers are human, very much human, a truth often forgotten by the angry shouters on the terraces and the callous cynics on the pub stools. Like a club tethered to the bottom of the table, the sense of relegation a tight noose around the neck, Lake sensed his fate even as he rehabbed. There was no coming back. But maybe this was never the ultimate prize. Perhaps his victory was the immense personal pride he took from knowing that when he had to keep working, he did, and when he was compelled to quit, he did not.

At his most vulnerable, both personally and professionally, Lake descended into depression. 'All the elements of my personality that had previously given me strength – my drive, my optimism, my humour – were suddenly snatched away', he confessed, 'leaving behind a dreadful sense of emptiness. I felt like one of those snakeskin exhibits often found in natural history museums: a hollow, fragile shell, the life and soul having slithered out and departed'.

In recent years, many high-profile athletes have spoken publicly about anxiety and depression. A multitude of football leagues and organisations have taken action to support their athletes' mental health and well-being, including the Premier League, the Football Association, and the Professional Footballers Association

(PFA). Their efforts are helping to lessen the stigma, prejudice, and discrimination that can be associated with mental health conditions. But when Lake was playing, there were no fellow footballers openly discussing how interconnected emotional wellness is with physical performance. There were no organisations offering a 24-hour helpline, creating a nationwide network of counsellors, or training coaches in mental health first aid – programmes that were recently launched by the PFA.

Lake found the courage to speak with his GP about his deteriorating mental state and received the necessary professional help. He visited the Manchester Priory once or twice a week for hour-long sessions with a psychotherapist. Together, they discussed the numerous factors that pose mental health risks to professional athletes: the unsustainable quest for perfection, the enormous public pressure to win, the lifestyle requirements and sacrifices, and how careers can end in the blink of an eye due to injuries. Lake's psychotherapist emphasised the profound impact his damaged knee was having on his psyche. 'Your injury's been like a bereavement, in a way', she told him. 'You're in shock. You're in mourning. You feel like a huge chunk of your life is missing'.

Here is an example of the massive social stigma that was attached to mental illness at that time: 'I was scared to death of bumping into a City fan,' Lake wrote in *I'm Not Really Here*, 'worried sick that news would leak out that Paul Lake was seeing a shrink. I'd cover this particular base by always going to the Priory with a spare cheque in my pocket that I'd scrawled on. If waylaid by someone in a sky blue shirt, my plan was always to wave the cheque quickly around before claiming that I was en route to present it to some mental health charity based at the centre'.

Lake had taken the first step on his long road to mental health recovery, a road that was just as difficult as the one he undertook for his right knee. He was prescribed antidepressants and continued therapy. In September 1996, nine months after retiring, he started attending 'A' level evening classes at South Trafford College. Early the next year, he began work on a sports therapy diploma. During the 1997 close season, he joined the City medical team as an academy physio, ready to begin a second career at Maine Road. 'For the past 20 years', Lake said, 'my life had revolved around that old stadium – it had been my home, my sanctuary, my social hub – and cutting loose seemed unthinkable. The emotional attachment to my mother-club was as strong as ever, the gravitational pull still as powerful, and I couldn't envision my daily commute being anything other than up Didsbury Road, down Kingsway, and along Wilbraham Road towards my Moss Side mecca'.

Lake never enjoyed the football career he envisioned for himself – derby day victories, a trophy case filled with winners' medals and caps for England, moments of individual brilliance – but by writing so honestly and so eloquently about his struggles in *I'm Not Really Here*, he helped normalise mental health in professional football. Thanks to his efforts and the efforts of many others, the superheroes of the sporting world are more comfortable removing their red capes, seeking professional help, and taking a break from competition if need be. And this legacy, not one rooted in football, will prove to be the more enduring.

'Catch a train from Plymouth to Inverness', wrote football correspondent Mike Langley in the January 7 edition of *The Observer*, 'detouring through Wales and East Anglia while scrutinising every full-time league from the Premier to the Scottish Second, and you will fail to uncover a more inept set of scorers than the group employed by Manchester City'. Langley's scathing yet amusing take came after City's 0-0 draw with Division One Leicester City in the third round of the FA Cup. Heading to the match, the club's paltry goal total was a British-low of 12 in 21 league matches. The squad managed two goals in a game only once: during a 2-1 home victory over West Ham United on New Year's Day.

Poor finishing plagued City all season. Fluffed sitters, players denied by the woodwork, dire misses from close range, penalty attempts blazed wide – the poor luck and ineptitude took many forms. Georgi Kinkladze, Steve Lomas, and Garry Flitcroft were an enterprising midfield trio, but six-foot-plus forwards Niall Quinn and Uwe Rösler often looked cumbersome and awkward playing in front of them. Pundits criticised City's monotonous attack: quick, deft work on the ground in midfield was followed by predictable, high, crosses from the wings for Quinn and Rösler. More than one pundit suggested that if manager Alan Ball could acquire a fleet-of-foot striker who could run on to a through ball, City's attack would reach another level.

Reinforcements were forthcoming. On January 19, the club signed forward/midfielder Nigel Clough from Liverpool for £1.2 million. Chairman Francis Lee financed the deal by offloading second-choice goalkeeper Tony Coton to Manchester United in a rare transfer between the cross-city rivals.

But results changed little, even with Clough's presence in the starting XI. City saw out January with a 1-0 loss at Tottenham Hotspur and consecutive 1-1 draws against Coventry City and Southampton. With little more than three months left in the season, Ball and his squad were sitting just outside the relegation zone, battling with five other clubs to dodge the trap door.

In February, focus shifted from the league to the FA Cup. After City's much-maligned attack netted five goals in the replay against the Foxes, the club travelled to Coventry for a fourth-round tie. A snowy night in the West Midlands ended 2-2, the Sky Blues' Dion Dublin equalising in stoppage time. One week later, goals from Quinn and Clough set up a highly anticipated fifth-round showdown with United.

For cash-strapped City, the opportunity to put one over on their rivals was not nearly as enticing as the financial windfall: a 45% share of the gate at Old Trafford, plus television receipts, meant a £400,000 sum for the visitors. The money ended up being a consolation prize, as United prevailed 2-1 thanks to a converted penalty by Eric Cantona (after a highly controversial foul call on Michael Frontzeck) and a Lee Sharpe goal with 13 minutes remaining. Eliminated from both cup competitions, City could now focus solely on ensuring their league safety.

The determination and energy the squad exhibited in a February 24 draw against top-of-the-table Newcastle United, dubbed 'the Entertainers' for their swashbuckling style of play, instilled supporters with hope. City dominated early and deservedly took the lead on 16 minutes. Scott Hiley made an impressive run down the left wing and fed the ball to Clough, camped just outside the penalty area. His fierce, low shot clipped Quinn's heel and fluttered past outstretched goalkeeper Pavel Srnicek.

One minute from the half, Philippe Albert's first-time finish tied the score. After the break, City grabbed the lead again. Kinkladze, who turned in one of his best per-

formances in sky blue, made a forward run through the left inside channel, cannoned a shot at the keeper, gathered the rebound, and chipped the ball perfectly to Quinn, who squeezed in a header from a tight angle. Newcastle proved they were worthy of their nickname when Faustino Asprilla poked in a match-equaliser in the 71st minute.

The goal set up a scintillating final act. With only 13 minutes to go, Rösler, darting toward the far post, steered in a shot-cum-cross from Steve Lomas. A desperate City began defending too deep and too desperately and paid the price when Albert placed a low, accurate shot past Eike Immel in the 81st minute. The gripping 3-3 draw was a match of the season candidate, but more importantly, the result – and sudden revival of City's moribund attack – had the players believing that they could muster enough points during their final 11 fixtures to avoid the drop.

'Even though our league position was precarious', Tony Curle said in reflecting on the 1995-96 campaign, 'we still felt confident that we could pull away from the bottom three. We just felt we needed that one performance, that one result to kick-start a run of good form because we'd been competitive in most of the games we'd played that season but were just on the wrong end of score lines'.

The familiar listlessness returned. March brought a 1-1 home draw with Blackburn Rovers, a 3-1 defeat at Arsenal – Gunners' manager Bruce Rioch did not even bother to attend; he was abroad scouting new talent – and another 1-1 draw one week later, this time at Chelsea. A Kinkladze brace – the second goal a thing of pure beauty, the Georgian zipping past defender after defender before elegantly chipping the ball over the keeper; even visiting Southampton fans applauded – powered City to a 2-1 victory on March 16 and three sorely needed points.

From his office as chairman, Lee had one eye on the league table and the other on City's accounts. The worsening financial strain on the club – according to the previous year's annual report, Manchester City had an accumulated debt of £18.7 million (even after receiving that hefty sum of £400,000 following the FA Cup match versus United) – forced Lee to move players that were essential to winning their relegation dogfight. The chairman informed Ball that he needed to contact Rovers' manager Ray Harford about selling Garry Flitcroft. When the manager refused, Lee informed him that the club needed £3.5 million or the banks would foreclose. 'He's got to go', the chairman insisted. 'He is the most saleable player we've got'. Lee won; Flitcroft was shipped off to Blackburn for £3.2 million on March 22.

A four-match winless run followed, including a 3-2 derby defeat at Maine Road. New signing Mikhail Kavelashvili – bought for £1 million, Lee having mollified the banks – and Rösler scored for City. It was the German's strike, not the Georgian's sterling debut, that generated the bigger headlines. Locked in a feud with Ball, Rösler celebrated his goal by dashing towards the bench to taunt his manager. Clough was on his heels and attempted to stop him. During a *Match of the Day* interview after the final whistle, Rösler was angrily blunt: 'I'm playing for this football club, my team, and our supporters but not for Alan Ball'.

City now sat 18th in the table, level on 31 points with Coventry and Southampton, but behind both clubs due to goal differential. Three matches remained, three opportunities to write a thrilling tale of survival and escape. Or for the fatalists – the supporters who firmly believed that when it came to City, if something *could* go wrong, it *would* go wrong – three chances to trip and fall before crossing the season's finish line.

At age 16, Niall Quinn caught the eye of Fulham manager Malcolm Macdonald. For Easter weekend, he was flown to London for a trial with the club. Buzzing with excitement – it was the young Irish player's first time on a plane – he was met by the Newcastle United legend at the airport and whisked away to the club's facilities in West London.

Quinn impressed in a few training sessions and performed well in a match for the youth team, earning him a spot with the reserves against Charlton in the Football Combination. 'I didn't get eaten alive', he remembered, 'but I certainly got nibbled daintily'. His next test was against the reserves for Queens Park Rangers. Quinn was playing at centre-back and was instructed to mark Clive Allen, who was a few seasons away from scoring a staggering 49 goals in all competitions for Tottenham Hotspur. On this afternoon, Allen netted five.

Sitting in Macdonald's office the next morning, Quinn was told straight away that he was being flown home. 'I'll give it to you the truthful way, son', the Fulham manager said. 'As long as you have a hole in your arse, you will never make a footballer'. Macdonald then handed Quinn an autographed ball and sent him on his way.

Macdonald was sacked by Huddersfield Town in 1988 and never managed in football again. Eight years later, Quinn was in his 14th season and on his way to becoming his country's all-time top scorer. The Irishman would have been forgiven had he sent the Fulham manager a written missive that stated, 'As long as you have a hole in your arse, you will never make a talent evaluator'.

Born on October 6, 1966, Quinn was raised in Crumlin, a suburb of Dublin. 'The place was an old-style mix of terraced and semi-detached houses', Quinn remembered, 'built at a time when people still valued space and green fields'. His mother was a teacher, his father, Billy, a star hurler who played in the 1952 and 1953 All-Ireland Minor Hurling Championship. The couple emigrated to England, settling in Strood, Kent, where his father worked as a steel erector. When they returned to Ireland in 1959, his father found employment at a Dublin bakery and began playing for a club hurling team on the weekends.

Quinn took up hurling, too, and Gaelic football. While attending Drimnagh Castle Secondary School in the Dublin suburb of Drimnagh, he also immersed himself in football and golf. Saturdays consisted of hurling at 11 a.m., Gaelic football at 1 p.m., and football later in the afternoon. On Sunday, he did it all over again.

Billy never wavered on what sporting path he wanted his son to choose. 'We remained a fundamentalist GAA [Gaelic Athletic Association] family', Quinn said, 'and hurling was the highest religion'. Years passed before his father learned he was playing football for Manortown United in nearby Perrystown. His mother smuggled him to matches.

Quinn's progress in football was matched by his development in hurling. During the summer of 1983, he earned a spot on the Dublin minor hurling team and was a standout on a side that advanced to the All-Ireland minor final, where it was soundly defeated by Galway. 'The light went out of the world for a few days', Quinn said of the loss. Days later, his mood brightened considerably when Bill Darby, longtime Dublin-based scout for Arsenal, knocked on the door to the family home in Crumlin. The Gunners wanted Quinn to travel to London for a two-week trial.

His playing experience with Arsenal was markedly different from his brief spell at Fulham. No humiliating encounters with star forwards, no dismissals, no autographed footballs. Placed on the club's under-18 team, Quinn was paired up top with another aspiring young forward: Paul Merson. In a 9-0 win over Southall, Quinn scored three times, his partner six. Against University College, London, he potted two goals and set up two more in a 4-0 victory. The next day, his 17th birthday, he trained with the first team.

Quinn signed professional forms with Arsenal in October 1983. He worked closely with former club legend and youth team coach Pat Rice, who helped tackle his self-doubt and instil in him the belief that he could be a successful footballer. Rice's workouts were ever demanding, always challenging: kicking a football against a wall 100 times without it hitting the ground, sprints to the top of Highbury's North Bank, cross-country runs while carrying a heavy sandbag.

After starring for the youth team and then the reserves, Quinn earned a spot in the first team's starting XI for a December 1985 home match against Liverpool. (The headline in *The Irish Independent* that morning: 'Hurling Star to Make Debut'.) He set up a Charlie Nicholas goal and then netted one of his own in a 2-0 Arsenal victory. The next season he was a regular – 48 total appearances, 12 goals – before his playing time dipped dramatically over the next few years. His game needed improvement, particularly when he had possession of the ball, and his time away from the pitch and the training ground were not spent wisely. 'I was a good drinker and a bad gambler', he said, 'and being out of the team most of the time for more than two years allowed me to improve my performances in both disciplines'. He was a ghost on Arsenal's thrilling 1988-89 title team, typically named as the 13th man in the squad, spending the entirety of matches on the bench. His lack of appearances meant he did not receive a championship medal. 'It wasn't so much the medal as the isolation that bugged me', Quinn admitted.

Towards the end of his career in North London, manager George Graham only played Quinn when forward Alan Smith needed a rest. He was sold to Manchester City for £800,000 during the 1989-1990 season. When he arrived in March, the club's state of dire poverty shocked him. 'At training, no Arsenal player could go out wearing a sock with a hole in it', Quinn said. 'Socks with holes were not the Arsenal way. No, sir. The Manchester City I joined was a hole in the sock sort of place'.

Quinn settled in nicely under manager Howard Kendall. He worked tirelessly in the Maine Road gym, improved his ball control, struck up a spirited head-tennis rivalry with Tony Book and physio Roy Bailey, and playfully bantered with team-mates over his exorbitant transfer fee. On the pitch, he brought a much-needed edge to an anaemic City attack. After Quinn's arrival, Kendall and his squad recorded just one loss over their final nine matches, propelling them from the relegation zone to 14th.

The Irish forward became a fixture in the starting XI over the next few seasons, always good for 30-something appearances and double-digit scoring totals. But Quinn forever endeared himself to the blue side of Manchester thanks to moments that had no connection to matches and statistics. One occurred during a pre-season tour of Penola, Italy, in the summer of 1992. Quinn was drunkenly boogieing in a nightclub wearing nothing but cut-off jeans when he was spied by travelling City supporters. A terrace anthem was born: 'Niall Quinn's disco pants are the best, They go up from his arse to his chest, They're better than Adam and the Ants, Niall Quinn's disco pants'.

Another memorable moment occurred during a fifth-round FA Cup tie against Manchester United on February 18, 1996. While battling for possession along the far touchline, Michael Brown, playing in only his second match for City, stamped Nicky Butt on the back. The ever-temperamental, always intimidating, Roy Keane took exception to the act and viciously berated Brown. Incensed by Keane's bullying, Quinn shoved his Irish national teammate before unleashing his own torrent of abuse. 'I have no excuses except it was City versus United', Quinn said, 'and for once I was up at a level of desire and intensity that might have matched Roy's'.

Perhaps his actions were also rooted in his frustration and resentment over irregular playing time and a frosty relationship with new manager Alan Ball. 'Alan and I never made it on to each other's Christmas card lists', Quinn said, 'and I hardly made it on to many of Alan's squad lists'. What he did make was the reserve squad, which was where Ball asked him to train for much of the winter of 1995-96. 'It's a strange feeling to be cold-shouldered by a club you love', Quinn later admitted.

Throughout that shambolic season, his final one with City, Quinn endured every obstacle with his usual grace, humour, and tenacity. When self-doubt took hold, he trained harder. When exhaustion wearied him, he focused on why he donned that sky-blue jersey. And when despair was ready to suffocate him, he reminded himself of the secret to being a successful footballer – a secret revealed in his autobiography – always be happy for the privilege of having your occupation be playing in a child's game. 'I was a workhorse', Quinn said of those final months of the 1995-96 campaign. 'I played on my own up front and ran my legs off. I did it because I am a professional, because even if they don't like me, they pay me and because City is a club with fans that deserve good things'.

For Quinn and his teammates, only three opportunities remained in the 1995-96 season to deliver these deserved good things. Stuck in the relegation zone, City hosted Sheffield Wednesday on April 13. Manager Alan Ball opted to return Uwe Rösler to the starting XI for the first time since March 23 – the German's exclusion was due to the pair's ongoing feud – and the decision paid dividends. In the 64th minute, Quinn received a throw-in from Martin Phillips, held off an Owl centre-back, and crossed for Rösler, who scored the match's only goal with a left-footed volley. 'Sometimes you have to drive your players to madness to get the right result', Ball said afterwards, likely alluding to the animosity that existed between him and several of his players.

Manchester City 1997/98: engineers of one of the most bizarre relegations in football history.

The euphoria over the hard-fought victory quickly faded when results started coming in from across the country. City's two relegation rivals also won: Coventry City defeated Queens Park Rangers and Southampton delivered a shock upset of table-leading Manchester United. More maddening was that the next round of fixtures produced similar results: Southampton nipped Bolton Wanderers, Coventry held off Wimbledon. Meanwhile, City overcame the flaws that plagued them all season – Georgi Kinkladze's tendency to drift in and out of matches, no attacking plan other than to hoist high balls to Quinn, missed scoring opportunities – to slip past host Aston Villa on a 69th-minute goal from Steve Lomas.

One week later, judgment day arrived: May 5 at Maine Road, an end-of-season match against Liverpool to determine City's Premier League fate. 'If we win next week, I'll bet we stay up', Ball declared after the win over Villa. Even the most resolutely optimistic City supporter would have hesitated to agree.

In today's age of instant information, constant connectivity, and uninterrupted communication, it is nearly impossible to imagine a scenario like the one that played out in Moss Side on this fateful Sunday afternoon. Since Manchester City were level on 37 points with Coventry City and Southampton, but trailing in goal difference, manager Alan Ball and his squad needed accurate updates on this pair of concurrent matches as much as they needed goals. Staying up was not only contingent on securing points, but also on how the relegation rivals fared.

In May 1996, there were no handheld devices to provide up-to-the-minute scores. Twitter was a transistor radio held to the ear. Years later, writer Tim Rich identified the source of the incorrect score line City received as well as detailed how quickly this one innocent falsehood found its way to the ears of the club's players, leading to one of the most dramatic – and bizarre – relegation moments in English football history.

Remarkably, only 20 minutes before the match's conclusion, City's relegation to Division One seemed so assured that updates from the Coventry and Southampton matches were unnecessary. Liverpool went ahead half a dozen minutes in when a low cross from Steve McManaman was inadvertently diverted into the net by last week's hero against Aston Villa, Steve Lomas. Niall Quinn wasted a pair of scoring opportunities six minutes apart and Uwe Rösler botched one of his own before Kop legend Ian Rush, playing in his last match for Liverpool, showed the two how to secure a spot on the scoresheet. His shot from outside the area deflected off Keith Curle's boot and into the right-hand corner.

The visitors remained two goals in front until the 71st minute when a nifty solo run by Georgi Kinkladze ended with him being fouled by Neil Ruddock in the penalty area. Rösler converted the spot kick. Seven minutes later, Martin Phillips, a second-half substitute for Quinn, delivered a cross to Kit Symons at the far post, who slotted home from close range. Then came the now infamous bit of misinformation.

City's bench received word that Southampton were trailing to Wimbledon, a result that meant Ball and his squad were safe and the Saints were in the relegation zone. Believing that a third goal was no longer needed, City's players utilised their best time-wasting tactics, including Lomas standing in the corner with the ball under his boot, holding off Liverpool players. Four minutes from stoppage time and still certain a draw kept them in the Premier League, City's coaching staff, bench, and nearby supporters then witnessed Quinn return to the pitch. The substituted striker learned from a police monitor in the tunnel that Southampton and Wimbledon were in fact drawing and that City required a third goal to save themselves. The juxtaposition of a frantic, running Quinn, decked out in his post-match attire of a yellow dress shirt and beige slacks, screaming at a group of kitted footballers, urging them to attack, made this one of the most indelible images in City's history. Lomas, later indulging in a bit of gallows humour, remarked that it was the fastest he had ever seen Quinn move.

In the 88th minute, that desperately needed third goal almost came. Kinkladze sent a ball into the area that Nicky Summerbee, stationed at the far post, headed back across goal. His delivery was just inches behind Mikhail Kavelashvili, who could not get a boot on the ball. The match ended 2-2, and soon after the final whistle, City learned that Coventry and Southampton drew as well.

In Rich's wonderful book, *Caught Beneath the Landslide: Manchester City in the 1990s,* David Horwich described how the calamitous final minutes unfolded. Horwich was watching the match from the directors' box with his father, Michael, who was a vice president at the club.

> *Just in front of me was a couple who I think were from Oldham. She always had a radio and would constantly give out the scores in every game. The guy next to her was the one responsible for the fuck-up. He shouted out to Francis Lee that Southampton were losing. Francis shouted the news to Martyn Margetson [the reserve goalkeeper] who was standing behind the City dug-out. Martyn passed the message on that we only needed to draw. Shortly afterwards, I tapped the woman with the radio on the shoulder and asked, 'Are Southampton losing?' and she replied, 'No. Defi-*

nitely drawing'. 'Definitely?' 'Definitely'. I then grabbed Franny Lee and said, 'Southampton are definitely drawing'. His face absolutely fell.

After being part of the funeral procession of supporters that departed Maine Road, Horwich met with clients at the Royal Oak pub in Didsbury. 'I was telling everyone the story of how "this wanker" had cost us relegation', he remembered, 'when this guy walked in and said, "I am so sorry". I told him it probably hadn't made any difference'.

Yes, after nearly nine months of dire performances on the pitch, erratic managing from Ball, and irresponsible decision-making from the board room, one mistaken score line likely did not make a difference.

On April 24, 1996, former Manchester City chairman Peter Swales suffered a massive heart attack. He was still recovering at Wythenshawe Hospital when he died on May 2. Three days later, prior to the start of the end-of-season match against Liverpool, both clubs and the Maine Road crowd observed a minute's silence for his passing. 'As everybody hung their heads', wrote David Conn in *Richer Than God: Manchester City, Modern Football, and Growing Up*, 'there was a sense of shame. We had hounded Swales out in an unforgiving public humiliation for a childhood hero, Francis Lee, who we believed would make us happy again. And here we all were, on the brink of relegation'.

There was worry that the silence would not be observed, that the booing and jeering that often emanated from these very stands when Swales was in charge would rain down once more. But the solemn stillness was never broken, the 31,436 supporters packed into Maine Road recognising that despite all the former chairman's flaws and mistakes, he was a man who bled sky blue, a fan who was truly City to the core.

During his takeover battle with Lee, Swales expressed his desire to preserve three seats in the directors' box and a table for four in the dining room. But by the time a settlement was reached – only two seats, no table – Swales made the decision to never again attend a match. 'I can't go to Maine Road', he confessed to club historian Dr. Gary James before he died. 'How would the fans treat me?'

1997-98: 'Are the Pies Really That Good?'

The essence of English football's first superstar is captured in a simple yet colourful early 20th-century cartoon. Kitted out in Manchester United red, Billy Meredith stands bowlegged, a toothpick jutting from his lips, a sack of money in his left hand. The toothpick was the Welshman's trademark, a callback to his adolescence working in the coal pits, where he developed a fondness for chewing tobacco, a messy habit he swapped for chomping on a toothpick when the Manchester City groundsmen began grumbling about the revolting mess he left on the Hyde Road pitch. His bowlegs – like a pair of calipers, one commentator remarked – were a feature of his hunched-over-the-ball playing style, an approach that allowed him to develop his legendary control and to emerge as the greatest right winger of his generation. And the sack of pounds? This was a sly reference to the massive financial scandal Meredith triggered, a turmoil that ended City's first period of sustained success and bolstered rival United's championship aspirations.

In the spring of 1904, Meredith was a leading figure in the increasingly popular world of professional football. Accounts of his brilliant performances filled English and Welsh sports pages. His likeness was captured in dozens of cartoons in the days before photography found widespread use among newspapers. He was a superb dribbler, 'magnetising the ball round his toes in a half-circle and then running down the field to the goal-line', wrote a *Manchester Guardian* scribe. When Meredith was not attacking the penalty area, he was hugging the touchline, darting past bewildered defenders to deliver pinpoint crosses into the box. In addition to his superior ball control and sublime passing accuracy, Meredith possessed a deft scoring touch, an inherent skill that set him apart from his wing-playing brethren. He was City's top scorer in four seasons out of five in the late 19th century.

At the 1904 FA Cup final, Meredith, calmly chewing on a toothpick, led City onto the pitch at London's Crystal Palace. The club's appearance marked the first time in the competition's 32-year history that a side from Manchester advanced to the final. Meredith ensured it was a memorable one for the thousands of supporters who made the rail trip from Lancashire. The Welshman tallied the match's only goal in the 23rd minute when he received a ball from teammate George Livingstone, dashed more than 30 yards down the right wing – and showcasing his exemplary dribbling ability – skipped past a Bolton Wanderers defender, and fired a shot into the Trotters' goal.

Football correspondents from *The Daily Graphic* newspaper felt that Billy Meredith was offside, and the goal should have been disallowed. The offside rule at the time stated that three players had to be goal side of the attacker when the ball was played. The writers believed this was not the case when Livingstone played the ball to Meredith. The debate over whether it was a goal or not continued for decades. Thirty years later, in the leadup to Manchester City's appearance in the 1934 FA Cup final, Meredith was asked if he was indeed offside. 'Nonsense', he replied. 'Not a single Bolton player made a murmur'.

Meredith's journey from the drudgery of heavy industry to the celebrity of professional football was not uncommon in the late 1800s and early 1900s, when generations of players picked up the sport to avoid the pit or the dole. Meredith was born on July 30, 1874, in Chirk, a small Welsh town located on the border with England. Chirk was situated in the heart of an important coal-mining area that supplied Lancashire's ever-expanding industrial machine. Throughout Meredith's childhood, there were two pits, Black Park and Brynkinalt, both operating behind the picturesque hills that overlooked the town. His father and older brothers worked at the former, and when Meredith turned 12, he did as well. He started at the bottom of the main shaft, unhooking tubs from the trains that hauled coal to the surface, progressed to driving the pit ponies that towed tubs of coal, and graduated to 'hutching', which involved pushing tubs along stretches of the shaft too difficult for the ponies to traverse.

Football became Meredith's escape from the subterranean misery of the coal mines, his love for the game nurtured by his three older brothers: Jim, a right full-back; Sam, a left full-back, made close to 50 appearances for Stoke City; and Elias, who brought Meredith to see the day's top English sides, often hoisting his younger brother onto his shoulders to give him a better view of the action on the pitch. During one trip with Elias, Meredith watched Preston North End's legendary 'Invincibles' side, which ended the season unbeaten and became the first to win a league and cup double. Many years later, he spoke of the great impact fleet-footed winger Jack Gordon made on his approach to the game.

Packed with local miners, Meredith's hometown club possessed one of the most successful working-class amateur sides of this era. He made his first-team debut with Chirk in September 1892 and spent the next season dividing his time between his local club, Northwich Victoria, and Wrexham. In November 1894, City – recently rechristened after seven seasons as Ardwick AFC – signed Meredith on amateur forms. The Welshman was enticed by the passion of the club's administrators and servants as well as the employment and domestic accommodations. He temporarily worked at W&J Galloway and Sons, a Manchester-based manufacturer of steam engines and boilers, the job fulfilling his passion for engineering. Meredith was also offered lodging on Clowes Street, a few hundred yards from City's ground, where he stayed in between return trips to Chirk.

The club was rewarded generously for its efforts to comfortably settle its big signing. Meredith tallied 12 goals during the 1894-95 campaign and 90 in total during his first six seasons, impressive figures for a winger. Equally noteworthy was his durability. The Welshman missed only seven league games during his first five seasons with City. Nicknamed 'Merry Meredith' by supporters, he became the club's most popular player and its most recognisable name at the national level. 'He was a crowd-pleaser', wrote John Harding in *Football Wizard: The Billy Meredith Story*. 'With his speed, his powerful long-range shooting which produced spectacular goals, and his baffling ball control that bemused many a heavily built full-back, he was perfectly equipped to give the people what they wanted, what all football fans have ever wanted: entertainment'.

But after the 1904-05 campaign, the City star found his name in national newspapers for reasons other than his on-the-pitch exploits. On April 29, the final Saturday of the season, Meredith and his teammates were scheduled to face Aston Villa at Villa Park. A victory coupled with a Newcastle United loss would give City their first-ever title. 'Our officials were very keen on us finishing with level points', Meredith remembered, 'and we were offered a good bonus [£100] if we managed to do this. Our blood was up, and the game wasn't the pleasantest'. In the second half, with the visitors trailing 3-1 and their title hopes all but gone, the match turned ugly when City's Sandy Turnbull struck Villa captain Alec Leake. Football correspondents covering the match disagreed on how the fight started but agreed that Turnbull got the better of his opponent.

During the close season, as accusations flew in local newspapers, the Football Association launched an investigation into the incident. On August 5, the FA announced its findings, and fans across the country were stunned to learn the report did more than address the players' misconduct. In addition to a suspension for Turnbull, Meredith was banned for the entirety of the 1905-06 campaign for bribery. A witness claimed he overheard a conversation during which Meredith offered Leake £10 to intentionally lose the match. From his wife's home in Chirk, the Welshman issued a sternly worded denial: 'Such an allegation as that of bribery is preposterous! I could never risk my reputation and future by such an action, and I repeat that I never made such an offer'. Newspaper articles supported him, declaring him a man of integrity, a sportsman of principle. Potential legal moves were discussed. In the end, the FA's ruling was final, and the winger had no choice but to serve the suspension.

Yet the matter did not end there. City's complaints over Meredith's punishment and the anti-Football Association comments appearing in northern newspapers angered the FA's councilors. An auditor named Tom Hindle was appointed to closely watch the club and report any suspicious activity. Hindle had just started his scrutiny of City when he discovered something out of the ordinary: while banned from all football-related activity, Meredith was still attending matches at Hyde Road and visiting the dressing room and club offices. More damning was the topics of conversation during the Welshman's visits. Having been with the club for over a decade, Meredith felt it was the board's duty to take care of him financially while he was not playing. 'At the beginning of the trouble it looked as if the club was going to recognise this', Meredith said, 'but later I found them shilly-shallying and putting me off until I got tired.' Meredith's visits to Hyde Road were marked by heated arguments with club secretary Tom Maley and club directors over the payment of his wages – arguments Hindle witnessed. Maley ultimately presented Meredith with a letter stating that he would always be a Blue but that he would have to 'lie low' until Hindle's shadowing of the club ended. Since the FA explicitly stated that City could not support the suspended player, this was in direct violation of its ruling.

Another FA commission was appointed, and City players and management were questioned about Meredith's alleged bribe against Villa as well as the possibility of illegal payments to players, a growing issue in the world of professional football. During the late 19th century, football's traditionalists and progressives squared off in a battle for the soul of the game. The former group felt that the Football League's burgeoning financial success was robbing football of its inherent 'sporting' values, that only amateur players were true 'sportsmen'; the latter welcomed the rise of professionalism and recognised that football was a business, one that was increasingly driven by large profits. A compromise was reached in 1901 when the Football League introduced a maximum wage of £4 per week and abolished the paying of all bonuses to players. But the sport's dirty little secret was that even after the introduction of these new financial rules, players were regularly paid under the table and given performance bonuses and extra pounds in their weekly wage packets.

Still incensed by the lack of compensation from his club, Meredith was more than willing to volunteer information about City's illegal pay practices. 'From 1902 I had been paid £6 a week', Meredith later confessed. 'I don't believe that any member of our team was paid less than I was, and the season we carried off the Cup [1903-04], I also received £53 in bonuses for games won and drawn. Some players drew more. Altogether, the club paid in bonuses £654 12s 6d. The team delivered the goods and the club paid for the goods delivered, and both sides were satisfied'.

In his dealings with the FA, Maley did not deny that City paid its players more than the maximum allowed, but he also stated that this was a common business practice among leading English clubs. Maley stated that if the FA examined the books of all 20 First Division clubs, not four would come out 'scatheless'. Unfortunately for City, they were the club under intense scrutiny and for their transgressions, they were harshly penalised.

On May 31, 1906, the FA issued its verdict. City and their players were both found guilty – the club for disregarding the sport's financial regulations, the footballers for having demanded the illegal payments. The punishments were harsh and unprecedented: 17 current and former players were suspended until January 1, 1907, Maley and former chairman Waltham Forrest were banned from English football sine die, and director John Allison was handed a seven-month suspension. Massive fines were also handed out: £250 for the club and a staggering £900 spread among the 17 players. Meredith and Livingstone, who was earning 10 shillings more a week than Meredith, were the most heavily fined with each required to pay £100.

The release of the FA's punishments brought an unceremonious end to City's first golden period, a four-year stretch during which the club captured the Second Division title in 1903, finished as runners-up in the league and won the FA Cup the next spring, and then claimed third and fifth in the table the next two seasons. Derby County secretary-manager Harry Newbould replaced the suspended Maley and was given the nigh-impossible task of rebuilding the stripped-bare, demoralised club. When he joined in July 1906, the squad had only 11 available players. Signing new talent meant draining the club's coffers, as rival First Division teams, aware of

Newbound's desperation, demanded exorbitant transfer fees for City's players. The club slumped to 17th in 1906-07 and were relegated two seasons later.

It should be noted that the conclusion of City's first golden period coincided with the start of Manchester United's first – which was no accident. After the Football Association's punishments in May 1906, four City players – Meredith, Turnbull, Herbert Burgess, and Jimmy Bannister – joined crosstown rivals United. The quartet made up the core of the sides that won the First Division in 1908 and the FA Cup one year later.

For the next 90 years, this financial scandal remained City's nadir; a woeful chapter in the club's history that left directors and players alike questioning the very future of football at Hyde Road, a moment of humiliation that filled longtime supporters with anger and despair. Ninety years later, during the summer of 1996, even the most intuitive City fan would not have foretold what the coming autumn would bring: a new club crisis, a new nadir, and new feelings of hopelessness.

During the nineties and noughties, *BBC Radio* deejays Marc Riley and Mark Radcliffe built up a cult following with their support for alternative music and penchant for offbeat humour. Both stalwart Blues, the pair recorded a spoof album under the stage name Shirehorses. One track was a takeoff of Nick Cave and The Bad Seeds' cover of the traditional folk song 'Henry Lee'. The lyrics resonated with Manchester City supporters:

Going down, going down, little Franny Lee,
Down to Division Three.
We've only one lad who isn't half bad,
And that's little George Kinkladze.
And at first the crowd roared,
But now they're just bored.
They go la-la-la-la-la, la-la-la-la-Lee,
This is the ballad of Franny Lee.

Much like Peter Swales before him, Francis Lee was now officially the subject of parody. And during the first five months of the 1996-97 season, his increasingly tumultuous and dysfunctional chairmanship became a study in absurdism.

Back for another go, manager Alan Ball continued to exhibit a blatant disregard for the art of understatement, declaring in August that he was 'on the cross' after the previous season's relegation. He was soon in the managerial unemployment line as well. After an August 24 loss to Stoke City and only days after signing Arsenal's Paul Dickov for £1 million, the former World Cup winner stated he was committed to returning City to the Premier League. But after discussions with his family and Lee, he changed course and resigned.

Asa Hartford, the club's 1979 Player of the Year, took over as caretaker while Lee searched for Ball's replacement. Former Arsenal boss George Graham, winner of all four domestic trophies during his time in North London, expressed interest in

Beleaguered Manchester City chairman Francis Lee.

the job, but after chatting with the City chairman, and discovering there was little money for new signings, decided against the move. Prior to the season-opening match against Ipswich Town, however, Manchester City chairman Francis Lee had stated, that although the club had not purchased so much as a goldfish during the summer, money was available to sign players. Other candidates included Bruce Rioch, Graham's successor at Arsenal, and former Republic of Ireland national team manager Jack Charlton.

As the search dragged on and additional big names were rumoured – including Crystal Palace's Dave Bassett and, most shocking of all, Howard Kendall, who walked out on City in November 1990 – Lee publicly discussed the possibility of hiring Hartford on a full time basis, only for the Scotsman to respond that even he had no interest in skippering a club that was struggling both financially and competitively. 'I have a contract as assistant manager', Hartford stated, 'and I am just taking temporary charge until someone is brought in'.

At Maine Road, supporters expressed their feelings on the extended vacancy with renditions of 'Nobody's Blue-and-White Army'. A sense of humour was certainly needed to process what was transpiring on the pitch. On September 17, City lost 4-1 to fourth-tier Lincoln City in the League Cup, a side that, according to a match report in *The Guardian*, 'boasted all the finesse of a pub team'. One week later, they were defeated again – this time 1-0 at home – and knocked out in the second round of this competition for the first time in 20 years.

The management job no one wanted finally went to former Manchester United winger Steve Coppell, who was appointed on October 7, six weeks after Ball stepped down. The move came less than 48 hours after a desperate Lee admitted that he was seriously considering taking control of first-team duties himself. In his first press conference with the media, Coppell deftly addressed his chairman's struggle to find a new manager and the fact that he spent most of his career wearing red. 'I am not bothered that other people did not want to take this job', he said, 'and the fact that I played for Manchester United is also irrelevant'.

Tact and diplomacy were certainly Coppell's strong suits. Supporters never quite learned if their new manager was equally adept at scouting, player selection, and match management. On November 8, his 33rd day on the job, Coppell stepped down, citing medical reasons and the pressures of modern football. 'Since my appointment', he stated during his final press conference for the club, 'this has completely overwhelmed me to such an extent that I cannot function in the job the way I would like to'. Shaken by the shock resignation and embittered by how the last managerial search transpired, Lee announced he would not immediately search for Coppell's replacement and that assistant Phil Neal was in charge for the foreseeable future.

Crushed by the extremely high standards he set for himself and the elevated expectations of supporters desperate to return to the Premier League, Coppell joined Kenny Dalglish, Terry Cooper, and Barry Fry as the latest manager to quit the game because of mental and physical health issues. His reign remains the shortest in club history.

Neal's first match in charge was a 3-2 loss to Oxford United. After the final whistle, a large contingent of the Maine Road crowd besieged the entrance to the ground, shouting angrily for the sacking of the board and the resignation of Lee. A Boxing Day loss at home to Port Vale was followed by more heated protests from fans. Three days later, Frank Clark, who resigned as Nottingham Forest boss less than two weeks earlier, became the fifth City manager in four months. He took over a club that was an estimated £15 million in debt, had dropped 15 of its first 25 league matches, and was only three spots from the bottom, the lowest standing in its long history.

Clark did not pick up his first league win until February 2, courtesy of a 4-1 drubbing of Oxford United, but the victory did right the ship. City lost only four of their remaining 17 matches and ended the season in 14th with 61 points. An unfortunate finish for a club aiming for an immediate return to the top flight but also a gratifying one considering where Clark's squad was positioned during the holiday period.

There were reasons for optimism heading into the 1997-98 campaign. Kinkladze signed a new three-year contract, making him the highest paid player in the club's history. 'We had to show our fans that we can compete with the very best', Lee stated, 'and we can pay wages to match'. Clark had delivered much-needed stability and confidence and during the close season, would be given the necessary funds to sign players that would better suit his system. History was on City's side as well. Since first earning promotion to the top flight in 1899, the club had only one stretch during which it played more than two seasons in the Second Division: 1963 to 1966.

City played in the Second Division during the 1938-39 and 1939-40 seasons and then when league play resumed after World War II, the 1946-47 season. However, the 1939-40 season was abandoned after only three matches.

Promotion was the goal and the only acceptable outcome. Failure to deliver on this objective and the vitriol directed toward the chairman would surpass anything Swales endured. Riley and Radcliffe's parody song would become a matchday staple at Maine Road. 'Going down, going down, little Franny Lee ...'

Manchester City's Georgi Kinkladze is unique among the hundreds of footballers who have pulled on the sky-blue jersey. There have been more prolific goal scorers, more precise passers, more deft dribblers, more tactically aware midfielders, more athletically gifted footballers, more talented all-around players. But none of them were Kinky, none were Gio, none regularly produced 'I was there when ...' moments for supporters or effortlessly crafted goals in contention for the greatest ever seen at Maine Road. During City's dark age, he was a slash of brilliant colour in a landscape of ashen grey. Similarly, no other club legend was a source of such divisiveness or was so equal parts maddening and mesmeric that he could elicit a comment like the one Everton manager Joe Royle made to former teammate Tony Book after a matchup with Gio and City: 'Kinkladze's a great talent, Booky, but he'll get you all the sack'.

For three seasons during the 1990s, two of which ended in relegation, Kinkladze was the centre of attention, the player under a beaming spotlight – supporters glorified his performances on the pitch, criticised him for his off-the-field controversies, and debated where he fitted into the squad tactically. 'Gio Kinkladze was all we had', wrote David Clayton in *Kinkladze: The Perfect 10*. 'He became like a piece of floating timber amidst the chaos of a shipwreck, in essence, something to cling to'.

Kinkladze was born on July 6, 1973, in Tbilisi, Georgia, then a Soviet Union republic. His father, Robizon, indulged his love for football by starting his son on a training regime at an early age. As soon as he could stand unaided, Robizon continuously rolled a ball to the toddler so he could learn to trap and kick. Daily workouts were fuelled by one-litre blends of apple, pear, pomegranate, and beetroot juices mixed by Robizon. 'He was never without a ball', his father remembered. 'We lived on the seventh floor, but I never let him go up in the lift. He had to bring the football up with his feet; he couldn't pick it up in his hands'.

Robizon's unconventional methods of training did not end there. He enrolled his son in regular classes for Mtiuluri, a traditional Georgian mountain dance, to improve his balance and footwork. Kinkladze's mother, Khatuna, wanted her son to give up football and dedicate himself to dance. So strong was this desire that Khatuna hid her son's boots when her husband was away on work commitments.

In the end, football won out. Robizon set up a mini gym in their home for daily exercise routines. Each night, after watching Kinkladze train at the Young Dinamo football school, he lectured his son on the mistakes he made that day and offered suggestions for improvement. 'Dad played a huge part in making Georgi a footballer', said older sister Marina. 'He was so dedicated and worked really hard with him'.

The deep commitment and endless preparation paid dividends. At age 16, Kinkladze made his professional debut with Mretebi Tbilisi, a club that he helped gain promotion to the Georgian Premier Division. From there, it was on to Dinamo Tbilisi, where he made an immediate impact: 14 goals in 30 appearances and 13 in 14 matches the next season. Kinkladze then struggled to find a permanent home, bouncing from Saarbrücken in Germany to Boca Juniors in Argentina and back to Dinamo. Ultimately, it was a performance for the Georgian national football team against Moldova in September 1994 that brought attention to his breathtaking talent. When the footage of this performance found its way to Francis Lee, the City chairman connected with Dinamo president Merab Jordania and was promised first refusal should Kinkladze become available – a brilliant tactic on Lee's part as two more international performances brought the Georgian wider acclaim.

In November 1994, Kinkladze ran Wales ragged in a 5-0 victory in the group stages of Georgia's 1996 Euro qualifying campaign. 'He ripped us apart in Georgia', said Welsh goalkeeper Neville Southall. 'He was a different class and the best player on the pitch by a mile. Everything went through Kinkladze that day and he was just as good in the return game in Wales'. In this match, Kinkladze scored the only goal on the afternoon in the 73rd minute: a cheeky chip from 25 yards out that sailed over the head of an out-of-position Southall. 'I recall booting one of the Georgians as they retrieved the ball out of the net', joked Southall, 'but I don't think it was Kinkladze'. City scout Jimmy Frizzell was in Cardiff to assess the Georgian and when he returned to Manchester, told Lee, 'If you've got an orchestra, he'll conduct it'.

On July 14, 1995, City completed the deal for Kinkladze, splashing out £2 million for the playmaking midfielder. The first Georgian to play in the Premier League, Kinkladze knew precious few words of English, prompting Lee to boast to journalists at the introductory press conference that he would soon be talking with his feet.

Across England that summer, similar press conferences were taking place at other top-flight clubs. After decades of signing primarily British and Irish players, chairmen were now regularly plucking talented footballers from Western and Eastern Europe. 'English soccer had always been suspicious of foreigners', wrote Joshua Robinson and Jonathan Clegg in *The Club: How the English Premier League Became the Wildest, Richest, Most Disruptive Force in Sports*, 'something about being an island in a post-empire age with a deeply ingrained skepticism of Europe and an unwavering conviction that Britain simply did things better, from its currency to its electrical plugs'. Case in point: The Premier League's first round of fixtures in August 1992 featured just thirteen foreign players – and half were Dutch or Scandinavian.

Three years later, with the eye-watering money and global exposure from *British Sky Broadcasting's* television deal having dramatically transformed the sport, Premier League clubs cast aside the decades-old xenophobic approach to recruiting talent and looked to the Continent for electrifying – and thus, expensive – talent. The arrival of Dutch stars Ruud Gullit and Dennis Bergkamp and Frenchman David Ginola during the summer of 1995 overshadowed Kinkladze's signing. The next year brought Gianfranco Zola, Gianluca Vialli, Ole Gunnar Solskjær, and Patrick Vieira. Foreign players were no longer viewed as curiosities – they were embraced as stars.

Which was the treatment Kinkladze received his first season at City. During his debut in sky blue on August 19, 1995, supporters passionately cheered his name and applauded his introduction – a reception that slightly embarrassed the Georgian. All throughout that day's 1-1 draw with Tottenham Hotspur, applause greeted every touch, pass, dummy, and shake of the hips. 'And what a gem the Blues have unearthed in little Kinkladze', wrote Paul Hince, City correspondent for *The Manchester Evening News*. 'Ball's first match as manager is likely to be the day a star was born'.

While Kinkladze struggled with the language barrier and cultural differences – his mother eventually moved to Manchester to cook and care for the unsettled Georgian, arriving with a suitcase stuffed with her son's favorite foods – he seamlessly assimilated into the squad. He set up Nicky Summerbee's winner against Bolton Wanderers on November 4 and sparkled again in a 1-1 draw at Sheffield Wednesday two weeks later. On November 25, the Georgian delivered his finest performance of the young season, using every trick in his extensive repertoire to unlock a formidable Aston Villa defence before scoring the match's only goal in the 85th minute.

By December, it was apparent that Kinkladze was the rare, hallowed footballer who could craft a moment of pure bliss, a player that delivered such a dizzying buzz you forgot or forgave every transgression and sin committed by their teammates on the pitch that afternoon. On the ninth of this month, during a dreary 4-1 away loss to Middlesbrough, the Georgian produced a goal-of-the-season candidate, brilliantly captured by Clayton in *Kinkladze: The Perfect 10*:

> *He received the ball from a [Ian] Brightwell throw-in just inside the Boro half and then wandered into the centre of the park before turning sharply towards goal, leaving two Boro midfielders in his wake. He then ghosted past another challenge 25 yards out, sold a dummy to two defenders just inside the box and then placed a shot accurately in at the far post with his left foot, just out of the reach of goalkeeper Gary Walsh.*

Boro supporters rewarded Kinkladze by voting him 'best opposing player' at the season's end. City fans blessed him with one of the most memorable terrace songs in club history, changing the chorus to Oasis' massive hit 'Wonderwall' to: 'And all the runs that Kinky makes are winding.... And all the goals that City score are blinding'.

A second never-to-be-forgotten moment came three months later on March 16, 1996. Fighting for their Premier League lives, City hosted fellow relegation battlers Southampton on a Manchester kind of afternoon: slate grey sky, mist in the air, a gnawing chill. Kinkladze appeared to care little for the difficult conditions. With 15 minutes gone, his blistering drive shook the water droplets off the Platt Lane end crossbar. Less than 20 minutes later, he put the hosts ahead: Nigel Clough's shot was palmed away by Saints keeper Dave Beasant and Kinkladze tapped in the rebound.

This goal was merely a prelude to the magic the Georgian served up next. Taking the ball from Steve Lomas just inside Southampton's half, Kinkladze pirouetted and darted toward goal while evading the clutches and grabs of Simon Charlton, slithered past the outstretched leg of Ken Monkou, hop-stepped over an attempted slide tackle, and then, surely breathless by now, toe-tapped deep into the penalty area, drew out a scrambling Beasant with breathtaking calm, and then delicately lifted the ball over the keeper's left shoulder. 'Oh, that's mesmeric', enthused

Match of the Day commentator Jon Champion, 'it's sublime, and it's typically Georgi Kinkladze!' This was a goal carefully crafted by a ballet artist working in the medium of football – or goal from a footballer infused with the soul of a dancer.

Kinkladze's wonder strike was the highlight of City's relegation season. The next season, with the club down in Nationwide League Division 1, the Georgian scored 12 times despite an endless glut of reckless challenges and rash tackles from the men marking him. By this time, the continuous meddling with the starting XI to discover the lineup that best emphasized Kinkladze's strengths – started by Alan Ball and continued with the club's carousel of coaches during the first five months of 1996 – became the bigger story.

'I knew I had a special talent in the team', said Steve Coppell, 'but the problem I had was working out how best to use him. If he wasn't creating, he wasn't producing. In that City side at the time, there was nobody who could do what he could do. Admittedly, he could have one good game, one average game, and maybe two bad games and get away with it, but I was trying to put the burden of responsibility back on his shoulders'.

Three months into his stint as manager at Maine Road, Frank Clark was still uncertain of Kinkladze's best position as well as how to properly utilize him. He spent the summer of 1997 attempting to develop a proper tactical plan – preparation that was necessary now that the Georgian had inked a three-year deal on May 17 and was returning. City's other headline move during the close season was paying £3.25 million to Portsmouth for England Under-21 striker Lee Bradbury, the most expensive signing in club history.

The 1997-98 campaign opened similarly to the previous two: with City in dreadful form. After a 2-2 draw against Portsmouth in the August 9 home opener, Clark and his squad were in Sunderland on August 15 for the christening of their new Stadium of Light. Old friend Niall Quinn tallied the opener as the visitors fell 3-1. One week later, a listless 1-1 home draw with Tranmere Rovers delivered boos and jeers – and the season's first bit of controversy. Striker Uwe Rösler reacted furiously to being subbed off by kicking a water bucket and throwing a sports drink to the ground. 'There are no problems', Rösler insisted after his outburst. 'I have a really good relationship with Frank Clark. He knows me, knows that I have a high temperament'.

Tantrums in the stands would have been the appropriate response after City's elimination from the League Cup on August 28. Having cancelled out third-tier Blackpool's first-leg advantage thanks to an 88th-minute goal from Kevin Horlock, the squad proceeded to hit the woodwork and the keeper during a 4-2 penalty shootout defeat. The less than 13,000 who turned up at Maine Road watched a City side that dominated in possession while looking woefully uncreative in the final third. A floundering Clark was left to grasp at straws. 'That's our first victory of the season and we have to take some heart from that'.

A 3-1 win over Nottingham Forest on September 3 eased a little of the pressure on the manager. Ged Brannan, a Clark signing in March 1997 for a fee of £750,000, recorded the only brace of his short City career. A struggling Bradbury helped set up Brannan's first goal.

Then results turned sour again. A meek Kinkladze penalty was saved in a 1-1 draw at newly promoted Bury on September 12. Eight days later, Bradbury finally opened his goal-scoring account for City in a 2-1 home loss to Norwich City, although by that stage fans had started referring to the £3 million Lee Bradbury without the Rs in his surname. He picked up his second in a 6-0 drubbing of Swindon Town on September 27 with Kinkladze, Horlock, and Paul Dickov joining him on the scoresheet. City failed to find the net in their next four matches, three of which ended in defeat. With Bradbury and Rösler injured, Dickov and Michael Brown were left to carry the goal-scoring burden, but their finishing was continually lacking.

With their club only three points from the bottom, City supporters found pleasure in matters off the pitch. In late September, a *Match of the Day* magazine survey of leading sports retail outlets in *selected* areas revealed that the top five replica shirts sold in Manchester were City home, City away, Liverpool, Italy, and Brazil. The results were fodder for passionate Blues who had long argued that their club claimed more supporters within the city limits than their hated rivals.

Few supporters were in a humourous mood after a 1-0 home loss to Stoke City on October 22. Fans staged an angry protest outside Maine Road, chanting 'Franny out' and 'We're shit and we're sick of it'. Stewards and police protected the directors' entrance with steel barriers. 'We are just crawling on our hands and knees at the moment', said Clark. For a manager barely ten months on the job, the stress and anxiety had become unimaginable. Except anyone familiar with the ex-Nottingham Forest star knew that cracking under this strain was not an option.

Frank Clark was approaching 32, had a reputation for being injury-prone, and most discouraging of all, was without a club. Released by Newcastle United, where he once worn the captain's armband, Clark received interest from Darlington, Doncaster Rovers, and Hartlepool United – all Fourth Division clubs – when the unlikeliest of managers rang him up, stated he was looking for an individual to organise his defence, and gave instructions to meet him at Scotch Corner on the A1.

'My car broke down on the way', Clark remembered. 'That was probably the only time I was ever late to meet Brian, but fortunately he waited, and we managed to get it sorted. He talked about his plans. He admitted they didn't have a very good team and that he desperately needed someone to play left-back, and he said I was the cheapest available. I knew all about his style – and I didn't have too many options'.

The Brian was Brian Clough, and over the course of the next four seasons, Clark did precisely what the legendary manager asked. He anchored Nottingham Forest's back four, played with unflappable calm and total confidence, faced down many an opposing attacker without going to ground (or, as teammate Kenny Burns put it, understanding that 'God didn't put studs in your arse'), and in the process, won First Division and European Cup medals. And while he toiled away under Clough, learned that a thick skin, a lack of ego, and a sense of perspective were keys to being a successful footballer – lessons he carried with him to the technical area. 'I like star players, special players', he told *The Independent* roughly three months after taking the City job, 'but I don't like that star attitude'.

Clark was an atypical manager: uncomfortable in the standard dress of his profession – whether tracksuit or three-piece suit – undemonstrative on the touchline, free of the self-created controversies that surrounded many of his colleagues.

'Always one of the most popular and engaging of managers', Paul Wilson wrote in *The Observer*, 'with a good line in droll self-deprecation'. For City, he was part of a dying breed, along with his successors, Joe Royle, Kevin Keegan, and Stuart Pearce – men who did not arrive at Maine Road or later, the Etihad Stadium, with sparkling managerial CVs, surnames recognised across Europe, or eight-figure salaries. Clark was a direct link to an age that was passing, to the sport that existed before the Premier League, lucrative television money, and Monday night pageantry.

Three months into the 1997-98 campaign, there were doubts that even a member of the old guard, one of the most respected managers in the English game, had the power to save City. Clark faced enormous expectations when the season kicked off, certainly bigger than usual on account of the club's year zero approach. Under the direction of Chief Executive Mike Turner, who replaced Colin Barlow the previous season, the club's souvenir shop – which, according to esteemed local photographer Kevin Cummins, contained nothing at all you would ever want to buy – was replaced by the City Superstore, erected on the spot of the old social club. City also ended their 63-year relationship with Umbro and signed a kit manufacturing deal with Kappa. The Italian sportswear company broke with tradition and changed the home colours to a deeper, hipper shade named 'laser blue'.

Equally as surprising was Turner's decision to redesign the club badge, which had been in place, albeit in varying different forms, since 1970. Inscribed with a Latin motto that translated to 'pride in battle' and dominated by a golden eagle and three decorative stars, the new badge was strongly derided by fans. Nonetheless, the club's suddenly modernised outlook and its willingness to turn its back on the past had supporters feeling optimistic.

By late October, a verdict had been reached: new look, same old club. After 12 matches, City had taken a paltry ten points and sat in the embarrassing position of 22nd, firmly entrenched in the relegation zone. 'Manchester City', wrote Jim White in *The Guardian*, 'the 24-hours-a-day, seven-days-a-week, 12-months-of-the-year crisis club'. The latest calamity occurred on October 28 when Georgi Kinkladze wrecked his £50,000 Ferrari 355 by slamming into a signpost and motorway bridge support. Miraculously, the midfielder walked away from the crash only needing 30 stiches. However, he did lose his place in the starting XI the next night at home to Crewe Alexandra. In a rare bit of good fortune for Clark, the player he selected to replace Kinkladze, debutante Chris Greenacre, scored the match's only goal.

The October 22 protest outside Maine Road demonstrated that supporters were furious and frustrated over the mounting losses. Yet the fans were not voting with their feet. Despite the poor run of form and the club's precarious position in the table, the Maine Road stands were mostly full: 30,474 for the season opener against Portsmouth, 27,258 versus Norwich City on September 20, 27,384 to see Crewe Alexandra, and crowds of more than 25,000 in four other home fixtures. While not a hard and fast rule, relegated clubs typically suffer noted declines in gate receipts. When Wolverhampton Wanderers, Sheffield Wednesday, and Birmingham City were sent down, their crowds shrank significantly. Stuck in the old Second Division basement, Newcastle United saw home attendances dwindle to less than 12,000. In recent English football history, there was no precedent for this brand of devotion. 'The support is marvelous', Clark said, 'but the expectation here is unreal. I've never known quite that combination before, but it's what makes the club what it is'.

Asked White in that piece in *The Guardian*, 'Is loyalty to City just a mark of stubborn differentness from Red-favoring friends and colleagues? Is the match merely an opportunity for group masochism? Or are the pies really that good?' Maybe the shared trauma resulting from the many years of relegation instilled in supporters the desire to be intimate, to be close to one another every other Saturday, to stand shoulder to shoulder in the Kippax. Maybe watching City provided fans with a much needed but similarly uncomfortable window into their own lives, an opportunity to examine their frailties, their vulnerabilities, and more than anything else, their humanity. Or maybe, just maybe, the Maine Road pies really *were* that good.

Whatever the case was, City supporters continued to journey to Moss Side, to crowd into Maine Road's four stands, to cheer wildly, boo noisily, sing lustily. 'City 'til I die! / I'm City 'til I die! / I know I am, I'm sure I am / I'm City 'til I die!' A simple song about a fan's complex relationship with their football club, a song that does not allude to past glories or triumphs to come, but simply declares that they are dedicated, will forever remain dedicated, and only death will erase their loyalty.

If there existed an all-time table for testing fan loyalty, Manchester City would unquestionably be perched at the top. The month of November delivered further defeats, fresh protests, new setbacks – and still, considerable crowds. A 3-2 home loss on November 4 prompted another post-match demonstration against chairman Francis Lee. City's woes increased when they learned Lee Bradbury, their £3 million signing over the summer, would be out until January due to a bone fracture in his back.

In perhaps one of the stranger fixture list coincidences, City's November 7 match was against Huddersfield Town, ten years to the day after thrashing them 10-1. Results favoured the Terriers this time, as the visitors departed with a 1-0 victory. A week later, City stole a point at Sheffield United thanks to Kevin Horlock's last-minute tap-in. Around this time, Lee uttered the quote of the season: 'I've played in the World Cup, sweated out multi-million-pound business deals. I've trained some good horses. I'm a father. And yet 90 minutes at Maine Road can make me feel like an old dish rag'. Never has a chairman sounded more like a tortured fan.

Further late-match heroics – this time a goal from Tony Vaughan – earned Clark and his men three home points against Bradford City on November 22. A 3-1 loss to Stockport County was followed by three more much-needed points versus West Bromwich Albion. In the 55th minute, Georgi Kinkladze skated across a slick, icy surface to send a cross to Paul Dickov, who flicked in the ball at the near post to give City their second away win of the season.

The hope was the season was poised to take a turn for the better. But this was City, whose ground had earned the unenviable nickname the Theatre of Comedy, a twisted play on Manchester United's Theatre of Dreams. At Maine Road, hope was snickered at and ridiculed. Another frenetic finish – three goals in the last ten minutes, including two in stoppage time – disguised a rather dull 2-1 Birmingham City victory. 'Perhaps the worst thing we did was to score the opening goal, as a goalless draw would have been acceptable to us in the circumstances', said Clark, having lost all sense of logic. Perhaps the pressures of the job were causing him to crack.

A 2-0 home win over Middlesbrough, the club's fourth against a top-seven opponent, was pushed to the back pages due to an announcement from Oasis' Noel Gallagher, a lifelong City supporter, that he had no intention of sinking his millions into the club. 'At the end of the day I am a fan', said the musician, 'and I don't want those scally City fans coming round my house putting my windows in when City are in the Third Division, blaming it all on me'.

After a particularly un-festive holiday period, relegation to the third tier appeared inevitable. City suffered a 1-0 away defeat to Crewe Alexandra on Boxing Day and then a 3-2 loss to Nottingham Forest at Maine Road on December 28. Continuing the season's trend, City played impressively in a 2-0 home win over Bradford in the third round of the FA Cup and a 3-0 away thrashing of Portsmouth. Two steps back, one step forward.

The New Year victories marked a return to form for Uwe Rösler, who was at loggerheads with Clark earlier in the season, first because of how he reacted to being substituted and later when he was hesitant to commit long-term to the club. An ever-dependable striker during a five-year stretch in which goals were at a premium, Rösler was a fixture in the starting XI during the most tumultuous chapter in the club's history. During a period of scarce standout talent for City, he was one of the few to lay claim to being a star. Unknown to him, his career in sky blue had entered its final act.

When he was a youngster, Uwe Rösler won selection to Leipzig's school of excellence, an academy of sorts for East German footballers, marksmen, swimmers, track and field athletes, weightlifters, and volleyball and handball players. Rösler and his roommates would listen to a C-60 cassette tape of England football fans singing terrace anthems – 'You'll Never Walk Alone', 'We're on the March', 'We Shall Not Be Moved ' – dreaming of the Saturday afternoons when they would be serenaded by supporters. 'We all loved English football', the German striker remembered, 'the passion of the fans, the tradition, and the stadiums'. Many years later, recovering from a severe ankle injury and wishing to take his career in a new direction, he had one destination in mind.

Rösler joined Manchester City on trial in March 1994. After a slow start, he notched five goals in eight matches. In the season finale, away at Sheffield Wednesday on May 7, he scored City's only goal in a 1-1 draw, and 5,000 fans who made the trip sang Rösler's name to the tune of 'Go West'. He arrived in Moss Side at a career nadir, his confidence and fitness levels low, his damaged ankle untested, and quickly he became the focus of his supporters' adulation. 'When I finally realised it was my name that was echoing around this famous old English stadium, it made the hairs stand up on the back of neck', Rösler said. 'All those years ago, as a kid, I'd listened on a tape to English songs being sung and now here I was, and it was happening to me'.

Rösler was born in Altenburg, East Germany, on November 15, 1968. He was raised in Starkenburg, a town of only 2,000 inhabitants, and was turned onto football by his father, an agricultural worker and the president of the local village club. His playing career was cut short by chronic asthma; still needing an outlet for his passion, he turned to coaching. From his father, Rösler inherited this love for the game. From

his mother, he received a tremendous work ethic and a desire for continuous improvement. He settled at the Leipzig school of excellence when he was 11, attending education classes and training sessions during the week and returning home to see his parents on the weekends. 'It was a huge decision for my parents because I was their only child', the German said, 'but they knew this was a fantastic opportunity for me'.

Rösler started as a midfielder, a box-to-box player who ran all day, before making the switch to striker. He took naturally to the new position, grew almost five inches in a year, and started scoring goals in bunches. A selection to the East German Under-18 national team came next before he signed his first contract with 1. FC Lokomotive Leipzig in 1987. Lok was one of East Germany's strongest sides, having reached the final of the European Cup Winners' Cup the previous season. Qualifying for Europe gave Rösler the opportunity to travel outside his country for the first time in his life, and the journeys to destinations across the Continent were eye-opening.

> East Germany was grey – grey buildings, grey cars, and people even wore grey clothing. There was a distinct lack of colour in our lives, so Sweden was a breath of fresh air. From the moment we got off the plane, I was fascinated with the country. Beautiful green hills and fauna, blue skies, fresh clean air, and houses brightly coloured in red, green, white, and blue. It was the least grey place I'd ever been to, and it couldn't have been more different from the dreary streets and cities back home.

As Rösler earned a reputation for being a dependable goal-scorer, so too did he develop one for being short-fused and rebellious. He signed with 1. FC Magdeburg for the 1989-90 season and during one of his first matches, squared off against his former club, Lok. Late in the game, he scored the winning goal and celebrated by dashing to the Lok bench and making an obscene gesture to an assistant coach that he felt had humiliated him on his first day with the senior squad. 'It was foolish because it wasn't exactly going to go unnoticed and caused a scandal in East German football', Rösler remembered. 'The game was live on TV so the whole country knew about what had happened'.

Except that in East Germany in the late 1980s, Saturday football controversies were often overshadowed by Monday's political events. Beginning in September 1989, Leipzig was the scene of massive peaceful protests against the socialist East German regime. Known as the Monday Demonstrations, they grew with each passing week. On September 4, approximately 1,000 people gathered outside Saint Nicholas's Church to demand more democratic freedoms. By early October, crowds swelled to over 100,000. Though many anticipated violent clashes with soldiers and armed police, such confrontations were rare. In the ensuing weeks, similar protests spread across the country. 'It was an unprecedented public show of defiance', Rösler said, 'as our people finally found their voice. We were in the middle of a revolution and with all the civil unrest, our concentration couldn't help but be affected'.

Over the next year, East Germans were amazed by one miracle after another, moments that had all the elements of a dream: the fall of the Berlin Wall, the establishment of a new government committed to liberalisation, the reunification of Germany. Like millions of other East Germans, Rösler's life was turned upside-down. West German sports agents flocked to the east, on the hunt for cheap football talent, offering hefty contracts and lavish lifestyles. Delighted with the new opportunities for his club career, Rösler was equally saddened by how reunification brought an end to his international career. He won his fifth and final cap in East Germany's last-ever game, a 2-0 win against Belgium on September 12, 1990. German reunified three weeks later. 'We were paid a massive bonus for winning', Rösler remembered, 'because the authorities had to get rid of all the currency, but I was just glad I was there and was part of it because it was still my country. I never felt less than proud to wear that jersey'.

Magdeburg sold him to Dynamo Dresden for two million marks, a record-breaking transfer fee between two East German clubs and one that brought heightened pressure from supporters and intense scrutiny from the media. Rösler struggled to produce during his two seasons and was sold to 1. FC Nürnberg, where his form went from poor to pitiful: 28 matches without a goal in the Bundesliga. The striker returned to Dresden on loan and saw his scoreless drought stretch to 40 games. Then came the successful trial at City, which essentially saved his club career. City paid £375,000 for him in the close season.

Hard-nosed and hard-working, Rösler established a strong bond with the Maine Road faithful, which instantly recognised his drive, toughness, and no-nonsense approach to the game. 'If you had the backing of the fans', the German said, 'they would carry you through any difficult periods you might encounter'. He also developed a keen appreciation for the club's history, an admiration often absent in an oft-travelled footballer. Rösler spoke glowingly of playing one final time before the Kippax, which was due to face the wrecking ball in the summer of 1994. In this April 30 match against Chelsea, he even found the back of the net.

The German striker proved that his successful trial was no fluke, scoring a team-best 22 times in only 36 starts during the 1994-95 season and earning City Player of the Year honors. His goal total dipped (13) the next season, but a pair of notable finishes against Manchester United forever endeared him to fans. In the fifth round of the FA Cup, the German executed a delightful scoop over the outstretched arm of Peter Schmeichel. Less than two months later, Rösler delivered a screamer from along the edge of the penalty area and then celebrated by running toward manager

Alan Ball – who he was locked in a feud with over playing time – and pointed to the name on his jersey. 'I've always worn my heart on my sleeve', the German said, 'it's just the way I'm made, and I didn't believe the world revolved around Uwe Rösler – far from it – but I should have known better'.

His form dipped during later seasons; his last with City, 1997-98, produced just seven goals. Only it was apparent by now that there was more to his legacy than finding the back of the net. Rösler and teammate Georgi Kinkladze represented the future – a future in which players from the Continent and beyond filled the starting XIs of English clubs. The pair were the first non-British and non-Irish stars at the club since Bert Trautmann, and their popularity further opened up the English game to others like them while opening up the minds of supporters who were familiar with a top flight dominated by footballers from the Home Nations.

The Netherlands' Gerard Wiekens joined the club for the 1997-98 campaign and was a first team regular for the next five seasons. Bermuda's Shaun Goater signed in March 1998 and went on to score 103 goals in 212 appearances for City. Costa Rica's Paulo Wanchope and Norway's Alfie Haaland came aboard for the 2000-01 season and were later joined by Algeria's Ali Benarbia, China's Sun Jihai, and France's Nicolas Anelka and Sylvain Distin. Like many other clubs in the Premier League, City became a melting pot of football talent.

In January 1998, after a bleak holiday period, the club needed all the help it could muster – foreign, English, or otherwise. After the 3-0 away win at Portsmouth, City's second-highest goal total so far that season, there was a spiritless 1-0 defeat at Maine Road to Sunderland, which counted old friends Peter Reid, Niall Quinn, and Nicky Summerbee among their ranks. City closed the book on January with a 2-1 loss to West Ham United in the FA Cup's fourth round, a 2-2 home draw with Charlton Athletic on the 28th, and a scoreless affair at Tranmere Rovers three days later in what was a relegation six-pointer.

'League tables don't lie', manager Frank Clark declared ahead of the cup clash. 'It is dangerous to assume we are too big or too good to go down'. Clark was vocalising the darkest thoughts of even the most positive of City supporters. Still, hearing it stated so plainly, in such a public forum, and from the man steering the ship brought fresh fears to an already terrified fanbase. There was a very real, very serious, possibility that this famous club would be relegated to the third tier of English football for the first time in their history.

In February 1998, the *Channel 4* paranormal television series *Fortean TV* investigated the legend that Manchester City's Maine Road was built on the site of an old Romani settlement, and because of this, a curse was laid on the ground by a member of the Romani people. In true City fashion, there was a second curse to blame for the club's misfortunes: while the pitch at Maine Road was being prepared for use in the early 1920s, a horse and cart fell into a deep pit close to the centre circle. The horse broke its leg, was shot where it lay, and covered with earth. A similar curse afflicted Birmingham City and when the club's run of form went from bad to worse, the Blues' chaplain performed exorcisms in the dressing rooms at St. Andrew's and on

Manchester City manager Frank Clark in happier times.

the field. When this did not reverse the club's fortunes, manager Barry Fry staged an exorcism of his own by urinating on all four corners of the pitch. Fry claimed this did the trick and recommended the procedure to any club similarly afflicted.

This is how City's 1997-98 season entered its final act.

Reinforcements arrived on February 17 in the form of Peter Beardsley, who joined on loan from Bolton Wanderers (Beardsley is the only player to make first-team appearances for Manchester City, Manchester United, Liverpool, and Everton.) The out-of-form England international made just six appearances for City. The day also ended with Bury drawing against Stoke City, a result that dropped City to 23rd in a 24-team Nationwide League Division 1.

Manager Frank Clark never had an opportunity to field the new arrival in a starting XI as he was sacked the next day. In typical City fashion, Clark learned of his dismissal in the most unprofessional way possible: through a voicemail from a journalist and a morning radio newscast. 'I'm disappointed about that', Clark said. 'I would have hoped for better treatment'.

His replacement was former City striker Joe Royle, fresh off an 11-month sabbatical from football. He became the sixth man to take charge in the last 18 months, the managerial carousel leaving the club on the brink of administration. Each new appointment had naturally sought to remake the first team in his own image and as a result, more than 50 professionals, accumulated at a cost of £33 million, were on the books. Royle was instructed to prune the squad as much as manage it.

City gave the new boss a quick taste of their trademark disappointment and dysfunction. Leading 1-0 against Ipswich Town, the team wilted during the match's final seven minutes. A low, innocuous shot from 30 yards out by substitute Bobby Petta found its way through a mass of bodies and into the net. Kieron Dyer nabbed the game winner two minutes into stoppage time, denying City a desperately needed three points.

Royle immediately set about improving the squad's fitness levels, a weakness he identified as the primary reason for the late-match defeats. He also shored up the squad's much-maligned defensive unit and scouted for talent that could be signed quickly and cheaply. Most important of all, he settled the endless debate over where to play Georgi Kinkladze, by dropping him from the starting XI. One match was needed to make this decision. In the loss to Ipswich, the Georgian created the opening goal for Kit Symons and then ignored every instruction delivered by Royle and his assistant, Willie Donachie. The inevitable new manager bounce ensued: a 3-1 win at Swindon Town thanks to a brace from Uwe Rösler and a rare Lee Bradbury goal; a 1-0 home victory over West Bromwich Albion in which Rösler scored again; and a 3-1 defeat of host Huddersfield Town.

City had a new manager in place, delivering sorely needed stability to the club, but their house was not in order quite yet. March 16 brought the announcement that Francis Lee was resigning as chairman after four years in charge. To members of the board, Lee's reign had essentially ended one month earlier, when David Makin, a director at City, called a *BBC Radio Manchester* phone-in to voice his displeasure with Lee, Clark, and the overall state of the club. Makin's harsh yet honest assessment shocked listeners. 'He [Francis Lee] overrides everybody', the director said. 'He tries to be dominant. I am in business and know that, if you haven't got a happy workplace, there are problems. I don't think City is a happy workplace and, frankly, there is a problem'. And then: 'I have had enough. I will be doing my best to remove the chairman because he is staying there, and I don't know if he is bloody minded or stubborn. He is being proud. If I was him, I would put on a moustache and a cap and hide'.

In the months leading up to these events, Lee's grip on the club had gradually eroded through a series of purchase agreements. JD Sports bought a 19% shareholding from Lee and his backers. The deal was funded by Makin and John Wardle, co-founders of the sports-fashion retail company. Stephen Boler boosted his shareholding to 30% and then switched his allegiance to the JD pair. The consequence of these moves was the ascension of Dennis Tueart, JD Sports' representative for its stake, to a more prominent role in the day-to-day operations of the club. The City legend demanded the replacement of Clark and then organised Lee's resignation.

In one of the club's most notorious backroom episodes, Paul Stanley, a small shareholder, asked Lee during a board meeting what the consequences were if the club was relegated to the third tier. 'I don't know because if we go down', said the chairman while gesturing to the window of the Kippax banqueting room, which overlooked the pitch, 'I'll jump off the top of this stand'. Exasperated by Lee's severe arrogance, many board members likely wished he kept his promise.

With David Bernstein, the club's financial director, now in charge as chairman, Royle was blessed with money to spend. On March 19, he made his first signing, plucking midfielder Jamie Pollock from Bolton for £1 million. The month was an especially cruel one as Royle's honeymoon period ended abruptly. Defeats to Oxford United, Port Vale, and Bradford City and a home draw with Sheffield United left the club winless in March.

As City prepared for their final six matches – six 'cup finals' to stave off an unprecedented relegation to England's third tier – one final signing was completed on transfer deadline day. His impact this season was minimal, but in the years to come, he emerged as one of the club's most beloved and respected players.

Shaun Goater's initial exposure to Manchester's football divide came during an innocent jaunt to a corner shop for a packet of wine gums. The Bermudan striker left Manchester United's Cliff training ground with fellow youth players Lee Sharpe and Giuliano Maiorano when a man approached them with a crowbar and shouted, 'I fucking hate Man United!' before angrily pursuing the trio down the street. 'Our Adidas tracksuits and proximity to the Cliff must have given away our identity as United youth players', Goater remembered. 'He started yelling that he was a City fan, and even as I was running away, I was thinking, "What the hell's the matter with this guy?" I was aware of the rivalry between United and City, but not of its intensity, although years later I would happily immerse myself in it'.

Born on February 25, 1970, Leonard Shaun Goater was raised in Hamilton, Bermuda, by his mom, Lynette, a pair of aunts, and his grandmother. Lynette was a footballer herself, having played for a local side known as the Bermudian Cosmos, named after the popular American club the New York Cosmos. In addition to passing on her footballing genes, she also gifted her son an intense competitive spirit, a quality she never lost. 'In later years', Goater said, 'her first words during a transatlantic phone call would be, "Did you win?"'

Growing up in the Marsh Folly section of Hamilton, Goater was taken under the wing of Andrew Bascome, a neighborhood footballer six years his senior. Bascome taught Goater the importance of tirelessly perfecting your football skills and, more importantly, worked with him on the life skills one needed away from the pitch, repeating mantras such as 'remember who you are and who you represent'. 'He was a parental figure', said Goater, 'and as I got older, he became more of a father-figure in my life, too. He was a perfect role-model for any young boy'.

Goater played for local league sides, chiefly North Village, where he worked his way up from the minors to the bantams to the junior team. Upon graduating from Whitney Institute, he was offered an athletic scholarship to Columbia High School in Maplewood, New Jersey. The goal was to attend and play football at an American university. Only an unexpected complication arose: playing for his high school team in Bermuda rendered him ineligible in the States.

Back home in Hamilton, a dejected Goater learned how swiftly fortunes can change for young, aspiring athletes but also how quickly opportunity can spring from crisis. 'On my return', Goater said, 'Manchester United just happened to be in Bermuda because of a week-long break in their league programme'. He played in a select XI against a Bermuda under-21 side prior to United's friendly with the national team. Content with being part of the support act that warmed up the crowd for the main event, Goater was shocked to discover that he had played well enough to impress the United scouts and earn himself a trial with the club.

Six months after his trial – a torturous six months during which there was no communication from United – Goater was in Haiti with the Bermudian national team for a World Cup qualifier when he learned that the English club had offered him a two-year deal. He signed with United in July 1988 and was contracted to earn approximately £40 a week, a sum that was, according to him, 'less money than

the schoolkids who packed groceries back home'. He approached manager Alex Ferguson, mentioned how he and his mother recently purchased a home, and requested a bump in his weekly earnings. Ferguson quadrupled his pay packet.

Satisfied with his wages, Goater grew increasingly frustrated with his lack of playing time, though this was largely the result of joining a United youth team loaded with talent. 'I never felt out of my depth', he admitted, 'though I also reckoned I wasn't any better than the players they already had at the club'. He did not train with the first team, was rarely included in match-day squads, and watched as mates like Sharpe found favour with Ferguson. 'Maybe I just wasn't ready to be thrown in at the deep end', Goater said. 'One thing I was sure of, however: there was no way I was going to leave England without having a real crack at it somewhere'.

That somewhere was Third Division Rotherham United, which signed the Bermudian prior to the 1989-90 campaign. Over the next seven seasons, Goater received the first-team action he desperately craved, scoring 86 goals in all competitions, and picked up a winner's medal in 1996 when the Millers won the Football League Trophy. And whether at the training ground or during a competitive match, his effervescent persona shone through, making him a popular player among teammates and supporters. 'I always used to play with a smile on my face', Goater admitted, 'and if I missed an easy chance I would grin and say to myself, "God, Shaun, how did you miss that?"' Dwight Yorke arrived at about the same time as I did, and he never lost his smile during his time at United. It was the laid-back culture we'd grown up in. I didn't find it funny that I had missed or treat it as a joke; it was just a chuckle at myself'.

At Rotherham, fans christened Goater with the nickname 'Lenny', and the weekly adulation he received from the terraces sent his confidence levels soaring. He was regularly the club's leading scorer and twice topped the 20-goal mark. Like any of the best strikers, Goater's attacking prowess was the result of both his mental and physical gifts. Short on long-distance stamina – 'Running to a tree three miles away and back just wasn't for me', he confessed – the Bermudian was quick off the mark and lightning-fast on sprints. Combine that with his intelligence and positioning and he was a footballer who was not going to dash past an opponent over ten or 20 yards but instead, beat them during those crucial first three. 'A lot of my goals were scored by being first to a ball', Goater said, 'which would give me the chance to maybe toe-poke the ball home ahead of the man who was marking me. Being sharp and alert helped me score a lot'.

During the summer of 1996, Goater moved to Bristol City for a fee of £175,000. He immediately fell in love with the West Country city and even more so with John

Ward, the club's manager. Understanding that Goater was not a striker who would chest down the ball and fire in a shot from long range, he focused on developing his strengths inside the penalty area, specifically on running past defenders to be on the end of crosses and through balls. Ward also made the Bermudian a more well-rounded striker by improving his build-up play. 'This was what I needed', he said. 'I knew my game was moving up a level. I watched highlights of games, saw goals I had scored as a direct result of the training we were doing, and it was altogether an exciting time'.

Goater upped his strike rate – 40 goals in 75 league appearances for the Robins – was named to the 1997-98 Professional Footballers' Association Second Division Team of the Year, and offered a new contract. He was pleased with his current situation, in love with both Bristol and the club, content with earning a living in the bottom two divisions of English football. So, when Manchester City manager Joe Royle came calling in the spring of 1998, he was hesitant to depart, even though the transfer could potentially fulfill his dream of playing in the top flight.

In the end, the move up north was too alluring. Goater joined City on a transfer deadline day for £400,000. During his journey to the club's facilities, he displayed his trademark short-distance swiftness from the driver's seat of his car: he received a speeding ticket. 'My first three points for the club', Goater joked. He quickly discovered that the atmosphere at the club was a stark contrast to the one he left at Bristol. The Robins were heading toward promotion; City were embroiled in a relegation scrap. Within a week, Goater's sky-high confidence levels plunged, largely due to the abuse hurled at him and his teammates while they trained at Platt Lane. 'Because it was so accessible, adjacent to two roads with see-through fences', Goater explained, 'people would pull up in their cars and holler abuse at the squad. "You're rubbish – you're not fit to wear the shirt" and suchlike. It was a dire situation for a team that was in need of encouragement. When Joe Royle later said he sometimes felt as if he were in a zoo when we trained, I knew exactly what he meant'.

Goater and fellow new signee Ian Bishop, back with the club after eight years at West Ham United, made their debuts on March 28 at Bradford City. The Bermudian had a pair of terrific chances but could not convert on either, prompting *The Guardian* to state that he was the latest victim of MSS – missing-sitters syndrome – a condition that afflicted City players all season. The visitors slumped 2-1 with Jeff Whitley scoring their lone goal.

Away from the pitch, the focus was on Georgi Kinkladze and a rumoured £5.5 million deal to Dutch giants Ajax. The Georgian, promised a transfer if the club did not gain promotion, had not played for City since a March 14 loss to Port Vale and did not feature in the starting XI again until the April 4 home clash with Stockport County. Unsurprisingly, Maine Road was at near capacity: the season's largest crowd (31,855) turned out to offer their full-throated, unequivocal support. They were rewarded with one of City's biggest victories of the season as opposing keeper Eric Nixon, who wore sky-blue in the 1980s, suffered through the most calamitous of afternoons. Nixon is also remembered for achieving the rare distinction of playing for clubs in all four divisions of the Football League in a single season. In August 1986, he was loaned to Fourth Division Wolverhampton Wanderers and made 16 league appearances. He then had a short loan spell with Second Division in November 1986 then a move to top-flight Southampton the next month. In January 1987,

Nixon went out on loan again, this time to Third Division Carlisle United, where he made 16 league appearances.

Goater opened his account for City five minutes into the match before Stockport tied the score shortly afterward. Nixon was felled by an injury midway through the first half, leaving stand-in Brett Angell in goal while the keeper received stiches for a mouth wound. After his return, Nixon's poor punch on a cross allowed Richard Jobson to head City into the lead. Lee Bradbury recorded his first brace for the club to complete the scoring.

The victory, Royle's fourth since taking charge on February 18, put City a point clear of the bottom three and gave the squad and supporters a shred of hope that they could save themselves over the final five matches. 'We reckoned two more wins would probably be enough to save us from the drop', Goater remembered.

City remained one point above the relegation zone after a 2-2 draw at Wolverhampton Wanderers on April 11. Leading 2-1 thanks to goals from Jamie Pollock and Kevin Horlock, City once again showed a bewildering inability to kill off games and surrendered a goal five minutes from time. Then came two lethargic performances in five days: a 1-0 loss to Birmingham City at Maine Road and a similar score line at Middlesbrough. The former defeat was especially exasperating since City had a man advantage for the entire second half after Steve Vickers was red carded for a dust-up with Bradbury. A pair of matches remained, two opportunities to avoid the most ignominious of relegations, two lifelines for this drowning, gasping football club.

When the moment is right, English football supporters will gladly show off their trademark senses of humour, one that runs the gamut from strange to mischievous to twisted. So, it is fair to state that at some point in the annals of the sport's history, a club's fan base had a bit of cheek and nominated an opponent for player of the season. But have supporters ever honored an opposing footballer for their historical impact? 'There was an online poll conducted on the Internet somewhere to vote for the most important man of the last millennium', Jamie Pollock remembered. 'QPR fans invaded it, and I ended up finishing above Jesus Christ. People were then understandably asking, "Who is this Jamie Pollock person?"'

Manchester City supporters surely knew the answer to this question. In the penultimate match of the 1997-98 season, at home to fellow struggler Queens Park Rangers, Pollock was responsible for perhaps the most famous gaffe in club history. For a generation of fans, the phrase 'Typical City' or the term 'Cityitis' evoked one image, one nightmarish and traumatic moment: Pollock racing back toward his own goal, eyes looking skyward as he chased down a chipped QPR pass, flicking the ball over an opposition forward, and then calmy sending a perfectly placed, first-time header over the outstretched arm of his flailing goalkeeper, Martyn Margetson.

'Sometimes you can get lucky', Pollock said, 'and your own goal doesn't come with any consequences, but that wasn't the case for me. I remember knocking it over [Mike] Sheron and thinking "Wahey!" – but then I put it in my own net. I just didn't see that Martyn had moved. It was the worst feeling ever. My teammates and the manager Joe Royle were brilliant. At halftime, Joe addressed the team and just said, "It was farcical. Let's just not do it again. Move on"'.

Had it gone into the correct net, it would have been a contender for goal of the season. Unfortunately for Pollock and City, it did not. Now trailing 2-1 and with three-quarters of the match still to play, City surged forward in a frantic attempt to equalise and if possible, by sheer determination, blind luck, or a catastrophe like the one that benefitted QPR, pull ahead and pick up the three points.

Pollock nearly redeemed himself less than ten minutes later, but his well-struck shot smacked the underside of the bar. Shortly thereafter, the woodwork saved QPR a second time when Kevin Horlock nicked the top of the bar after a scramble in the penalty area. In keeping with the season's theme, Lee Bradbury missed several golden opportunities before finally netting the equaliser three minutes after the break. But that was it – City could not muster a third.

For QPR, the draw virtually guaranteed their safety and made a cult figure out of Pollock. 'I was informed not long after that game that I'd been voted QPR's player of the year', he remembered. 'Their fans sent me Christmas cards as well. I was back at QPR the following year [1999-2000 campaign] and I was on the bench. Their fans were shouting, "Get on the pitch, Jamie! Get us a goal". To be fair they were brilliant – I didn't mind'.

One fixture remained: at Stoke City on May 3. A match – no matter what the outcome, no matter who the victor – that would surely live in the memories of City supporters. Quite simply, a final day to end all final days.

'A breezy Sunday afternoon in May', opened the game preview in the official club programme. 'What will the circumstances be? It hardly bears thinking about'. The anxiety was certainly justified. City entered the match knowing that even a victory might not be enough to save them from what would be the club's greatest humiliation. Royle and his squad also needed either Port Vale or Portsmouth, managed by old friend Alan Ball, to drop points in their away games at Huddersfield Town and Bradford City respectively. Further adding to the afternoon's drama was that Stoke were also fighting to avoid the relegation trapdoor. The basement of the Nationwide League Division 1 table looked like this:

	P	**W**	**D**	**L**	**GF**	**GA**	**Pts**
QPR	45	10	19	16	51	62	49
Port Vale	45	12	10	23	52	66	46
Portsmouth	45	12	10	23	48	62	46
Stoke	45	11	13	21	42	69	46
City	**45**	**11**	**12**	**22**	**51**	**55**	**45**
Reading	45	11	9	25	39	77	42

In the days leading up to the match, City's sense of desperation was best illustrated by their decision to hire a private jet to fly Georgi Kinkladze back from Georgia's international match in Tunisia. The midfielder returned to the starting XI against QPR, Royle determining that a relegation dogfight was no longer the time to vex over where to employ his most controversial footballer. The other big news for the showdown with Stoke was that Horlock and Gerard Wiekens passed late fitness tests and were in the lineup. Match day found City at full strength.

The relegation stage was set, the curtain poised to raise on another English football drama. The emotions were too much for the day's audiences to bear. Perhaps it was the fury over how their clubs performed this season, or the helplessness from relying on results from other matches, or the loathing from knowing they would still support these footballers next season no matter what the outcome. Whatever the reason, there were violent skirmishes between City and Stoke supporters before the match, during play, and until the final whistle. Police reported that 300 were ejected and another 25 treated for injuries. The worst incident involved fans throwing bricks, leaving two with fractured cheekbones.

Ultimately, both clubs were consigned to the same fate, the same punishment. It was difficult to determine when fans became aware of score lines from the Vale and Portsmouth matches, but when City's travelling contingent started singing – in what has become one of the most oft-cited examples of just how somber, sardonic, and self-aware the club's supporters are – 'Are you watching, Macclesfield?' it was clear the news had spread. (During the 1998-99 campaign, the Manchester derby was Manchester City versus Macclesfield Town. City won both matches.)

Ball's Portsmouth won 3-1, and Vale cruised to a 4-0 victory. City were relegated despite scoring five times on the afternoon, including two from Shaun Goater. 'We are going down, however', said Royle, 'not for one month or for one year but for what has happened over a number of years'.

During the close season, the manager and his assistant, former City left-back Willie Donachie, set targets of removing 20 names from the playing staff and slicing the £7 million wage bill by half. Ian Brightwell, who made 337 appearances for the club, was given a testimonial match and a free transfer. Margetson was released. Kinkladze was sold to Ajax for £5 million. Kit Symons left by mutual consent after refusing to accept a pay cut.

In early September, *The Guardian* ran an extensive piece on the club's inexorable decline. Buried in the story was an anecdote involving a 36-year-old City fan named Chris Morris. After a match-winning goal by Bury, Morris tore up his season ticket in frustration, an act of defiance applauded by other members of the Maine Road faithful. The ticket was returned to him in the post the next Tuesday. 'It seems you can't get away from the club', he said, 'no matter how hard you try. So, I'm going back to Maine Road for the West Brom game next Saturday and looking forward to it'.

In the 1998-99 season opener, a little more than three months after being relegated, City played Blackpool at Maine Road, their first league match against the club in more than 27 years. Goater, Bradbury, and Kakhaber Tskhadadze all scored as the hosts won 3-0. The announced attendance was 32,134.

City 'til they die – they're City 'til they die. They know they are, they're sure they are, they're City 'til they die.

Epilogue: City of Lost Souls

For several decades now, the first verse of 'Blue Moon' has cascaded down from the terraces and stands at Maine Road, City of Manchester Stadium, the original and new Wembley Stadiums, and countless grounds across England and Europe. No club anthem so perfectly captures the mindset of its fanbase.

'The enigma of City fans will go on', wrote Mark Hodkinson in *Blue Moon: Down Among the Dead Men With Manchester City.* 'They are every character Shakespeare created, but all in the same person: foolish, loyal, proud, dogged, sentimental, and headstrong. They are the type of people who still cry at re-runs of *The Incredible Journey*. Happy or sad, they howl, "Blue Moon, you saw me standing alone", to the night sky or the pub landlady. It is a beautiful song. When they sing it, they are the sailor drifting down the Ship Canal after too many years at sea. They didn't get the girl, but what the hell, City beat Gillingham – Division One here we come!'

Yet, for all the heartbreak and loneliness articulated in its opening words, 'Blue Moon' is a song of love, hope, and deliverance. 'And then they suddenly appeared before me', goes the third verse. 'The only one my arms will ever hold / I heard somebody whisper, "Please adore me" / And when I looked, the moon had turned to gold'. At long last, the forlorn figure found what they desperately craved, and their world is no longer blue. Where there was once despair, now there is happiness.

During the second half of 1996, two significant club developments occurred. Though both were relegated to the back pages of local newspapers, they set City on a course for the unimaginable success they enjoy today. On July 10, as part of a board restructuring, London-based member David Bernstein was named financial director and given the unenviable task of revitalizing the relegated club's dire finances. Five months later, discussions kicked off regarding City becoming tenants of a soon-to-be-constructed 60,000-seat stadium for the 2002 Commonwealth Games. Change was coming.

In December 1997, another boardroom shakeup resulted in Bernstein taking over as deputy chairman. Six months later, Francis Lee stepped down, and Bernstein took his place. Unlike Lee, who boasted of champagne and singing until hoarse, the new chairman embraced a more pragmatic approach. 'The key is to reconcile the balance of the squad with a sensible financial situation', he said on the eve of City's first-ever season in the third tier.

When City were relegated in May 1998, *The Manchester Evening News* ran a photograph of a young supporter wiping away tears. Bernstein requested a copy of the picture and hung it in the boardroom at Maine Road. He told guests the photo was a reminder that the club must never put their fans through the same torturous ordeal again. For the first time in years, Maine Road was a looking-forward sort of place.

Slowly but steadily, Bernstein straightened out City's finances. Players were transferred out, others outright released. In November 1999 – six months after the momentous victory over Gillingham – it was announced that Rupert Murdoch's *BSkyB* had agreed to pay £5.5 million for a 9.9% stake in City, filling the coffers with much-needed cash. As part of the deal, the club stood to collect an additional £5.5 million after agreeing to appoint Sky Sports Ventures as its media agent.

The stadium deal was even sweeter. Following the conclusion of the Commonwealth Games, City of Manchester Stadium was converted from a 38,000-capacity arena to a 48,000-seat football stadium at a cost to Manchester's city council and the club. Dubbed 'the Wembley of the north' by *The Guardian*, much like Maine Road was 80 years prior, the £110 million stadium was an absolute gem with its high exterior masts, towering circular stairways, and undulating roof lines. Locals joked that it looked like a giant, upturned spacecraft being held in place by the structure's numerous cables. City were truly about to enter the space age.

On May 11, 2003, the club hosted its last-ever match at Maine Road. Southampton won 1-0 with Michael Svensson scoring the final goal. Demolition of City's beloved home – so aptly described in Colin Schindler's novel, *The Worst of Friends: Malcolm Allison, Joe Mercer, and Manchester City*, as a stadium that 'rose out of these mean narrow streets like a cathedral, towering over the tiny dwellings of the impoverished people who formed its congregation' – began later that year. Eighty years of memories were dissembled in 10 months.

'The stale concoction of beer, smoke, and urine made the gangways of Maine Road an intoxicating place for a kid', wrote Will Unwin for The Set Pieces website. 'Football was my first look into the adult world: seeing the anxiety, joy, anger, and despair that I was only infrequently acquainted with at home'. After eight decades of football that elicited as many tears as it did smiles and produced the most dedicated, self-deprecating supporters in the game, the old club was moving to a new home. Unbeknownst to fans, they had very likely witnessed the last relegation of their lifetimes.

Bibliography

The Manchester Guardian / The Guardian

The Observer

Bluemoon-mcfc.co.uk

Alan Ball: The Man in White Boots, David Tossell, Hodder & Stoughton (2017)

And He's the Left-Back, Remember?, Simon Curtis & Howard Hockin, CreateSpace Independent Publishing (2015)

The Autobiography of Don Revie: Soccer's Happy Wanderer, Don Revie, Museum Press (1955)

The Ball is Round: A Global History of Football, David Goldblatt, Riverhead Books (2008)

Big Mal: The High Life and Hard Times of Malcolm Allison, Football Legend, David Tossell, Mainstream Publishing (2008)

Blue Heaven: Manchester City's Greatest Games, Ian Penney, Mainstream Publishing (1996)

Blue Moon: Down Among the Dead Men with Manchester City, Mark Hodkinson, Mainstream Publishing (1999)

Bobby Johnstone: The Passing of an Age, John Leigh, Breedon Books Publishing (2007)

Catch a Falling Star: The Autobiography of Neil Young, Neil Young and Dante Friend, Empire Publications (2004)

Caught Beneath the Landslide: Manchester City in the 1990s, Tim Rich, deCoubertin Books (2018)

The Club: How the English Premier League Became the Wildest, Richest, Most Disruptive Force in Sports, Joshua Robinson & Jonathan Clegg, Houghton Mifflin Harcourt (2018)

Cups for Cock-Ups: The Extraordinary Story of Manchester City F.C., Ashley Shaw, Empire Publications (1998)

Don Revie: Portrait of a Footballing Enigma, Andrew Mourant, Mainstream Publishing (2003)

The Essential History of Manchester City, Ian Penney, Headline Book Publishing (2002)

Everything Under the Blue Moon: The Complete Book of Manchester City F.C. and More!, David Clayton, Mainstream Publishing (2002)

Feed the Goat: The Shaun Goater Story, Shaun Goater and David Clayton, The History Press (2006)

Football from the Goalmouth, Frank Swift, Sporting Handbooks (1948)

The Football Man: People & Passions in Soccer, Arthur Hopcraft, Aurum Press (2013)

Football Wizard: The Billy Meredith Story, John Harding, Robson Books (1998)

Forever Boys: The Days of Citizens and Heroes, James Lawton, Wisden Sports Writing (2015)

Frank Swift: Manchester City and England Legend, Mark Metcalf, DB Publishing (2013)

I Believe in Miracles: The Remarkable Story of Brian Clough's European Cup-Winning Team, Daniel Taylor, Headline Book Publishing (2015)

I'm Not Really Here: A Life of Two Halves, Paul Lake, Century (2011)

Images of Sport: Manchester City Football Club, David Saffer, Tempus Publishing (2000)

Inverting the Pyramid, Jonathan Wilson, The Orion Publishing Group (2009)

Joe Mercer, OBE: Football With a Smile, Gary James, James Ward (2010)

Kinkladze: The Perfect 10, David Clayton, Parrs Wood Press (2005)
The Legends of Manchester City, Ian Penney, Breedon Books Publishing (2002)
Manchester City: Meredith to Mercer and the FA Cup, Eric Thornton, Hale (1969)
Manchester City on This Day: History, Facts & Figures from Every Day of the Year, David Clayton, Pitch Publishing (2011)
Manchester City: 20 Defining Matches, The Guardian, Guardian Books (2012)
Manchester the City Years 1857-2012: The Most Comprehensive History of Manchester City Football Club, Gary James, James Ward (2012)
McIlvanney on Football, Hugh McIlvanney, Mainstream Sport (1999)
The Mixer: The Story of Premier League Tactics from Route One to False Nines, Michael Cox, HarperCollins Publishers (2018)
One in a Million, Trevor Francis & Keith Dixon, Pitch Publishing (2019)
Pitch Black: The Story of Black British Footballers, Emy Onuora, Biteback Publishing (2015)
Rejoice! Rejoice! Britain in the 1980s, Alwyn Turner, Aurum Press (2010)
Richer Than God: Manchester City, Modern Football and Growing Up, David Conn, Quercus Publishing (2016)
Spirit of '58: The Incredible Untold Story of Northern Ireland's Greatest Football Team, Evan Marshall, Blackstaff Press (2016)
Spotlight on Football, Peter Doherty, Art & Educational Publishers (1948)
Steppes to Wembley: The Autobiography of Bert Trautmann, Bert Trautmann, Robert Hale (1956)
The Title: The Story of the First Division, Scott Murray, Bloomsbury Sport (2018)
This Simple Game: The Footballing Life of Peter Barnes, Peter Barnes and Jimmy Wagg, Empire Publications (2000)
Trautmann: The Biography, Alan Rowlands, Breedon Books Publishing (2012)
Uwe Rösler: Knocking Down Walls, Uwe Rösler, Trinity Mirror Sport Media (2013)
Who Said City Couldn't Play!, Philip Neale, Shutlingsloe Publishing (2013)
The World to Play For, Trevor Francis with David Miller, HarperCollins Distribution Services (1983)
The Worst of Friends: Malcolm Allison, Joe Mercer, and Manchester City, Colin Schindler, Mainstream Publishing (2009)

Thank you, Kristen, Aidan, Liam, Quinn, Nolan & Siobhan. For your love, support, and patience - and for allowing there to be "Dadz is working" time.

The photos used in this book are from a Manchester City fan's private collection and from Alamy.

'When they are great again, City will have shown that they are worth their extraordinary fans. To this day these fans will walk a million miles for one of Joe Mercer's smiles. They'll sing a million songs waiting for some new Mercer-like magic. Because they are City, and Christ do they know they're born'.

Paul Morley, November 1998